ALEXANDER POPE
THE POET IN THE POEMS

ALEXANDER POPE

THE POET
IN THE POEMS

Dustin H. Griffin

PRINCETON UNIVERSITY PRESS
Princeton, New Jersey

Copyright © 1978 by Princeton University Press

Published by Princeton University Press,
Princeton, New Jersey

In the United Kingdom: Princeton University Press,
Guildford, Surrey

Library of Congress Cataloging in Publication Data will be
found on the last printed page of this book

Publication of this book has been aided by a grant
from The Andrew W. Mellon Foundation

This book has been composed in VIP Baskerville

Clothbound editions of Princeton University Press books
are printed on acid-free paper, and binding materials are
chosen for strength and durability.

Printed in the United States of America
by Princeton University Press,
Princeton, New Jersey

For
my mother
and father

Contents

Abbreviations

Corr.	*The Correspondence of Alexander Pope*, ed. George Sherburn, 5 vols. (Oxford, 1956)
The Garden and the City	Maynard Mack, *The Garden and the City: Retirement and Politics in the Later Poetry of Pope, 1731-43* (Toronto, 1969)
"Life of Pope"	Samuel Johnson, "Life of Pope," in *Lives of the English Poets*, ed. G. B. Hill, III (Oxford, 1905)
Pamphlet Attacks	J. V. Guerinot, ed., *Pamphlet Attacks on Alexander Pope, 1711-1744, A Descriptive Bibliography* (London, 1969)
Poems	The Twickenham Edition of *The Poems of Alexander Pope*, ed. John Butt et al., 11 vols. (New Haven and London, 1939-1969)
Pope Bibliography	R. H. Griffith, ed., *Alexander Pope: A Bibliography*, 2 vols. (Austin, Tex., 1922-1927)
Spence	Joseph Spence, *Observations, Anecdotes, and Characters of Books and Men*, ed. J. M. Osborn, 2 vols. (Oxford, 1966)
This Dark Estate	Thomas Edwards, *This Dark Estate: A Reading of Pope* (Berkeley, 1963)
Works of Pope	*The Works of Alexander Pope*, ed. Whitwell Elwin and W. J. Courthope, 10 vols. (London, 1871-1889)

Preface

I have attempted in this book to offer an interpretation of one dimension of Pope's poetry: the various ways in which his poems can be said to be self-expressive. I wanted to examine poems from the whole range of Pope's career, and different kinds of poems, not just the *Horatian Imitations*, the poems most obviously suited to my approach. Some readers may be surprised to find a chapter on *An Essay on Man*. It is included because in my view the poem centers on the figure of the narrator. Like *The Dunciad*, the *Essay on Man* charts Pope-the-narrator's attempt to present and master a body of material. Some readers may be disappointed to find no extended discussion of *The Rape of the Lock*, *Eloisa to Abelard*, or the *Moral Essays*. I can only say that I do not pretend to present a comprehensive account of Pope's poetry, but rather a reading of the poems from one particular perspective. Some poems, as I see it, participate to a lesser degree in the pattern I discern. I have limited myself to poems which clearly reflect the historical Pope or in which the narrator is prominent.

Readers of this book will recognize some of my debts. The work of Maynard Mack and Thomas Edwards has prompted much of my thinking about Pope. I have tried to record specific obligations, and I take this opportunity to declare my general indebtedness and to express my gratitude. Other debts are invisible: Charles Frey, Frank Stack, Thomas Brooks, and especially my wife, Gale Griffin, I thank for their careful and helpful comments on earlier drafts of individual chapters. Christopher Ricks read the manuscript at an earlier stage and gave valuable and challenging suggestions. Maynard Mack read a subsequent version and helped provoke a late set of revisions. To my friend and former colleague Gardner Stout, who gave very generously of his time and advice, I am particularly grateful. His steady encouragement helped keep me going at a difficult time. Others helped make the writing of the book easier. Leonard Hansen generously made available his fine collection of rare books. A Humanities Research Fellowship from the Regents of the University of California freed me from teaching duties in 1974. Grace O'Connell, as always, flawlessly and speedily performed the duties of typist.

I wish to thank Oxford University Press for permission to quote from *The Correspondence of Alexander Pope*, edited by George Sherburn, and Methuen & Co. Ltd. for permission to quote from the Twickenham Edition of *The Poems of Alexander Pope* and from J. V. Guerinot, *Pamphlet Attacks on Alexander Pope, 1711-1744, A Descriptive Bibliography*. Finally, I thank my Princeton University Press editor, Mrs. Marjorie Sherwood, who did more for my manuscript than any author could expect, and my copyeditor, Gretchen Oberfranc, whose sharp eyes and good sense helped prepare it for the printer.

Introduction

Yes, while I live, no rich or noble knave
Shall walk the World, in credit, to his grave.
To VIRTUE ONLY AND HER FRIENDS, A FRIEND,
The World beside may murmur, or commend.
Know, all the distant Din that World can keep
Rolls o'er my *Grotto*, and but sooths my Sleep.
There, my Retreat the best Companions grace,
Chiefs, out of War, and Statesmen, out of Place.
There *St. John* mingles with my friendly Bowl,
The Feast of Reason and the Flow of Soul.[1]

This familiar passage displays one of the most distinctive characteristics of Pope's verse: the presence of a voice, speaking in the first person, that identifies itself one way or another as "Pope." The voice is a recurrent one, not only in the four full-scale satirist's apologies (the poems to Fortescue and Arbuthnot, and the two "1738" Dialogues),[2] but also in the remaining *Horatian Imitations*, in the series of familiar epistles, and in other early poems. It is present too in his epic and didactic works, particularly in the *Essay on Man*, with its intimate address to Bolingbroke at the opening and close—"Awake, my St. John! . . . Come then, my Friend, my Genius, come along, / Oh master of the poet, and the song!"—and in the *Dunciad*, the greatest "personal

---

[1] *Imit. Hor. Sat.* II.i.119-28. Here and throughout I cite from the Twickenham edition of *The Poems of Alexander Pope*, ed. John Butt ed al., 11 vols. (New Haven and London, 1939-1969) (hereafter cited as *Poems*).

[2] *Imit. Hor. Sat.* II.i; *An Epistle to Dr. Arbuthnot*; *Epilogue to the Satires*; Dialogues I and II. To these may be added the Preface to the 1717 *Works* and the prose *Letter to a Noble Lord*, which was addressed to Hervey, written and printed in 1733, but not published until 1751. It is reprinted in *The Works of Alexander Pope*, ed. Whitwell Elwin and W. J. Courthope, 10 vols. (London, 1871-1889), v, 423-40 (hereafter cited as *Works of Pope*). As Warburton notes, the letter "bears the same place in our author's prose that the 'Epistle to Dr. Arbuthnot' does in his poetry"—that is, both are apologies, "vindications of his moral character" (ibid., 423n.).

satire" in the language. To these we can add a vast collection of highly self-conscious letters and the prefaces to his published volumes that deal with the man as well as his works. Most of these pieces have for one of their subjects, and often the deepest subject, the temperament, morals, and artistic or satiric powers of the figure whose voice we hear.

Most of Pope's readers for two hundred and fifty years have felt encouraged, furthermore, to link this "Pope" closely with the historical Alexander Pope of Twickenham and to sense from the "eagerness and intensity" of his lines that "in his poetry [they] are in contact with the nature of the man himself."[3] By reestablishing and clarifying the nature of this intimate link—not quite an identity—between "Pope" and Pope, a link still partly obscured by what is beginning to look like an episode of New Critical domination, we can recover some of the personal energy that invigorates Pope's greatest poems and makes them vividly self-expressive products of an imagination intrigued with and often at odds with itself, and yet more sharply at odds with the world.

Such, in brief, is the argument of this book. To substantiate its different parts will require some excursuses into Pope's life and art and their interinanimations. The initial chapter seeks to demonstrate Pope's constant concern in letters and poems with self-revelation, and to disarm the objection, without denying the fact, that Pope was simply not the paragon that in some poems he claims to be. In the second chapter I explore the conflicting ways in which Pope conceived his self in letters and poems, and how his selves in some respects resolve into a single, rich conception, the Friend of Virtue, his consciously approved self-image. The third chapter treats the poems of the 1717 volume, in which Pope frequently appears, reflecting on his concerns as poet, and particularly on the troubling problem of fame. The fourth chapter takes up another series of

[3] Courthope, in *Works of Pope*, III, 26.

early poems, the familiar epistles, in which Pope focuses his subject, usually an elegiac one, by means of personal experience. The fifth chapter deals with the *Essay on Man*. In that poem Pope sketches a "general Map of Man," wherein the lineaments of his own experience are mirrored, and he exercises his powers as poet-expositor to clarify man's special place in the "maze"/"plan" of the universe. The subject of the sixth chapter is the openly autobiographical *Horatian Imitations*, in which Pope's aggressive and retiring impulses conflict and in some respects resolve. The last chapter explores the ways in which *The Dunciad*, a powerfully personal satire, though not an autobiographical poem, celebrates the witty triumph of Pope himself, its half-hidden hero.

What is the precise relation between the "Pope" of the poems and the Pope of history? The most sophisticated recent answer comes from Maynard Mack, who argues, for example, that the autobiographical speaker of the 1730s poems is a symbolic figure, a Roman poet-moralist, a Cowleyan exemplar of retirement, and at the same time "very plainly a version of the historical Alexander Pope." "It was . . . through an intense engagement of his own personality and situation with the traditional topics and situations of satire that Pope always found his distinctive rhetorical voice. . . . The elements of the self-projection were such as required him to recreate his limited personal being by drawing on a large historical identity."[4]

My concern will be to look closely at that "version" of Pope given in his poems. What kind of version is it? In what precise ways can we say that the poems are self-expressive? The subject is hedged round with difficulties: is the version a self-idealization, and if so, what relation does the idealized self bear to the historical one? In proclaiming himself a moral paragon is Pope fooling other people, or

---

[4] Mack, *The Garden and the City: Retirement and Politics in the Later Poetry of Pope, 1731-43* (Toronto, 1969), pp. vii-viii, 110-11 (hereafter cited as *The Garden and the City*); see also pp. 8, 100.

himself? The public act of proclamation should also make us cautious. Virtually every self-descriptive statement in Pope's letters and poems is in large part a calculated public utterance, designed to persuade an audience, to create an effect. But calculated utterance is not *ipso facto* factitious. In some of the most interesting poems self-promotion or self-advertisement seems less Pope's interest than what we may call self-analysis or self-exploration—conducted, to be sure, in public, with the knowledge that people are listening. At such moments, however, Pope allows into his verse a wider range of his personality. Self-exploration can serve the ends of apology, but in some cases (*The Dunciad*, for example) it may be conducted for its own sake.

Just as a number of readers in the past sought to uncover moral discrepancies between the historical Pope and the deliberate, conscious "Pope," so some present-day readers will look behind the conscious "Pope" to find the unconscious Pope. A purely psychoanalytic reading of Pope might proceed on the principles, as enunciated by a recent proponent, that works of art express a writer's innermost preoccupations, that these unconscious motives and emotional conflicts may produce latent or buried themes, and that although conscious and unconscious purposes may be at odds, underlying conflict may be given "logical and social coherence through conscious elaboration," through, that is, an artist's creative mastery.[5] In Pope's case, to probe beyond the conscious level might produce valuable insights, particularly with a poem like *Eloisa to Abelard*, where dramatic impersonality might allow the poem to express elements within Pope (especially strong and ambivalent sexual feeling) that he might hesitate or be unable to reveal *in propria persona*.

The nature of the bulk of Pope's poetry has suggested to me an approach compatible with these principles, yet different in an important respect. For Pope seems to have

[5] F. C. Crews, "Literature and Psychology," in *Relations of Literary Study*, ed. J. Thorpe (New York, 1967), pp. 73-88.

brought to the surface (the manifest level) emotional conflicts that animate his poetry. As I will argue, he displays lively recognition of a fragmented, chaotic self and of conflicting impulses within himself toward retirement and toward fierce engagement. He quite openly confronts the fervent moral idealism that produces an exalted self-conception with the powerfully aggressive and vindictive feelings that he releases through the "lash," "brand," and "pointed pen" (Pope's terms) of satire. Without denying the probable role of the unconscious motives and other emotional conflicts, the self-deceptive defenses and rationalizations that characterize the autobiographical utterances of all civilized men, I will concentrate on the various motives and impulses that Pope brings to consciousness. In some cases (for example, *The Dunciad*), I explore motives—Pope's attraction to Dulness and anarchy, for example—not fully brought to consciousness, yet richly present in the verse. I then examine two different and sometimes only loosely related ways in which Pope's poems may be said to be self-expressive or self-presentational: first, Pope as poet-protagonist in the poems, in which his role is manifestly expressed and shaped by conscious artistic, rhetorical, and autobiographical demands; and second, Pope as private person, whose special imaginative and psychological concerns emerge publicly—because at some level Pope *expresses* them—in the texture of the verse, especially if the poems are read in light of Pope's entire career.

Such an examination necessarily entails a kind of myopia and distortion. In order to bring out what I take to be a significant dimension of Pope's poems, I focus on certain passages and certain aspects of those passages, and perhaps exaggerate their importance in any comprehensive interpretation of the poetry. (I largely ignore, for example, the poem's political implications.) I argue not so much for a full reinterpretation as for wider recognition of one dimension: Pope's presence in the poems.

POPE THE MAN

·◄【1】►·

An Approach
to Pope

Self-Revelation

Pope was plainly one of his own favorite subjects, and nowhere so obtrusively as in his letters. His disposition toward self-revelation can be observed in the Horatian poems of the 1730s, but we can study that disposition and the motives that prompted it more clearly in his correspondence dating from 1710 and even earlier, when he began to develop the habit of "pouring himself out on paper." The letters throughout his career are characterized by regular, self-disclosing, informal, but "sincere" (the word is a recurrent one) communication, couched not in wit but, to use one of Pope's favorite phrases, "the language of the heart."[1] "All the pleasure or use of familiar letters is to give us the assurance of a friend's welfare, at least 'tis all I know, who am a mortal enemy and despiser of what they call fine letters."[2] His subject is himself, in all his daily "motions" (both the movements of the body and the vicissitudes of the spirit). "You have often rebuked me for talking too much of myself & my own Motions," Pope

---

[1] Pope to Trumbull, 1714, in George Sherburn, "Letters of Alexander Pope, Chiefly to Sir William Trumbull," *Review of English Studies*, n.s., 9 (1958), 401; *Epistle to Dr. Arbuthnot*, 399; *Epistle to Augustus*, 78; Pope to Bolingbroke, 1740, *The Correspondence of Alexander Pope*, ed. George Sherburn, 5 vols. (Oxford, 1956), IV, 261 (hereafter cited as *Corr.*). In the *Epistle to Augustus* Pope perhaps has in mind the easy, intimate self-reference of Cowley's *Essays* (e.g., "Of Myself") and the elegy on the death of his friend Harvey, as opposed to the "pointed wit" of his songs and pindarics.

[2] *Corr.*, II, 41. "The Use of writing Letters resolves wholly into the Gratification given & received in the knowledge of each others Welfare" (ibid., IV, 356).

writes to Martha Blount (*Corr.*, III, 187), but he insists on passing on word of his most ephemeral moods and movements.

The style of a personal letter, in like manner, is designed to convey the "self" most effectively. Although he began his career as a correspondent by exchanging witty banter and pieces of "fine writing," sounding in many of the early letters like a latter-day Restoration wit, Pope seems shortly to have become dissatisfied with the inauthenticity of such a stance and began to ask instead for honest, natural communication.[3] His familiar conception of a letter as "talking on paper" first appears as early as 1710: "You see, sir, with what freedom I write or rather talk upon paper to you."[4] In the same year he first cites the commonplace—"They say a letter should be a natural image of the mind of the writer" (*Corr.*, I, 94)—that he would in later letters reanimate with personal conviction. He would speak, for example, of his letters as "these shadows of me," as "the most impartial Representations of a free heart, and the truest Copies you ever saw."[5]

The desire to convey a "true picture" is sometimes supplanted in Pope's letters by the expressed desire to reveal the naked original itself, as if no use of language, even the most scrupulous, could fail somehow to distort. "You see my letters are scribbled with all the carelessness and inattention imaginable: my style, like my soul, appears in its natural undress before my friend" (*Corr.*, I, 155-56). The wishful fantasy of unmediated communication even takes a mythic form: "The old project of a Window in the bosom, to render the soul of man visible, is what every honest

[3] See Pope to Wycherley, March 1705, *Corr.*, I, 5, quoted in Chap. 2 below, p. 43.

[4] *Corr.*, I, 94; see also I, 105, 238, 353, III, 433.

[5] *Corr.*, I, 355, 352-53. A melancholy letter can convey a "peevish image of my Soul" or "a true Picture of my own Heart, as far as I know it myself" (ibid., IV, 106). See also Pope to Caryll: "so fairly and faithfully have I set down in 'em [my letters to you] from time to time the true and undisguised state of my mind" (ibid., I, 161).

friend has manifold reason to wish for" (*Corr.*, II, 23).
Pope's fanciful longing is given perhaps its most elaborate
expression in a letter to Lady Mary Wortley Montagu:

> If Momus his project had taken of having Windows in
> our breasts, I should be for carrying it further and
> making those windows Casements: that while a Man
> showd his Heart to all the world, he might do some-
> thing more for his friends, e'en take it out, and trust it
> to their handling. . . . But since Jupiter will not have it
> so, I must be content to show my taste in Life as I do
> my taste in Painting, by loving to have as little Drapery
> as possible.[6]

In subsequent letters the baroque excess of the exposed or
removed heart is tempered. Pope occasionally writes of
"opening" himself or his heart: to the Blounts, "Let me
open my whole heart to you"; to Caryll, "with what openness I unfold my whole heart in confidence of your friendship"; and later, to Bethel, "I am so awkward at writing letters, to such as expect me to write like a wit, that I take any
course to avoid it. 'Tis to you only, and a few such plain
honest men, I like to open myself with the same freedom,
and as free from all disguises, not only of sentiment, but of
style, as they themselves."[7]

Just as the wish to convey a "true picture" leads Pope, in
hyperbole, to speak of offering a sight or touch of the
naked original, so his idea of talking on paper develops
from the transcription of his *words* into the idea of "throwing" *himself* out on paper: "I resume my old liberty of

[6] *Corr.*, I, 353. In the same letter he imagines what a fine sight the naked
Lady Mary might make. See also: "I have a burning desire to see your
Soul stark naked, for I am confident 'tis the prettiest kind of white Soul, in
the universe" (ibid., I, 494); and "So much Candour & Good Nature as I
know are in your mind, would draw out one's most naked Sentiments,
without any Care about the cloathing them. And I am heartily sorry I
can't expose myself to you alone" (ibid., IV, 16).

[7] *Corr.*, I, 456, 132, III, 519; see also I, 232, II, 501, III, 14. "Opening oneself" seems to have been a cliché of letter writing of the period, but a
cliché that Pope adopted and developed.

throwing out my self upon paper to you, and making what thoughts float uppermost in my head, the subject of a letter."[8] Dissatisfaction with the connotations of a strenuous and enforced effort in "throw" may have led Pope to another term, "flowing," suggesting a gentle spontaneity. This is especially apparent in letters to intimate friends: "The natural overflowing and Warmth of the . . . Heart"; "In these Overflowings of my heart. . . ."[9]

From this perspective one can see that such phrases as "I love to pour out all myself, as plain / As downright Shippen, or as old Montagne" and "The Feast of Reason and the Flow of Soul"[10] have a long prehistory in Pope's correspondence, and that the stance of honest self-revelation that "Pope" adopts quite consciously in the Horatian poems is a stance that had become "nature" to the Pope of the letters.[11] Significantly, the "pour out" and "flow" of the poem to Fortescue have no equivalent in the Horatian original; indeed, Horace speaks not of "pouring out" but of "shutting up": "me pedibus delectat claudere verba" ("my own delight is to shut up words in feet").[12] Closer to the spirit of Pope's lines and his "open" temperament is the garrulous egotism of "old Montagne." He too professes "Freedom, Simplicity, and Plainness" in his manner, which makes him walk, he says, "with my Head erect, my Face

[8] *Corr.*, I, 111. Cf. "Methinks when I write to you, I am making a confession, I have got (I can't tell how) such a custom of throwing my self out upon paper without reserve," and "If I don't take care, I shall write my self all out to you": ibid., I, 274, 383.

[9] *Corr.*, I, 383, 268. One might speculate that "opening the heart" first suggested to Pope uncovering or exposing, and then, perhaps subconsciously, making an opening (c.f., "open a vein") to permit the metaphorical "flow" of blood.

[10] *Imit. Hor. Sat.* II.i.51-52, 128.

[11] Cf. *Corr.*, IV, 334: "You would be the person I should oftenest pour myself out to." "The Feast of Reason and the Flow of Soul"—a quintessentially Popean line—has another prehistory. It was in fact borrowed from an anonymous poem, *Dawley Farm* (1731), possibly by Pope; see *Poems*, VI, 452-55.

[12] *Sat.* II.i.28, and Pope, *Imit. Hor. Sat.* II.i.51. For "flow of soul" Horace has "nugari . . . et discincti ludere" ("sporting and trifling with unbuttoned [literally, ungirdled] ease"): *Sat.* II.i.73, and Pope, *Imit. Hor. Sat.* II.i.128.

and my Heart open"; "my natural way is proper for Communication, and apt to lay me open; I am all without and in sight, born for Society and Friendship."[13] With openness, for Montaigne as for Pope, comes the desire to speak out candidly, scorning reserve: "I expose myself in my true Opinion." Like Aristippus, Montaigne will "abandon myself to Candor, always to speak as I think." He himself is the "matter" of his book, the "Argument and Subject" of his *Essays*: "I look into my self, I have no other business but my self, I am eternally meditating upon my self."[14] To whatever degree self-revelation answered needs within Pope, it must have been encouraged from without by the example of Montaigne.

When Pope came to publish an official edition of his letters in 1737, he described them in the Preface in terms that had become familiar to him: except for the early effusions of wit, the letters are "by no means Efforts of the Genius but Emanations of the Heart. . . . Many of them having been written on the most trying occurrences, and all in the openness of friendship, are a proof what were his real Sentiments, as they flow'd warm from the heart, and fresh from the occasion" (*Corr.*, I, xxxvii, xxxviii-ix). But elsewhere in the Preface and in letters from this period, though he continued to conceive of his letters as self-revelation, Pope began to see self-revelation in a new light.

Pope's official reason for the publication of his letters was of course the usual subterfuge of authors: Curll's unauthorized edition of 1735—which we now know Pope instigated—required Pope to publish a "correct" version. Doubtless Pope shared with every author the hope of glory; even his friend Swift suspected that Pope had long nurtured "Schemes" of "Epistolary fame" (*Corr.*, III, 92).

---

[13] Montaigne, "Of Profit and Honesty" and "Of Three Commerces," in Montaigne, *Essays*, trans. Charles Cotton, 3 vols. (London, 1685-1686), III, 6, 59.

[14] Montaigne, "Of Profit and Honesty," "Of Presumption," and "Of the Affection of Fathers to their Children," in ibid., III, 4, II, 510, 525, 91. Cf. Pope's "With Aristippus . . . indulge my candour" (*Imit. Hor. Ep.* 1.i.31-32).

But fame in the ordinary sense seems not to have been Pope's sole motive. He was aware that a published letter has a new audience, the reading public, who were likely to be familiar with Pope through his published poems. Many of them would have formed what in Pope's mind was a mistaken picture of him—as a malicious, ill-natured, envious wasp, the image publicized by his enemies. Publication of the letters gave Pope an opportunity to defend his character by proving the charges wrong, by proving himself a virtuous man and, especially, a faithful friend of Virtue and her friends. In 1726, more than ten years before the letters were published in his own edition, Pope wrote to Caryll, as he did to other friends, asking for the return of his letters, especially any "as would serve to bear testimony of my own love for good men, or theirs for me."[15]

But Pope's contemporaries were not his only imagined audience, or even his most important one. The letters began as the warm overflow of the heart, the outpourings of his soul to private friends, and served next as a "proof" of his nature and "testimony" to his love of virtue. (Pope was fond of legal metaphors in his self-disclosures: the *Epistle to Dr. Arbuthnot* was announced as a "Bill of Complaint" in the court of his contemporaries.) They would stand finally, so Pope came to think, as an enduring "monument" for posterity.[16] He hopes

> to erect such a *Particular* & so *Minute* a Monument of his & my Friendship, as shall put to shame any of those Casual & cold Memorandums we see given by most ancient & Modern Authors, of their Regard for each other, & which yet Posterity have thought exemplary.

[15] *Corr.*, II, 419. See Pope to Allen, ibid., IV, 19, which clearly indicates that Pope, although he affected otherwise, hoped that publication of the letters would do some "advantage" to "my own character," particularly his character "as a Man." In preparing the Pope-Swift letters for publication in 1740, Pope noted that the edition "will only show, that such and such Men were my friends" (ibid., IV, 53).

[16] Note that one of the meanings of "monument" is a legal instrument (OED, s.v. "monument," 2).

I love him beyond all Forms of Wit & Art, & would
show how much more the *Heart* of a sincere Esteemer
& Honourer of Worth & Sense can do, than the
Tongue or Pen of a ready writer, in representing him
to the world. (*Corr.*, IV, 64)

So Pope wrote in 1740 in preparing for publication his letters to and from Swift. The term "monument," which occurs more than once in Pope's discussions of his published
letters and poems,[17] suggests not only "reminder" or
"memorial," but may also imply the qualities of art: an enduring structure, composed, like a poem, of words, intended not only for its own day, but for all time.[18] When
Pope rejoiced with Swift that "the strict Friendship we have
borne each other so long, is thus made known to all mankind" (*Corr.*, IV, 337), he was perhaps thinking not just of
the men of their own day. As early as December 1726,
when he was calling in verses and letters in the possession
of his friends, Pope gave as his reason that he wished "to
settle my whole accounts with posterity" (*Corr.*, II, 418-19).
A year later the concern for posterity emerges strongly but
indirectly in a letter to Samuel Buckley in praise of the latter's forthcoming edition of the historian Thuanus. He
imagines the comfort men like Thuanus must feel "to see
so much worthy Pains taken, to right them after their
Deaths, & set their Labours in the fullest and fairest light:
And I believe, the Care of such an Editor as yourself, is All
the Reward an honest & faithful Historian ever did, or
could, hope to receive for his integrity." He goes on to contrast such men who "wrote for Posterity, and are of use to
all Ages" with others like himself, who "write only for the

[17] "It is not to Vanity but to Friendship that he intends this Monument":
Preface to the 1737 edition of Pope's letters, in *Corr.*, I, xxxix. See also
ibid., IV, 337. Pope also refers to *The Dunciad* as a monument: "In this
Monument they [the dunces] must expect to survive" ("Publisher's Preface"). See below, p. 267. In the Preface to his 1717 *Works* Pope considers
that he may be "building a monument"; see below, Chap. 3.

[18] The term may have been chosen with one of Horace's odes in mind:
"Exegi monumentum aere perennius . . ." (*Odes* III. 30).

present Ear" (*Corr.*, II, 471-72). It is plain of course that Pope is affecting the amateur's carelessness. He too wrote for posterity and hoped to be of use to all ages. Does he not here long for the same kind of editorial care that Buckley accorded Thuanus? Was he not himself planning, in effect, to be his own editor?

As with Pope's letters, so with his poems. Pope liked to think of them too as speaking out about himself and his opinions, as defending his own character, as addressing posterity. Upon the publication of the Pope-Swift *Miscellany* in 1727, he wrote to his joint-author:

> I am prodigiously pleas'd with this joint-volume, in which methinks we look like friends, side by side, serious and merry by turns, conversing interchangeably, and walking down hand in hand to posterity; not in the stiff forms of learned Authors, flattering each other, and setting the rest of mankind at nought: but in a free, un-important, natural, easy manner; diverting others just as we diverted ourselves. (*Corr.*, II, 426)

A month later Pope wrote to Swift that their names "shall stand linked as friends to posterity," both in the verse *Dunciad Variorum* and in the prose *Miscellanies*, "and (as Tully calls it) *in consuetudine studiorum*" (*Corr.*, II, 480).

As Pope grew older, as that "long disease" his life brought him closer to death, he thought more and more often about leaving an image of himself for posterity. Such thoughts were apparently prompted by the illness and death of friends, who fell one by one before him—Gay, the poet's own mother, Arbuthnot. After the death of their mutual friend Gay, Pope wrote to Swift with memorials and monuments in mind:

> There is nothing of late which I think of more than mortality, and what you mention of collecting the best monuments we can of our friends, their own images in their writings: (for those are the best, when their

minds are such as Mr. Gay's was, and as yours is). I am preparing also for my own; and have nothing so much at heart, as to shew the silly world that men of Wit, or even Poets, may be the most moral of mankind. (*Corr.*, III, 347)

Some two years later the deaths of Gay and of old Mrs. Pope, and the impending death of Arbuthnot, all contributed to the sober and melancholy tone of Pope's most comprehensive image of himself, the *Epistle to Arbuthnot*.

In the Preface to his *Works* (1735), in which the epistle was included, Pope wrote that "All I have to say of my *Writings* is contained in my *Preface* to the first of these volumes," that is, in the 1717 Preface. "And all I have to say of Myself," he continued, "will be found in my last Epistle," the *Epistle to Dr. Arbuthnot*. More privately, he wrote to Arbuthnot in terms that accord to the poetic epistle the same status he accorded to his own published letters. He refers to "the Poem I told you of, which I hope may be the best Memorial I can leave, both of my Friendship to you, & of my own Character being such as you need not be ashamd of that Friendship. The apology is a bold one, but True: and it is Truth and a clear Conscience that I think will set me above all my Enemies, and make no Honest man repent of having been my Friend" (*Corr.*, III, 431).

A few years later, in 1739, when Pope, then past fifty, was seriously ill, he wrote to his friend Fortescue, who was also ailing. Though dying, Pope still worries about the imperiled "Publick Weal." And though "no Child of mine (but a Poem or two) is to live after me," he still thinks of the name he leaves: "I never had any ambition, but this one, that what I left behind me (if it chanced to survive me) should shew its parent was no Dishonest, or Partial, Man, who owed not a Sixpence to any Party, nor any sort of advantage to any Mean or mercenary Methods" (*Corr.*, IV, 169). Not unlike a dying man who looks on his children as a way of gaining some power over death (images of the parent, they "extend his breath," as Pope himself extended the breath or life of his mother),[19] Pope, whose spouse, so he liked to think, was his muse,[20] and whose children were his poems,[21] holds some hope that those children will survive to give a good report of him. Near the end of his life, indeed, he takes comfort that "my Works have not dy'd before me" (*Corr.*, IV, 364). They lived to testify to contemporaries and to posterity that Pope-the-poet was a good man.

The metaphor of testimony—a recurrent one in his letters—serves best to characterize Pope's autobiographical impulse. Self-revelation in his poems and letters is almost always a carefully calculated performance, acted out in a public arena and designed to persuade an audience. Pope's particular kind of rhetoric, especially in the later poems, is defensive: apology for his works and person. Even when he claims to write only to please himself and his conscience, he implicitly appeals for the approval of his readers. Gray makes an illustrative contrast. He too speaks *in propria persona* and in accents, though still and small, that are no less calculated. But Gray speaks as a little-known poet with very little sense of or confidence in a public audience, addressing chiefly himself and a few friends, and with ambivalence about publishing or even being understood. A private poet, Gray more nearly inclines toward self-expression for its own sake. As autobiographer he approaches confession: "this is who I am, how I see the world." Pope, though always personal, is never private. He writes apology: "this proves my integrity."[22] Not surprisingly, Gray imagines no

---

[19] *Epistle to Dr. Arbuthnot*, 410.   [20] *Corr.*, I, 243, 292, 293, II, 227.

[21] The "Letter to the Publisher" refers to the *Dunciad* as "an orphan of so much genius and spirit, which its parent seems to have abandoned": *Poems*, V, 11. Pope's enemies made use of the same trope: "The author of the *Dunciad* has now oblig'd himself, and is perfectly happy in beholding his illustrious Brat, the just semblance of his sweet temper'd Parent, make his appearance" (*Pope Alexander's Supremacy and Infallibility examin'd* [1729], p. 1).

[22] I borrow the distinction between confession and apology from Francis Hart, "Notes for an Anatomy of Modern Autobiography," in *New Directions in Literary History*, ed. Ralph Cohen (Baltimore, 1974), p. 227. Note

social function for himself as poet. The Elegist and Bard bear no relation to society; they withdraw into themselves or feel actively alienated. Pope, by contrast, even when alienated, acts as social-moral-political critic or constructs in virtuous retirement an alternate society from which he keeps the world in view. Likewise, self-revelation for Pope always means keeping an audience in view, even in his most apparently self-absorbed moments.

"Life" vs. "Book"

About a man who always keeps an eye on his audience, we inevitably ask whether he is telling the truth. Since Plato, rhetoricians have been suspect. When Pope declares, at the end of his life, that he "never had any uneasy Desire of Fame, or keen Resentment of Injuries" (*Corr.*, IV, 364), is he to be believed? Despite the pose of detachment, Pope was by no means indifferent to the fate of his writings. He took great care that his works would endure well beyond his death, correcting and preparing for the press his "deathbed" edition, procuring the services of William Warburton as editor and commentator. Few students of Pope's character have doubted that, like most poets, he sought (to use his own phrase) an "honest fame" or that he smarted when his poems and particularly his morals were attacked.[23] No man indifferent to "injuries" would have put together with such assiduity the bibliography of personal attacks published in the *Dunciad Variorum*.[24] In assess-

---

his distinction: "confession as an intention of impulse places the self relative to nature, reality; apology places the self relative to social and/or moral law." For a discussion of Gray's sense of his audience, see my "Gray's Audiences," *Essays in Criticism*, 28 (1978), 208-15.

[23] On Pope's pretended insensitivity to criticism, see Johnson, "Life of Pope," in *Lives of the English Poets*, ed. G. B. Hill, 3 vols. (Oxford, 1905), III, 188, 209 (hereafter cited as "Life of Pope"). See also *Corr.*, III, 11-12, and Sutherland's preface to *Poems*, v, xxvi.

[24] "A List of Books, Papers, and Verses, in which our Author was abused, printed before the publication of the *Dunciad*: with the true names of the authors," with an appended list of attacks, "After the Dunciad, 1728."

ing the relation between Pope and "Pope," we know that in the course of his daily life he was not the man of virtue that in letters and poems he claimed to be. Discrepancies between Pope's behavior as a professional man of letters and the image of himself he liked to project have been part of the public record since Pope's lifetime. A selection of them need only be enumerated to be recalled: apart from the numerous quarrels where he was on occasion the aggressor, Pope, by his own admission, "equivocated pretty genteely" in denying authorship of the paraphrase of the First Psalm;[25] he dealt with his *Odyssey* cotranslators in a way that seemed to them, and to most of Pope's subsequent critics, less than above-board; he engaged in a series of devious, unscrupulous maneuvers in order to arrange the publication of his letters by Curll in 1735 and (more reprehensibly) the publication of the Pope-Swift letters in 1740.[26]

Such discrepancies between Pope's actions and his claims about himself are not simply a moral problem for him or for his reader, or a matter to be left to the biographer. Because of Pope's constant habit of self-revelation in letters and poems, because of his conception of himself in letters and poems as a man of virtue, because of his repeated claim that he had "stooped to truth and moralized his song"—it becomes very difficult to distinguish between "biographical" and "critical" matters, and virtually impossible to distinguish the "purely moral" and the "purely aesthetic."

How then is the reader of Pope's poems to view the disparities between Pope's claims and acts? To many early readers the answer was simply that Pope was a hypocrite. In a versified pamphlet published after the *New Dunciad* in 1742, transparently entitled *The Difference between Verbal*

[25] See *Corr.*, I, 350.

[26] He could even write to his dear and dying absent friend, Swift, artlessly declare the tenderness of his heart and the steadiness of his affections, and in the next breath maintain the pretense that the publication of their letters is somehow due to Swift ("not of my erecting, but yours"): *Corr.*, IV, 337.

and Practical Virtue, Pope appears, along with Horace, Seneca, and Sallust, as an exemplum of an old truth:

> What awkward Judgments must they make of Men,
> Who think their Hearts are pictur'd by their Pen;
> That *this* observes the Rules which *that* approves,
> And what one praises, that the other loves.
> Few Authors tread the Paths they recommend,
> Or when they shew the Road, pursue the End;
> Few give Examples, whilst they give advice,
> Or tho' they scourge the vicious, shun the Vice.
>
> (P. 1)

The charge of hypocrisy was an old one; in fact, it was one of the standard attacks against the man and poet who dared to proclaim that he was Virtue's friend:

> *To Virtue only, and her Friends, a Friend*;[27]
> But him so bless'd, to hear, it wou'd offend.
> For when that Virtue is indeed possess'd,
> It is in Silence, and the Owner's bless'd. . . .
> You say, *impartially your Muse intends*
> *Fair to expose yourself, your Foes, and Friends*.
> And Leaf by Leaf your writings I have turn'd
> To find the Page wherein your Faults are mourn'd;
> Still self-blown Praise presents itself to view.[28]

Against this simple answer—that Pope was plainly a hypocrite—we can set the numerous tributes to his works and character made by friends and literary allies and by biographers such as Ruffhead. Many of these tributes are no doubt subject to the usual discount that applies to flattery, but it is not so easy to dismiss the lofty tributes from friends of Pope who were great men in their own right. From Pope's letters, Swift said, might be collected "the best

---

[27] As J. V. Guerinot notes, "no other line more infuriated the dunces; it was for them Pope's ultimate hypocrisy": *Pamphlet Attacks on Alexander Pope, 1711-1744, A Descriptive Bibliography* (London, 1969), p. xlviii (hereafter cited as *Pamphlet Attacks*).

[28] *An Epistle to the Little Satyrist of Twickenham* (London, 1733), p. 8.

System that ever was wrote for the Conduct of human life." The man himself, furthermore, might stand as an exemplar of virtue: "May God always protect you, and preserve you long, for a pattern of Piety and Virtue."[29] The testimony from most of Pope's defenders and adulators is just as much an oversimplification as are the attacks from his enemies. But Swift's praise, it should be noted, might leave some room for distinction between word and deed, between a man's epistolary self in all its quotidian variety and perhaps irrelevant concrete detail, and a "system" or "pattern" that might be *collected* or derived from the epistolary record.

The inadequacy of resting content with the simple notion of hypocrisy is most forcefully expressed by Johnson, who saw clearly that Pope's "life" and his "book" reflected different images, and who brought to bear on the problem his own deep moral and psychological understanding of resolution and performance:

> Nothing is more unjust, however common, than to charge with hypocrisy him that expresses zeal for those virtues, which he neglects to practise; since he may be sincerely convinced of the advantages of conquering his passions, without having yet obtained the victory, as a man may be confident of the advantages of a voyage, or a journey, without having courage or industry to undertake it, and may honestly recommend to others, those attempts which he neglects himself.[30]

[29] *Corr.*, IV, 77, 78. Earlier Swift had praised him: "I will take my oath that you have more Virtue in an hour, than I in seven years; for you despise the follies, and hate the vices of mankind, without the least ill effect on your temper; and with regard to particular men, you are inclin'd always to think the better, whereas with me it is always directly contrary" (ibid., II, 497).

[30] Johnson, *Rambler* 14, in *Works of Samuel Johnson*, ed. W. J. Bate and A. B. Strauss (New Haven, Conn., 1969), III, 76. Cf. Maynard Mack: "perhaps the will to virtue in Pope was genuine, only the act a slave to limit" (*The Garden and the City*, p. 30). Mack also speaks of "a genuine moral concern which (as with the rest of us) was no less genuine for his own lapses" (p. 187).

Even in the case of autobiographical writing, where a man not only recommends virtues, but also locates them in himself, hypocrisy and even self-deception may be terms too blunt:

> To charge those favourable representations, which men give of their own minds, with the guilt of hypocritical falsehood, would show more severity than knowledge. The writer commonly believes himself. Almost every man's thoughts, while they are general, are right; and most hearts are pure while temptation is away. It is easy to awaken generous sentiments in privacy; to despise death when there is no danger; to glow with benevolence when there is nothing to be given. While such ideas are formed they are felt, and self-love does not suspect the gleam of virtue to be the meteor of fancy.[31]

Pope, it is easy to imagine, might well in the act of writing have believed himself the Friend of Virtue.[32] But did he not, as an acutely self-conscious and self-analytical writer, consider the disparity between professions of virtue and "genteel equivocations"? Can he possibly have blinded himself to his own lapses? Johnson almost suggests as much:

> When Pope murmurs at the world, when he professes contempt of fame, when he speaks of riches and poverty, of success and disappointment, with negligent indifference, he certainly does not express his habitual and settled sentiments, but either wilfully disguises his own character, or, what is more likely, invests himself with temporary qualities, and sallies out in the colours

---

[31] "Life of Pope," pp. 207-8. Courthope likewise rejects the simple explanation of hypocrisy: "it will not do simply to brand him as a hypocrite" (*Works of Pope*, III, 25-26).

[32] Courthope refers to Pope's "self-deception" (*Works of Pope*, V, 299), but notes that the *Epistle to Dr. Arbuthnot* is "plainly full of an ardour, an enthusiasm, a conviction, which could never have been commanded by one who did not for the moment feel what he professed" (ibid., 270).

of the present moment. His hopes and fears, his joys and sorrows, acted strongly upon his mind.[33]

Perhaps, however, the conception of himself as the Friend of Virtue was so deeply engraved as to become convincing. In writing of Pope's letters, Johnson noted that "It is indeed not easy to distinguish affectation from habit; he that has once studiously formed a style rarely writes afterwards with complete ease."[34] What he said of the letters may have been true of Pope's style of life. The master conception, his favorite way of thinking of himself, may have mastered him.[35]

The Best Self

Perhaps the matter of Pope's hypocrisy or self-deception should be left there, but it remains to consider some evidence which confirms my suspicion that so self-conscious a man as Pope was aware of his lapses, and yet genuinely believed that the highly moral "Pope" of the poems and letters was a fair representation of his best self.

To begin with, the very frequency and insistent tone of Pope's protests that he speaks from the heart might naturally arouse our suspicion that this "natural" openness is willed or artificial. "I know in my heart (a very Uncorrupt Witness) that I was constantly the thing I profess'd myself to be, to you" (*Corr.*, II, 25). Pope may have borne such suspicions himself, as his very denial of them suggests: "It is the Point upon which I can bear no suspicion, & in which above all I desire to be thought serious. It would be most vexatious of all Tyranny, if you should pretend to take for Raillery, what is the mere disguise of a discontented heart" (*Corr.*, I, 383). His repeated longing to speak without a

---

[33] "Life of Pope," pp. 212-13.   [34] Ibid., p. 160.

[35] Cf. John Butt: "Pope himself may not have known how precisely to distinguish the historical portrait from the literary one" ("Pope: The Man and the Poet," in *Of Books and Humankind*, ed. J. Butt [London, 1964], p. 79). See also Courthope: "it is natural for men to mistake the conceptions they cherish for the reflection of themselves" (*Works of Pope*, V, 273).

mask may express his uneasy sense that it is almost impossible not to adopt some pose: "I cannot be *Sub-Persona* [literally, beneath a mask] before a man I love; and not to laugh with honesty, when Nature prompts . . . is but a knavish hypocritical way of making a mask of one's own face" (*Corr.*, I, 112). The fear of failure clearly suggests the *need* to display the undisguised self.[36] The ultimate end may be to prove to his friends (and perhaps, above all, to himself) the transparency of his mind. He is even prepared to reveal a few warts in order to validate the truth of the picture. Or, in Pope's recurrent metaphor, "the clearness and purity of one's mind is never better prov'd, than in discovering its own faults at first view: as when a Stream shows the dirt at its bottom, it shows also the transparency of the water" (*Corr.*, I, 274). This idea obsessed Pope: he repeats it in his private *Thoughts on Various Subjects* and in the familiar couplet from the Fortescue poem: "In me what Spots (for Spots I have) appear, / Will prove at least the Medium must be clear."[37] Is this perhaps a claim (or wish?) that, despite occasional lapses (graver lapses than he was ready to admit openly), the mind itself, the deliberate self, the medium of thoughts and actions, was clear?

Pope seems to have reflected often on the disparity between what he urged for himself and what he in fact achieved. In an early letter, for example, he notes that "when a man is conscious that he does no good himself, the next thing is to cause others to do some: I may claim some merit this way" (*Corr.*, I, 333). In the 1720s, writing in praise of sincerity, he tells Bethel: "next to possessing the best of qualities is the esteeming and distinguishing those who possess it" (*Corr.*, II, 501). Some years later he again remarks to Bethel: "It is all a poor poet can do, to bear testimony to the virtue he cannot reach" (*Corr.*, III, 381). In his

---

[36] See below, p. 43.

[37] *Thoughts on Various Subjects*, in *Works of Pope*, X, 551; *Imit. Hor. Sat.* II.i.55-56. See also a letter written in 1705: "Spots and Blemishes you know are never so plainly discovered as in the brightest Sunshine" (*Corr.*, I, 5).

poems too Pope occasionally dwells on the difference between real and ideal. In the epistle to Bethel (*Imit. Hor. Sat.* ii.ii), for example, he accords praise (touched with a slight condescending irony) to the man of temperance, pure, simple, and moderate in all things. Bethel becomes a kind of model for a poet who, whatever his devotion to temperance and moderation, would never be the simple soul that Bethel was: "His equal mind I copy what I can, / And as I love, would imitate the Man" (ii.131-32). These lines suggest a smiling admission that the act inevitably falls short of the will. One finds a similar situation at the end of the *Epistle to Dr. Arbuthnot*, where Pope holds up his father as a model for himself: the elder Pope lived quietly (a "Stranger to Civil and Religious Rage"), simply ("unlearn'd, he knew no Schoolman's Subtle Art, / No Language, but the Language of the Heart"), temperately ("His Life, tho' long, to sickness past unknown"). "O grant me thus to live," exclaims his son. The full force of this idealized portrait, drawn after the lineaments of the Horatian "happy man,"[38] depends on our seeing that Pope, presented elsewhere in this very poem as a warrior for truth and defender of virtue, whose life had already been one "long disease," who dared to "affront the great"—that he had never been, and could never be, the good, "innoxious" man who held it a "sin to call our neighbour fool."[39]

Consider last the *Epistle to Bolingbroke* (*Imit. Hor. Ep.* i.i), which likewise ends with a suggestion that Pope knows he falls short of his own exalted self-conceptions. He turns to address Bolingbroke:

Is this my Guide, Philosopher, and Friend?
This, He who loves me, and who ought to mend?
Who ought to make me (what he can, or none,)
That Man divine whom Wisdom calls her own,

[38] *The Garden and the City*, p. 106.

[39] Despite this impossibility, Pope later wrote to Fortescue that his real "Disposition," though the world thinks him a satirist, has always been to "Walk gently and inoffensively . . . out of this world, without any Animosity to any Creature in it" (*Corr.*, iv, 202-3).

Great without Title, without Fortune bless'd,
Rich ev'n when plunder'd, honour'd while oppress'd,
Lov'd without youth, and follow'd without power,
At home tho' exiled, free, tho' in the Tower.
In short, that reas'ning, high, immortal Thing,
Just less than Jove, and much above a King,
Nay half in Heav'n—except (what's mighty odd)
A fit of Vapours clouds this Demi-God.

The poem thus concludes with a charming, even moving, picture of human limitation, Pope's failure to make himself into his model.

An exalted self-conception, however, even where it exceeds the facts, is not necessarily rendered invalid for Pope or for his reader. Perhaps, in order to write autobiographical poetry that achieved some shape and coherence, Pope, like any autobiographer, was required to "assume a role": "An autobiography can scarcely be composed without assuming a role; the author 'plays his part' by selecting certain of his past actions for emphasis and omitting others, by manipulating his presentation of past episodes so as to show himself in a particular light, and by the overall tone of his narrative."[40] Not only does autobiography require adoption of a role or point of view, selection and conscious arrangement of material, and even some misrepresentation,[41] but, as Roy Pascal has written, the autobiographer discovers and presents his "innermost self":

[40] Paul Delany, *British Autobiography in the Seventeenth Century* (London, 1969), p. 174. Compare Roy Pascal on the "truth" of autobiography: "It will not be an objective truth, but the truth in the confines of a limited purpose, a purpose that grows out of the author's life and imposes itself on him as his specific quality, and thus determines his choice of events, and the manner of his treatment and expression" (*Design and Truth in Autobiography* [Cambridge, Mass., 1960], p. 83). On the need to select, see also Francis Hart, "Notes for an Anatomy of Modern Autobiography," pp. 228-30.

[41] Pascal notes misrepresentation, both conscious (reticence, deception, protection of self or others) and unconscious (tricks of memory, anachronistic distortions). See his chapter, "The Elusiveness of Truth," in *Design and Truth*.

The autobiographer is not simply uncovering facts and relationships that an outsider must necessarily be unacquainted with, but presenting an order of values that is his own. He must necessarily establish a sort of ideal image of himself. . . . Not that he idealises himself, sees himself as better than he might appear to others; but that he establishes an over-riding purpose, which he finds, perhaps to his surprise, has become expressed and grasped in the shape of his life. He presents an inner core, a self beneath the personality that appears to the world, that is his most precious reality since it gives meaning to his life.[42]

In Pope's autobiographical writings (both letters and poems) this process of self-discovery is also one of self-formation, a determination, as it were, to make himself into his best self, the image of which he shows the world.

Pope's acute self-consciousness, as man and as artist, his idealized conception of himself and his effort to portray himself in that image, might lead a psychologically minded critic less toward Freud than toward some modern social psychologists who see man as the role-taking animal, consciously adopting roles in order to achieve a self.[43] Putting far more emphasis than Freud on the self as a conscious product, role psychologists also stress the interaction between external and internal forces, between socially derived roles and individual psyche. Moreover, the notions of "role conception" and "role acceptance" suggest a more intimate relation between self and role than Pope's rhetorical critics have allowed.[44] A role may be derived from the public world, but it can be redefined and embraced in accordance with the needs of the psyche so as to become an integral part of one's "nature." The etymology of "persona"

[42] Ibid., p. 193.
[43] See, for example, George Herbert Mead, *Mind, Self, and Society* (Chicago, 1934), and Erving Goffman, *The Presentation of Self in Everyday Life* (Garden City, N.Y., 1959).
[44] See G. W. Allport, *Pattern and Growth in Personality* (New York, 1961), pp. 184-85.

might have suggested as much. It meant originally the mouthpiece of a stage mask (perhaps from *per + sona*, "to sound through") used to concentrate and amplify the voice of a speaker, then by extension the mask itself, and then, in classical Latin, a role or person represented by an actor, the part anyone plays in the drama of life, and even one's personality or character.

Not suprisingly, literary men have given the most resonant accounts of the function of the mask or role, especially the idealized self-conception, in shaping the innermost self and revealing it. As H. G. Wells put it in his autobiography, the persona or mask acts as a "standard" by which a man "judges what he may do, what he ought to do." It may be a "structure of mere compensatory delusions," but it is not necessarily self-deceiving. "A man who tries to behave as he conceives he should behave, may be satisfactorily honest in restraining, ignoring, and disavowing many of his innate motives and dispositions." A mask can become "the true face." Wells's own persona, he says, "may be an exaggeration of one aspect of my being, but I believe that it is a ruling aspect. It may be a magnification, but it is not a fantasy."[45]

Yeats too wrote of the mask as a means to achieve a deliberate or "active" virtue:

> If we cannot imagine ourselves as different from what we are and assume that second self, we cannot impose a discipline upon ourselves, though we may accept one from others. Active virtue as distinguished from the passive acceptance of a current code is therefore theatrical, consciously dramatic, the wearing of a mask. It is a condition of arduous full life.[46]

[45] Wells, *Experiment in Autobiography* (New York, 1934), pp. 10-11. The term "persona" is adopted from C. G. Jung (*Collected Works*, ed. H. Read et al., 17 vols. [New York, 1953-1960], VII, 154-60, 193, IX, 1, 122-23), but given significant reinterpretation. For the most part, Jung sees the persona as a mask derived from the collective psyche; usually a false and (self-)deceiving mask, it must be shed in the process of individuation.

[46] *The Autobiography of William Butler Yeats* (Garden City, N.Y., 1958), p. 317.

And no one has put more clearly the idea of two selves—
one ordinary, the other deliberate—than Matthew Arnold,
whose later essays are marked by a concern to distinguish
the "transient" self from the "permanent" self, the former
being "a movement of man's ordinary or passing self, of
sense, appetite, desire, the other, a movement of reflection
and more voluntary, leading us to submit inclination to
some rule, and called generally a movement of man's
higher or enduring self, or reason, spirit, will." This higher
self Arnold also calls the "best self."[47]

Pope no doubt felt that his "deliberate character," the
identity he projected in letters and poems, was his "best"
and deepest self. He could have found encouragement for
thinking so in the work of some contemporary moralists.
Shaftesbury defines the "real self" as "thy firm and stated
principles, thy cool thoughts and reasonings . . . such certain judgments, such certain opinions, and only such certain ones, for if they are not those thou hast approved and
confirmed, it is a wrong self, a nothing, a lie." For Bishop
Butler too, one's true character consists of one's powers of
reflection and approval, which produce the principles
"from which men would act, if occasions and circumstances
gave them power."[48] Thus the self is not located in actions
but in one's approved principles, which may or may not
eventuate in principled action. As Pope wrote to Bathurst,
"my life in thought and imagination is as much superior to
my life in action and reality as the best soul can be to the
best body" (*Corr.*, III, 156). A "life in thought and imagination" may encompass not only the poet's reverie or the
poet's creation of a world, but also his creation or recre-

---

[47] Arnold, Preface to *Last Essays*, in Arnold, *Complete Prose Works*, ed.
R. H. Super (Ann Arbor, Mich., 1962-1973), VIII, 154. The "best self" is
especially prominent in *Literature and Dogma* and in *Culture and Anarchy*.

[48] Shaftesbury, *Philosophical Regimen*, in *The Life, Unpublished Letters and
Philosophical Regimen*, ed. B. Rand (London, 1900), pp. 140, 136; Butler,
"Of the Nature of Virtue," appended to his *Analogy of Religion*, in Butler,
Works, 2 vols. (Oxford, 1849), I, 314-15. Though she has escaped Lovelace
again, after the rape Clarissa laments, "*I, my best self*, have *not* escap'd!"
(Clarissa to Anna Howe, June 28, *Clarissa*).

ation of himself. The best self is, then, as Arnold emphasizes, a product of will or choice. This was perhaps true of Pope, who took particular care to recreate or compose himself into the "Pope" who speaks to us from the Horatian poems of the 1730s.[49]

Self-Formation

"Pope may be said to write always with his reputation in his head." "He hardly drank tea without a stratagem."[50] Johnson's phrases point to a quality that has always been recognized in Pope: his calculation, his acute self-consciousness about himself and his actions. He was preoccupied with "images" of himself: the grotesque image, propagated by his literary enemies, of Pope Alexander, the wasp of Twickenham, the malignant humpbacked ape, *mens curva in curvo corpore*; and the flattering image of the many portraits he sat for. In describing the dozens of contemporary paintings, drawings, and engravings of the poet, W. K. Wimsatt has noted "the importance to [Pope] of having an adequate image of himself made public, and his apparently persistent efforts toward that end."[51] An adequate image, Pope would have known from his own study of painting, requires considerable care and attention on the part of the painter. More so perhaps for a man who would present his own image, for he must sit to himself.

Pope indeed seems to have been aware of his self, almost

[49] For Arnold, the "best self" tends to be the higher self of mankind in general (e.g., the Christian *novus homo*). Since his concern is ultimately social, he shows little interest in differences between one man's best self and another's. Pope's best self, I argue, is individualized, but his predominant moral concerns inevitably mean that he shares features with other "virtuous men."

[50] "Life of Pope," pp. 160, 200.

[51] Wimsatt, *The Portraits of Alexander Pope* (New Haven, Conn., 1965), p. xv. See also Wimsatt's "An Image of Pope," in *From Sensibility to Romanticism*, ed. F. W. Hilles and H. Bloom (New York, 1961): "All during his career as a man of letters Pope was a notably successful opportunist in the promotion of his own fame and the projection of the correct public image of himself" (p. 52).

as if it were a thing apart from him. Late in his life, for example, he complains that law, sickness, and company "Alienate me from my Friends, from my Pleasures, from my Studies, from my Self" (*Corr.*, IV, 78). The very passing of time is such as to wear away the self, as the features of a stone statue are effaced by wind and rain: "Not our friends only, but so much of our selves is gone by the mere flux and course of years, that were the same Friends to be restored to us, we could not be restored to ourselves, to enjoy them" (*Corr.*, IV, 50). Elsewhere the self is, so to speak, an object to be studied, nourished, developed, composed, retired into, cultivated, like the *hortus conclusus* (a medieval symbol of the Christian soul). In an early letter to Trumbull, Pope wrote: "I daily meet here in my Walks with numbers of people who have all their Lives been rambling out of their Nature, into one Business or other, and ought to be sent into Solitude to Study themselves over again."[52] To expose oneself, to be in the world, indeed, is to lack a self: "A man that lives so much in the world does but translate other men; he is nothing of his own. Our customs, our tempers, our enjoyments, our distastes are not so properly effects of our natural constitution, as distempers catched by contagion" (*Corr.*, II, 302). Or as he put it in a later poem, "Who there [in London] his Muse, or Self, or Soul attends?" (*Imit. Hor. Ep.* II.ii.90). When he had spent too much time in town, in the world, Pope often found it necessary to withdraw, to retire into the country, into study ("A Glutt of Study & Retirement in the first part of my Life cast me into this, & this I begin to see will throw me again into Study & Retirement" [*Corr.*, II, 185]), into himself: "I've been so long from home, that I must retire into myself a while, to recover a disposition to Study or thinking" (*Corr.*, II, 194).

It is characteristic of Pope to set self against the world and to pretend to ignore the latter in favor of preserving

[52] Pope to Trumbull, in A. C. Lunn, "A New Letter in the Trumbull Correspondence," *Review of English Studies*, n.s., 24 (1973), 312.

the health and, above all, the integrity of the former: "In my politicks, I think no further than how to preserve the peace of my life, in any government under which I live; nor in my religion, than to preserve the peace of my conscience in any Church with which I communicate" (*Corr.*, I, 454). He commends Swift for valuing "no man's civility above your own dignity," and urges him not to write for party, or indeed about politics at all, but to nurture and care for his "integrity": "If you must needs write about Politicks at all, (but perhaps 'tis full as wise to play the fool any other way) surely it ought to be so as to preserve the dignity and integrity of your character with those times to come, which will most impartially judge of them" (*Corr.*, II, 412-13). The self must be nourished and preserved, but it too may act to protect or to comfort. When the world threatens to invade his self—the symbolic action with which the *Epistle to Dr. Arbuthnot* opens—Pope retires further within his objectified robes of righteousness: "*Virtute meâ, me involvo*, as Horace expresses it: I wrap myself up in the conscience of my integrity, and sleep after it as quietly as I can" (*Corr.*, I, 162). "As for myself, I resolve to go on in my quiet, calm, moral course, taking no sort of notice of men's, or women's anger, or scandal, with virtue in my eyes, and truth upon my tongue":[53] "*All* honest Company is a rarity, but principally among Gentlemen. I think this one Sentence includes a General account of all Publick affairs. I have seen and heard, what makes me shut my Eyes, & Ears, and retire inward into my own Heart; where I find Something to comfort me, in knowing it is possible some men may have some Principles."[54]

[53] *Corr.*, III, 327. Compare the epigraph to the *Epistle to Dr. Arbuthnot*, from Cicero's *De Re Publica* VI.xxiii: "Do not attend to the common talk of the mob, nor place your hope in human rewards for your deeds; it is proper that virtue itself, by her own charms, draw you to true glory. Let others talk about you as they choose, for they will talk in any case" (Aubrey Williams's translation, in *Poetry and Prose of Alexander Pope*, ed. Williams [Boston, 1969], p. 198).

[54] *Corr.*, IV, 437. The letter continues: "I wish I had been nowhere but in my Garden; but my weak Frame will not endure it; or nowhere but in my

Although the topic of human identity has always interested mankind, Pope's active attention to the nature of his self marks him as a man of his Lockean age. "There has been very great Reason on several Accounts," says Mr. Spectator in 1711, "for the learned World to Endeavour at settling what it was that might be said to compose Personal Identity."[55] "Let us examine this thing of personality," says Shaftesbury's Theocles, "and consider how you, Philocles, are you, and I am myself."[56] Lexical evidence too suggests a new interest in what defines the self. About 1700, new meanings of "self" as a noun began to be needed, as designating not only the authentic person, but also an identity that might vary from time to time or might be divided against itself.[57] This renewed interest, as the *Spectator* notes, was largely prompted by Locke, who proposed, against the traditional notion of self as rational *substance*, that personal identity consists in consciousness.[58] And since the mind, in Locke's view, is a receptacle receiving im-

Study; but my weak Eyes cannot read all the Evening." The repeated phrases "into my own Heart . . . in my Garden . . . in my Study" suggest that Pope associated his "self," his heart (to be nourished, cultivated, and studied), with his garden and study at Twickenham.

[55] Eustace Budgell, in *The Spectator*, ed. D. F. Bond (Oxford, 1965), IV, 575 (no. 578). Cf. Hume's *Treatise of Human Nature* (1739): "We now proceed to explain the nature of personal identity, which has become so great a question in philosophy, especially of late years, in England" (I.iv.6).

[56] Shaftesbury, *Characteristics*, ed. J. M. Robertson, 2 vols. (London, 1900), II, 100-101.

[57] *OED*, s.v., "self," sb. C4: "that which in a person is really and intrinsically *he* (in contradistinction to what is adventitious)," from 1674 (Locke is among the earliest users); C4a: "What one is at a particular time or in a particular aspect or relation," from 1697; C4b: "an assemblage of characteristics and dispositions which may be conceived as constituting one of various conflicts or personalities within a human being," from 1703 (excluding a single "inward self" in Spenser).

[58] "Self is that conscious thinking thing, whatever substance made up of (whether spiritual or material, simple or compounded, it matters not), which is sensible or conscious of pleasure and pain, capable of happiness or misery, and so is concerned for itself, so far as that consciousness extends": Locke, *Essay Concerning Human Understanding* (1690), II.xxvii.17; see also par. 9, 19.

pressions and storing them in the memory, the self is simply the accumulated ideas.[59] These might theoretically add up to a single comprehensive self, but likewise, the self might change as ideas are added or forgotten. Anti-Lockeans found objectionable this denial of a permanent identity underlying and receiving all impressions, and they insisted on some innate attributes, whether depravity or a moral sense, or some persisting personality, "a perceiving, active being," an "indivisible thing which I call myself."[60] For Pope, however, attaining selfhood was not simply a Lockean matter of accumulating experience, of building up a self out of a lifetime's impressions; nor was it the discovery of an individuating essence, the "indivisible centre of the soul or mind."[61] Although his conceptions of himself may reflect elements of these competing views of selfhood,[62] he seems to have viewed the attainment of self as a process of deliberate choice, of willed self-formation,[63] or, as he put it in the Prologue to Addison's *Cato*, of "conscious virtue." In an early epistle he conceived of his life as a work of art, to be shaped and ordered like a stage play:

[59] Strictly speaking, the Lockean self is the impressions together with consciousness, the power to receive impressions (sensation) and "take notice" of them (reflection): *Essay*, ii.i.3-4. Locke even allows room for a permanent self that receives the impressions. A "person," he writes, is a "thinking, intelligent being, that has reason and reflection, and considers itself as itself, the same thinking thing in different times and places" (*Essay*, ii.xxvii.11). But in effect, as Ernest Tuveson notes, "Locke . . . transferred the clear identity from the ego to the separate ideas, the simple impressions": Tuveson, *The Imagination as a Means of Grace: Locke and the Aesthetics of Romanticism* (Berkeley, 1960), p. 29.

[60] Berkeley, *Principles of Human Knowledge* (1710), in Berkeley, *Works*, ed. A. C. Fraser, 4 vols. (Oxford, 1871), i, 156; Thomas Reid, "Of Identity," in Reid, *Essays on the Intellectual Powers of Man* (1785), ed. A. D. Woozley (London, 1941), p. 26. On the controversy between Lockeans and innatists, see J. A. Passmore, "The Malleability of Man in Eighteenth Century Thought," in *Aspects of the Eighteenth Century*, ed. E. Wasserman (Baltimore, 1965), pp. 21-46.

[61] Berkeley, *Siris* (1744), in *Works*, ii, 500.　　　　[62] See below, chap. 2.

[63] For some cogent remarks on these modes of self-conception, see Robert M. Adams, *The Roman Stamp* (Berkeley, 1974), pp. 1-4.

> Let the strict Life of graver Mortals be
> A long, exact, and serious Comedy,
> In ev'ry Scene some Moral let it teach,
> And, if it can, at once both Please and Preach:
> Let mine, like Voiture's, a gay Farce appear,
> And more Diverting still than Regular,
> Have Humour, Wit, a native Ease and Grace;
> No matter for the Rules of Time and Place.[64]

One may think too of the many poems which end with a prayer or with Pope's wish that he might make himself over in the lines of models held up for imitation:

> *Thus* [i.e., after this pattern] let me live, unseen,
>   unknown. . . .
>
> > *(Ode on Solitude)*

> Oh may some Spark of *your* Coelestial Fire,
> The last, the meanest of your Sons inspire. . . .
>
> > *(An Essay on Criticism)*

> Then teach me, Heaven! to scorn the guilty Bays;
> Drive from my Breast that wretched Lust of Praise. . . .
>
> > *(The Temple of Fame)*

> Teach me to feel another's Woe. . . .
>
> > *(The Universal Prayer)*

> Teach me, like thee, in various nature wise,
> To fall with dignity, with temper rise;
> Form'd by thy converse, happily to steer
> From grave to gay. . . .
>
> > *(An Essay on Man)*

Pope displays his familiarity too with the Horatian ideas that the wise man learns to provide himself with a balanced mind (*aequus animus*)[65] and that the self, like a poem, must be given the proper shape and measure:

[64] *To a Young Lady, with the Works of Voiture*. I cite the 1712 version. Pope made several changes in the text after 1726.
[65] *Ep.* I.18.112. Cf. *Corr.*, I, 275.

To Rules of Poetry no more confin'd,
I learn to smooth and harmonize my Mind,
Teach ev'ry Thought within its bounds to roll,
And keep the equal Measure of the Soul.[66]

Add to these the satires from the 1730s in which Pope would imitate Bethel (*Imit. Hor. Sat.* ii.ii), his own father (*Epistle to Dr. Arbuthnot*), and Bolingbroke (*Imit. Hor. Ep.* i.i), and one has a series of poems, ranging from Pope's earliest years until the latest part of his life, in which he envisioned a self into which he might be formed or shaped with the help of Heaven, or friends, or his own will.[67]

Especially in the case of Pope—imprisoned within a crazy carcass, a body that could never be shaped into a thing of beauty; endowed with a mind and body that were wretchedly ill-matched and a temperament as variable as April weather—the notion that the self, the mind and soul, might be new shaped, "smoothed" and "harmonized," must have been especially appealing. That recreated self might thus be a perfected version of the original self. Norman Ault speculates that Pope's lifelong aim of literary perfection (to "write well, lastingly well, immortally well," to be a "correct" poet) was in part his attempt to compensate for an imperfect body.[68] We may perhaps extend this principle of compensation and find it at work not only in Pope's literary goals. One senses Pope's consistent need to

---

[66] *Imit. Hor. Ep.* ii.2.202-5. Cf. the Horatian original: "sed verae numerosque modosque ediscere vitae" ("not to search out words that will fit the music of the Latin lyre, but to master the rhythms and measures of a genuine life"). See also Pope's remark about Wycherley: "Our Friend ended much in the Character he had lived in: and Horace's Rule for a Play, may well be apply'd to him as a Playwright" (*Corr.*, 1, 329). Pope then alludes to the *Ars Poetica*, 126-27: "if you care to fashion a new character, have it kept to the end even as it came forth at the first, and have it self-consistent."

[67] One should perhaps include in this list Horace and Montaigne; see below, Chap. 2, n. 38. Reuben Brower has spoken of Pope's entire career as "progressively an Imitatio Horatii": *Alexander Pope: The Poetry of Allusion* (Oxford, 1959), p. 165.

[68] Ault, *New Light on Pope* (London, 1949), p. 6.

recreate himself as the "Pope" of his poems, the Friend of Virtue, the Good Man and Good Poet, a more perfect or "correct" version of the historical Pope.[69]

Correcting the self, like correcting a poem, was for Pope a matter of editing, rearranging, polishing, adjusting, and, in some cases, reinventing. Consider first the rearrangements of the letters. In a few cases Pope's major alterations may be set down as an attempt to conceal or distort some discreditable act. But most of the changes, as George Sherburn notes, are aimed at paring away irrelevancy and incidental carelessness (*Corr.*, I, xv). Many of the early letters to Caryll, a Catholic friend from his private life, are transferred to recipients—Addison and Congreve—who were men in public life. Pope no doubt wished to show the world that he had long been friends with men of distinction. Perhaps because he had no copies of some letters once sent to Addison and other public men, he recreated the lost letters by readdressing to such men letters not unlike those he may originally have sent.[70] This kind of editing might simply produce a closer approximation to the historical fact. Another kind—inventing of letters—might likewise reveal the real. The Pope-Addison letters may perhaps be a wholly invented correspondence.[71] Yet the letters as a group may be designed to present the truth, as Pope understood it, of his quarrel with Addison over the rival versions of the *Iliad*. The letters all date from the period 1713-1714, just before and after Pope's agreement with Lintot to produce an English Homer. In them Pope shows

[69] See W. J. Bate on the classical conception of poetry (derived from Aristotle's emphasis on plot), as opposed to the Romantic, "that poetry should seek less to arouse and give voice to the personal associations and feelings of the observer than to guide them, and to impose upon them a finished ideal": Bate, *From Classic to Romantic* (New York, 1961), pp. 18-19.

[70] Pope, like many active correspondents, not infrequently repeated substantially the same "news" in several letters sent at about the same time. See, for example, *Corr.*, I, 158.

[71] Sherburn has included seven of these in his edition of the *Correspondence*. Five of the seven are proven fabrications (four are drawn from letters to Caryll). The other two are available only in Pope's printings and may well be fabrications or elaborations.

his friendship for Addison and his unreserved trust in Addison's good nature. He appears in undress, revealing his follies and inconsistencies in all artlessness. He tells Addison of his work on the translation. Addison, in return, offers friendship and warm encouragement and wishes for the forthcoming *Iliad*. In a final letter, dated October 1714, Pope sarcastically breaks off the relationship. The series of letters clearly suggests that Addison early gave Pope friendly encouragement, and in effect betrayed his former friend in 1715 by publicly praising Tickell's rival translation. Pope's version of the incident seems substantially true.[72] The invented letters thus served, so it may have seemed to Pope in later years, as supporting evidence for a case he knew to be true but could not demonstrate with authentic evidence.

Invention could do more than present the truth of a historical event. It might also reveal the felt truth of an event which circumstance did not in fact permit to happen.[73] Roy Pascal notes how fictionalized autobiography can often reveal the hidden or unrealized parts of a man's life more effectively than straightforward confession: "Invented situations can reveal potential reality. . . . if the right circumstances are not there, certain characteristics must remain for ever unknown, even unsuspected."[74] On one major occasion Pope took the liberty of rearranging events of his life for the purpose of presenting a public view of his best self. The *Epistle to Dr. Arbuthnot*, published in 1735, closes with the poet at his mother's deathbed. Yet, as Pope's friends knew well, and as Pope himself announced to the world in a footnote, his mother had died in 1733. The poem as we know it in fact consists of a series of fragments composed and published over a period of twenty years "by

[72] See Ault, *New Light on Pope*, Chap. 6.

[73] "What he sought to impose on the world was less an intentionally fictitious portrait than an accurate representation of the man he had always wished to be—the man he knew he might have been in happier circumstances of mind and body": Peter Quennell, *Alexander Pope: The Education of Genius* (New York, 1968), p. 236.

[74] Pascal, *Design and Truth*, pp. 176, 178.

snatches" (Pope's "Advertisement"). In its final form the epistle in 1735 abandons temporal distinctions. Events concern Pope and interest us not because they constitute the temporal sequence of his life, but because they continue to occupy a place in his mind. Addison's petty tyranny (c. 1714), Gay's death (1732), Mrs. Pope's deathbed (1733), and Arbuthnot's approaching death (1735) are all equally present to the poet.

The goal of Pope's rearrangement, composition, and creation of self, as with his careful composition and correction of poems, would appear to have been the propagation of an image that might endure, that might achieve the solidity and the permanence denied to flesh and the evanescent word. I have referred already to Pope's interest in portraits of himself. He succeeded as well as any Englishman of the eighteenth century in preserving the features of his flesh for posterity. To be sure, Pope took care that his "not displeasing" face (Johnson's phrase) should dominate the portrait, and that his small stature and hunchback be discreetly concealed.[75] Of the eighty-one portraits in Wimsatt's catalogue, only three of the nonsatiric images are full-length profiles, and of these, two were surreptitiously drawn.[76] I have noted too Pope's lifelong concern to "fix and preserve a few lasting, dependable friendships" (*Corr.*, III, 138), and his intention that his published letters be a "monument" to friendship. Likewise, his house and garden at Twickenham, hung thickly with portraits of his friends, was indeed "a memorial to friends."[77]

Finally, may one not perhaps see in Pope's labors as his own editor his special concern for self-formation, self-composition, for the perpetuation of a perfect image? At the precocious age of twenty-nine he saw through the press the *Works of Mr. Alexander Pope* (1717), with an engraving of a Jervas portrait as the frontispiece. When the volume

[75] As Joseph Warton noted, "He was too sensible of the Deformity of his Person to allow the Whole of it to be represented": Warton's edition of Pope's *Works* (1797), p. ix, quoted in Wimsatt, *Portraits of Pope*, p. 299.
[76] Wimsatt, *Portraits of Pope*, p. xxiv.   [77] *The Garden and the City*, p. 31.

appeared, he sent it off to Lady Mary in Turkey with the
remark, "You have all I am worth, that is, my Workes"
(*Corr.*, 1, 407). He dealt at first with booksellers, but after
1728 he worked directly with printers, displaying such interest in the procedures of publishing that his bibliog-
rapher has called him "the greatest advertiser and publisher among English poets."[78] In the mid-1730s he took
great pains to ensure the publication of a "correct" edition
of his personal correspondence, when, as Johnson suggests, it was relatively rare to publish personal letters, much
less for a man to publish his own.[79] His *Works* were published again in 1735; but numerous revisions after 1735, as
well as new poems, made him feel the need for a new complete edition. He procured Warburton's services as commentator and editor in the expressed hope that, significantly, both Pope and the poems would be enhanced: "I
have a particular reason to make you Interest yourself in
Me & my writings. It will cause *both them & me* to make a
better figure to Posterity."[80] Even in his last months Pope
was once again composing and arranging his poems, leaving them in proper order: "I *must* make a perfect edition of
my works, and then I shall have nothing to do but die."[81]
He was in effect composing the features of the self-image
he planned to leave for posterity. Indeed, his remark
suggests that his life's goal was nothing more or less than to
leave a "perfect edition."[82] In that perfect edition ("con-

[78] R. H. Griffith, *Alexander Pope: A Bibliography*, 2 vols. (Austin, Tex.,
1922-1927), 1, pt. 2, xli-xlii, xlvi-xlvii (hereafter cited as *Pope Bibliography*).

[79] "Life of Pope," p. 159.

[80] *Corr.*, IV, 428, emphasis added. See a later letter to Warburton: "no
hand can set them in so good a light, or so well turn their best side to the
day, as your own" (ibid., 501). See also ibid., 362.

[81] Pope's emphasis, quoted in Joseph Spence, *Observations, Anecdotes,
and Characters of Books and Men*, ed. James M. Osborn, 2 vols. (Oxford,
1966), 1, 258 (no. 622, Jan. 1744) (hereafter cited as Spence). "My works
are now all well laid out": ibid. (no. 621, Apr. 1742). Pope "corrected and
prepared for the press just before his death" an edition of the *Moral Essays: Poems*, III, pt. 2, xiv.

[82] As it turned out, the "deathbed edition" was suppressed and not published until after Pope's death. See *Poems*, III, pt. 2, xii-xiv.

substantial with its author," as Montaigne would have said)
Pope himself would appear as he wanted to appear: the
Friend of Virtue and her Friends, shorn of all irrelevant,
incidental, or uncharacteristic detail.

Maynard Mack describes Pope's grotto as an artful imitation of nature, as an exemplum of the conviction that " 'nature' is discovered in (and also brought to) her perfection
only by means of art."[83] One may perhaps say the same of
Pope himself: the moral image he offered was an artful imitation. His own nature was brought to its perfection in his
best self.

To take Pope's overt self-description at face value, one
might think the best self to be Pope's true, deepest self. As
Johnson noticed, "of his social qualities, if an estimate be
made from his Letters, and opinion too favourable cannot
easily be formed; they exhibit a perpetual and unclouded
effulgence of general benevolence and particular fondness.
There is nothing but liberality, gratitude, constancy, and
tenderness."[84] Pope's most ardent defenders have tended
to reflect his own self-estimate. But Johnson rightly refused to take the idealized self-image for the whole man, and
no reader now looking for the man in the poems need
feel reluctant or apologetic about exploring other elements
in Pope's imagination. The best self, though a major constituent of Pope's moral and poetic imagination, is not his
only self.

As I have noted, Pope knew well that he often fell short
of his ideal. Although the letters tend to present a moral
paragon, the poems reveal a richer and more various Pope.
By his own admission, Pope can be aggressive and vindictive, can delight in punishing. He can take an amoral delight too in his witty superiority over the dunces of the
world. And when he is not being so consciously autobiographical, other dimensions of Pope's imagination manifest themselves: a delicate aesthetic sensibility, responsive
to textures and polished surfaces; a visionary impulse (still

[83] *The Garden and the City*, p. 60.   [84] "Life of Pope," p. 206.

inadequately recognized by critics) prompting him to prophecy and fantasy; an attraction to disagreeables— pain, excrement, freaks and monsters,[85] even chaos and dulness.[86]

Moral idealism of course remains strong in everything Pope wrote, and the critic needs to pay full attention to the idealized self-image that governs the poems. But he needs to consider as well the tension between the best self and the other elements of Pope's literary personality. As I shall argue, Pope's self, even in his own mind, was not single and clearly defined. From his earliest years Pope conceived of himself in various ways, selected various identities for possible adoption. Some selves he seems to have outgrown; others came into serious conflict with one another. One self-image—the "incoherent" mind—persisted to the end, even after Pope had arrived at a central conception—"To Virtue only, and her Friends, a Friend"—that seems to include and harmonize many, but not all, impulses earlier in conflict.

[85] After visiting a hermaphrodite, Pope wrote: "few proficients have a greater genius for Monsters than my self" (*Corr.*, 1, 277).

[86] In a valuable essay I saw only after completing this book, S. L. Goldberg speaks of "an attraction in Pope towards chaos, disorder, and eccentricity, quite as powerful as that towards order, form, and moral rationality": "Integrity and Life in Pope's Poetry," in *Studies in the Eighteenth Century*, ed. R. F. Brissenden and J. C. Eade (Toronto, 1976), p. 192.

··◌❨2❩◌··

Pope's Selves: A View of
His Literary Personality

To whatever degree Pope may have arrived in his later letters and poems at a clearly defined self-image, it is plain
that such a self was the end product not of a simple and
linear process of maturation, but of a continuing drama.
By "drama" I mean to imply conflict, but not a fully theatrical view of the self.[1] In his early years Pope showed some
interest in the old metaphor of the world's stage—"a true
Modern Life is like a true Modern Play, neither Tragedy,
Comedy, nor Farce, nor one, nor all of these"[2]—but he
generally treats the metaphor facetiously, with an eye for
incongruity and farce. Likewise, a related metaphor and
Stoic commonplace—life as a game to be played as well as
possible—seems to have held little interest for Pope after
his early years.[3] Playing, for him, meant finding and choos-
ing a role that fit.

Wit, Rake, Lover

By temperament an "atmospherical creature," quick to re-

---

[1] For a discussion of theatrical and antitheatrical views of the self, see
two articles by Jonas Barish: "The Antitheatrical Prejudice," *Critical Quarterly*, 8 (1966), 329-48, and "Exhibitionism and Antitheatrical Prejudice,"
ELH, 37 (1969), 1-29. But Pope appears to elude categorization. He is an
exhibitionist, but not (for long) a role player; a man who prizes rectitude,
integrity, sincerity, but also variety and versatility of response.

[2] *Corr.*, I, 71. See also *To a Young Lady, with the Works of Voiture* and *Imit.
Hor. Ep.* II.ii.323-25.

[3] See *Corr.*, I, 42: "Human Life (as Plutarch just now told me, is like a
Game at Tables, where every one may wish for the best Cast; but after all
he is to make his best of that which happens, and go on contentedly." See
also ibid., 147, where this sentence reappears, only slightly modified, in
another letter.

spond to pressures and influences, and determined from an early age to be a poet, the young Pope experimented with a variety of available poetic roles or selves. He began his career by imitating the style of admired poets from the previous age—Waller, Cowley, Rochester, Dorset—models both fashionable and within the reach or range of a talented young poet, and by translating or paraphrasing the works of the English and ancient classics—Chaucer, Ovid, Statius, Homer—models more distant in time and in genius. In later years, as is often pointed out, he followed in the tracks of Virgil and Horace. As his career proceeded in imitation of theirs, it is natural to suppose that Pope thought of himself in their terms and that he kept the pictures of Dryden, Milton, Shakespeare, and others in his chamber, not only to keep him "always humble,"[4] but also to provide pictorial reminders of the poet he was trying to become.[5]

Because this aspect of Pope's conception of himself has been adequately recognized, I turn quickly to other, lesser-known selves that he seems quite consciously to have tried on. As the adolescent Pope looked about for particular models in the first decade of the eighteenth century, he fell between two eras: the witty, rakish Restoration world had not yet been replaced by the more decorous and moral world of the *Tatler* and *Spectator*. It is perhaps not surprising that in the relative isolation of Binfield he found a model in the Restoration stage wit and in the conversation of older men—Walsh, Wycherley, Congreve, Henry Cromwell—who had grown up in and remained a part of the Restoration wit tradition, a tradition of aristocratic detachment, quick repartee, slangy ease, and mildly indecorous jesting. In the early letters one hears a Pope who sounds like any number of stage Dorimants, Sparkishes, or Wouldwits, flinging off strings of epigrams and witty con-

---

[4] *Corr.*, I, 120.

[5] On this aspect of Pope's identity, see John Paul Russo, *Alexander Pope: Tradition and Identity* (Cambridge, Mass., 1972), esp. Chap. I.

ceits,[6] heaping scorn on dull fools,[7] and dabbling in bawd-ry.[8] The pose persists in the 1717 Preface, where Pope affects to describe poetry as "the affair of idle men who write in their closets." Like some gentleman amateur, he "writ because it amused me."[9]

A related role or self is that of the rake: "How gladly wou'd I give all I am worth, that is to say, my *Pastorals* for *one* of their *Maidenheads*" (*Corr.*, I, 137), he writes to Cromwell in 1711. As late as 1715, long after he had begun the Homer translation, Pope still liked to think of himself, playfully no doubt, as a "modern rake": "I sit up till one or two a clock every night over burgundy and champagne, and am become so much a modern rake that I shall be ashamed in a short time to be thought to do any sort of business. I must get the gout by drinking, as above said, purely for a fashionable pretence to sit still long enough to translate four books of Homer" (*Corr.*, I, 289). Pope gave a more finished picture of the rake torn between harlots and Homer in his *Farewell to London, in the Year 1715*:

> Dear, damn'd, distracting Town, farewell!
>   Thy Fools no more I'll teize:
> This Year in Peace, ye Critics, dwell,
>   Ye Harlots, sleep at Ease!
>
> . . . .
>
> Why should I stay? Both Parties rage;
>   My vixen Mistress squalls;

---

[6] *Corr.*, I, 5.

[7] "I find no other difference than this, betwixt the common Town-Wits, and the downright Country Fools; that the first are pertly in the Wrong, with a little more Flourish and Gaiety, and the last neither in the Right nor the Wrong, but confirmed in a stupid, settled Medium betwixt both": *Corr.*, I, 11.

[8] See, for example, the squib on Drury Lane whores sent to Cromwell: "But the well-worn Paths of the Nymphs of Drury / Are large & wide; *Tydcomb* and I assure ye" (*Corr.*, I, 47). Pope continued to dabble in bawdry in light verse. See the *Roman Catholick Version of the First Psalm*, and, of course, *The Rape of the Lock*.

[9] Elsewhere in the Preface Pope abandons this pose; see below, p. 92.

The Wits in Envious Feuds engage;
  And *Homer* (damn him!) calls.
· ·
Still idle, with a busy Air,
  Deep Whimsies to contrive;
The gayest Valetudinaire,
  Most thinking Rake alive.

The witty detachment of the poem suggests what we might suspect on other grounds: the role of rake did not really suit Pope.[10] Neither his health nor his serious attention to Homer permitted it.[11]

Furthermore, Pope's notion of himself as lover seems usually, and especially after 1715, to have taken the more decorous form of humble servitor. The period 1716-1718 encompasses his passionate letters to Lady Mary Wortley Montagu, romantically inaccessible because married and halfway across Europe. During the same period he is writing frequently to the Blount sisters, whom he loves, he says, "sincerely and passionately," signing himself "your most faithfull insignificant humble servant" (*Corr.*, I, 409). He affects a variety of stances: for example, the facetiously indifferent wit ("I know no Two Things I would change you for, . . . except Two good Melons" [*Corr.*, I, 409]) and the warm and easy companion ("I long to see you both; and love you so very well" [*Corr.*, I, 379]). But a favorite one is that of the rejected lover, the "wretched person in the abject condition of lying at a Lady's feet" (*Corr.*, I, 430): "think as well as you are able of one whose imperfections are so manifest, and who thinks so little of himself, as to think ten times more of either of you" (*Corr.*, I, 431).

As with Pope's descriptions of himself as rake, his declarations of devoted, humble love all have about them an air of artifice or affectation. We will probably never know the

[10] Pope later told Spence, " 'Tis vanity which makes the rake at twenty": Spence, I, 238.
[11] See Cibber's witty note on Pope's health in his narrative of the "Tom-Tit" episode: *A Letter from Mr. Cibber to Mr. Pope* (1742), pp. 48-49.

whole story of his relations with Lady Mary and the Blount sisters, and to what extent we should take his letters, with their open declarations and their hints ("The Epistle of Eloise grows warm, and begins to have some Breathings of the Heart in it, which may make posterity think I was in love" [*Corr.*, 1, 338]), as evidence of his authentic feelings. It would appear that at some time around 1720 he left off thinking of himself, or at least describing himself, as a lover. His palinodes at times convey the rough note of independence: "I have some times found myself inclined to be in love with you: and as I have reason to know from your Temper & Conduct how miserably I should be used in that circumstance, it is worth my while to avoid it: It is enough to be Disagreeable, without adding Fool to it, by constant Slavery" (*Corr.*, 1, 456). At other times he ruefully admits that for a man with his "deformities" and "manifest imperfections," the role of lover will not fit.[12] His most polished goodbye to all that may be the *Hymn Written in Windsor Forest*:

> All hail! once pleasing, once inspiring Shade,
>   Scene of my youthful Loves, and happier hours!
> Where the kind Muses met me as I stray'd,
>   And gently pressed my hand, and said, Be Ours!—
> Take all thou e're shalt have, a constant Muse:
>   At Court thou may'st be lik'd, but nothing gain;
> Stocks thou mays't buy and sell, but always lose;
>   And love the brightest eyes, but love in vain![13]

As with the *Farewell to London*, Pope says goodbye not only to a place, but perhaps also to a phase of his life and to a version of self that he now deems to be impossible.[14]

---

[12] Pope occasionally used the word "deformities" in writing to the Blounts. See, for example, *Corr.*, 1, 431.

[13] This poem was written in 1717 and sent in a letter to the Blounts. The letter hints at its close that Pope thinks of them: "I made a Hymn as I past thro' these Groves; it ended with a deep Sigh, which I will not tell you the meaning of" (*Corr.*, 1, 428).

[14] For further discussion of this topic, see Maynard Mack, "Mr. Pope:

Man of Sincerity, Philosopher, "Little Man"

The roles Pope ultimately abandoned—man of wit, rake, lover—seem never to have fitted comfortably. To us, and probably to Pope as well, they appear affected and assumed with some strain. What is more, each is challenged by another role—the man of sincerity, the philosopher, the "little man"—quite incompatible with the first. Even in the midst of florid, witty compliment, Pope pauses to ask for honest, sincere speech: "I must blame you for treating me with so much Compliment, which is at best but the Smoak of Friendship. I neither write, nor converse with you, to gain your Praise but your Affection" (*Corr.*, I, 5). From his earliest years his longing for "sincerity" (a frequent term of value in Pope's letters) never let him rest easy with the kind of artificial wit divorced from authentic speech: "I know no condition so miserable and blind as that of a young fellow who labors under the misfortune of being thought to think himself a wit; he must from that moment expect to hear no more truth than a prince or an emperor."[15]

Pope's delight in playing the rake likewise met regular challenge from the rival conception of himself as philosopher or contemplative. An early reader of the "Moralists," particularly Plutarch and Seneca, he no doubt found in the Stoics "some cold Consolation for the Inconveniences of this life, & the Incertainty of human Affairs" (*Corr.*, I, 66). "I am really a greater philosopher than I have the vanity to describe to you" (*Corr.*, I, 327). Acutely aware that he had, in Wycherley's words, a "great, Vigorous, and active Mind" lodged in a "little, tender, and crazy Carcase" (*Corr.*, I, 55),

---

His Person and His Poems," delivered as the last of four Northcliffe Lectures (May 1972, in London) and as a Clark Library seminar paper (January 1974, Los Angeles), to be published in a forthcoming collection of essays on Pope.

[15] *Corr.*, I, 94. See an early letter to Caryll: "For my part, there are some things I would be thought besides a wit; as a Christian, a friend, a frank companion, and a well natured fellow" (ibid., 155-56). Later, Pope came to think wit ("ingenious Natures," men "distinguished in capacity") compatible with sincerity. See ibid., II, 139.

he no doubt saw himself better suited for mental than for bodily pleasures, for a contemplative rather than an active life: "If I could bring myself to fancy, what I think you do but fancy, that I have any talents for active life, I want health for it; and besides it is a real truth, I have less Inclination (if possible) than Ability. Contemplative life is not only my scene, but it is my habit too" (*Corr.*, I, 454). And yet he is drawn in opposite directions. A few days later he writes: "I am something so much between a Philosopher and a Lover" (*Corr.*, I, 470), that is, one role interferes with the other.[16]

The lover, of course, had to yield to the same disability as the rake. His deformity may have seemed less disabling to him than his stature. Could a "little man" be taken seriously as a sexual creature? For a time Pope perhaps thought so. Upon a lady "who rally'd his person" he gained revenge with a rondeau translated from Voiture:

> You know where you did despise
> (T'other day) my little eyes,
> Little legs, and little thighs,
> And some things of little size,
> > You know where.

> You, 'tis true, have fine black eyes,
> Taper legs, and tempting thighs,
> Yet what more than all we prize
> Is a thing of little size,
> > You know where.[17]

Pope's tactic is to admit the physical deficiency and then compensate for it with a witty thrust. The same tactic appears to operate in Pope's more public, slyly sexualized de-

[16] For an amusing confrontation of philosopher and rake, see Pope's description of a coach ride with a pretty, sick woman (*Corr.*, I, 66-67).

[17] *Corr.*, I, 90. Pope, who describes the poem as revenge for a "total subversion of my Countenance," later omitted it from his published letters, referring simply to "the foolish Rondeau . . . upon my own Littleness." I quote the version given in *Poems*, VI.

scription in the *Guardian* of "The Club of Little Men": "a Sett of us have formed a Society, who are sworn to *Dare to be Short*, and boldly bear out the Dignity of Littleness under the Noses of those Enormous Engrossers of Manhood, those Hyperbolical Monsters of the Species, the tall Fellows that overlook us."[18] Here, as later in his career, Pope sought to extract "ornament" from "inconvenience," to convert the deficiencies of nature into strengths.[19] We may properly sense the same impulse to bold, grandiose self-assertion that characterizes the later poems of a little man who dares to stand up against a world of villainy. But in the description of the club, Pope is primarily facetious and maintains throughout a sense of the ridiculous. The president of the club is the "little Poet," Dick Distick, who dresses in black and "stoops as he walks": "The Figure of the Man is odd enough; he is a lively little Creature, with long Arms and Legs: A Spider is no ill Emblem of him. He has been taken at a Distance for a *small Windmill*."[20] The "little Poet" is no doubt a version of Pope himself, as is the "little hero," the "little politician," and the "little lover" who contracts assignations with tall ladies. Despite the compensatory wit, Pope here and later seems to concede his own ridiculousness as a sexual creature. Writing to Caryll at about the same time, he suggests that he has adopted the same view of himself that tall ladies might: " 'Tis certain the greatest magnifying glasses in the world are a mans own eyes, when they look upon his own person; yet even in those, I appear not the great Alexander Mr Caryll is so civil

[18] *Guardian*, nos. 91-92, in Norman Ault, ed., *The Prose Works of Alexander Pope*, Vol. 1, *The Earlier Works, 1711-1720* (Oxford, 1936), 121-29.

[19] Cf. Johnson's remark on Pope's grotto: "Life of Pope," p. 135. See also Maynard Mack's illuminating extension of the principle to Pope's entire career, in *The Garden and the City*, pp. 61-63.

[20] *Guardian*, no. 92, in Ault, ed., *Prose Works*, I, 125. Cibber may recall this description in his narrative of an episode alleged to have taken place about 1715, when he claimed to have rescued Pope, whom he compares with a Tom-Tit, "a pretty . . . little Creature," from a bout with a whore: "with a finger and a thumb, picked off thy small round Body, by thy long Legs, like a Spider, making Love in a Cobweb . . . a human insect" (*Another Occasional Letter from Mr. Cibber to Mr. Pope* [1744], p. 52).

to, but that little Alexander the women laugh at" (*Corr.*, I, 114). The same witty self-deprecation colors his romantic overtures to women. In proposing to meet Lady Mary, he suggests Lombardy, "the Scene of those celebrated Amours between the fair Princess and her Dwarf."[21] It is perhaps no coincidence that the men in the *Rape of the Lock* (which is contemporary with these letters and with the *Guardian* essays) are strikingly ineffectual and weak creatures, imaged as beaus and witlings, spluttering fools, sylphs (though once a woman, Ariel is apparently now "male"), or reduced by strong, assertive women to the status of monkeys and lap dogs.

Mr. Pope in Greece

The process of trying out potential selves seems to go on quite consciously in Pope's early letters and poems. It may even go on less consciously in an unsuspected place: the translation of Homer. Maynard Mack has conjectured that Pope's "imagination of his life and role at Twickenham" may draw some "nourishment" from the Homeric world of gardens and caves, feasts and vaunts. To illustrate the way Pope and Homer "interpenetrate," he cites Axylus, the hospitable "Friend to Human Race," whose "ever-open Door / Oblig'd the Wealthy, and reliev'd the Poor" (*Iliad* VI.18-19). Homer's lines, so Mack suggests, have been retouched so as to serve in part "as one of those exemplary images which linger in every man's mind of his own ideal identity."[22] But the interpenetration may have been much more general. Absorbed in his ten long years' labor, or, as he put it, his thoughts withdrawn from the present world

---

[21] *Corr.*, I, 365. In another wish-fantasy, Pope recognizes another disability. Writing to Lady Mary, he thinks of India, "where they tell us the Women like best the Ugliest fellows, as the most admirable productions of nature, and look upon Deformities as the Signature of divine Favour" (ibid., I, 364).

[22] *Poems*, Vols. VII and VIII, *The Iliad of Homer*, ed. Maynard Mack et al., VII, ccxxvii.

"to be fully possest and absorpt in the past" (*Corr.*, I, 240),
Pope may have seen in Homer's chief heroes the lineaments of possible lives, or in turn may have described those
heroes so as to reflect his unsettled notions of his own identity. Although Homer's text acted as a natural limit on any
shadowy self-projection, the notes Pope supplied or super-
vised left him more free.[23] In his commentary on the texts,
while he reflects on and contrasts the chief heroes, Pope
seems to separate out for closer analysis the elements that
intertwine themselves in the Homeric warrior and in his
own developing nature. As the young Pope fought his way
through the wit's "warfare on earth," through literary
quarrels, and later through the "war against the dunces"
and the war against Walpole's England, did he perhaps
imagine himself as an epic hero, armed with the strength
of valiant Achilles, pious Hector, or wily Ulysses?

Achilles, so reads Pope's note introducing him, is "compounded of Courage and Anger; one who finds himself
almost invincible, and assumes an uncontroul'd Carriage
upon the Self-Consciousness of his Worth" (*Iliad* 1.155n.).
Constant and violent in friendship, he is also revengeful
and implacable,[24] "obstinate in resentment" (*Iliad* IX.
806n.). He dares to speak his mind regardless of the consequences, or to set himself against a world of enemies. His
highest loyalty is to himself and his own honor. Can we
perhaps hear Achilles in the heroic satirist who refuses
counsel of caution or prudence, insists on speaking out, is
proud to see "men not afraid of God afraid of me?"

Hector, by contrast, is an "accomplish'd Character of
Valour unruffled by Rage and Anger, and uniting his
People by his Prudence and Example" (*Iliad* III.53n.). Al-
though his cause is not as good as Achilles', he is "the most

---

[23] Pope revised "every sheet" of the work done by his collaborators; see
Broome's final note to the *Odyssey* (*Poems*, Vols. IX and X, *The Odyssey of
Homer*, X, 378).

[24] These terms appear in Pope's "Poetical Index" to the *Iliad*, where the
leading attributes of each character are indexed.

amiable" of Homer's heroes. "Love of his Country . . . appears his principal Passion, and the Motive of all his Actions. . . . The Affection he bears to his Parents and Kindred, and his desire of defending them, incites him to do his utmost for their Safety" (*Iliad* III.53n.). Milder than Achilles, less enraged, Hector is pious, "tender to his parents, wife, child, and friends" ("Poetical Index"). We can perhaps find an echo of this figure as well in Pope, the poet whose *pietas* likewise displays itself in love of country, honor to his parents, and a passion for friendship.

Without suggesting that Pope consciously thought of Achilles or Hector as models (there is no evidence that he did), one might speculate that they may have come to represent two contrasting ways of life that Pope himself was considering: man in his individuality, fulfilled through himself alone; and man in his relatedness, fulfilled through family and friends. As Pope pondered the dangers of literary war, Ulysses may have represented a third and more appropriate kind of heroic life. Ulysses is "The Man, for Wisdom's various arts renown'd" (*Odyssey* I.1), "Artful in speech, in action, and in mind," and skilled in "useful craft" (*Odyssey* XIII.334-35). Homer calls him *polytropon*, says Pope, to denote his "prudent dissimulation, which disguised him in so many ways, and put him upon taking so many shapes" (*Odyssey* I.1n.).[25] Because his dissimulation is always combined with prudence, it is not "criminal."[26] Pope's defense of Ulysses denies any taint of low cunning or treachery. Without prudence and "such artifice as is suggested by Wisdom" (*Odyssey* XIII.338n.), his craft "might

[25] This interpretation of *polytropon* is traditional. Indeed, it is taken word for word from Le Bossu, "Of the Characters of Achilles, Ulysses, and Aeneas," *Treatise of the Epick Poem*, trans. "W.J." (1695), Bk. IV, Chap. 9, in *Le Bossu and Voltaire on the Epic*, ed. Stuart Curran (Gainesville, Fla., 1970), p. 193.

[26] "Prudence, with Dissimulation" is his commanding quality, as Pope notes repeatedly: *Poems*, IX, 20, 22, 27, X, 363. Pope views more favorably than Le Bossu Ulysses' deceitfulness. "Dissimulation," says Le Bossu, "is a wrong Method. We bear but little love to a Man we distrust": *Treatise of the Epick Poem*, p. 194.

have degenerated into Wickedness, and Double-dealing."[27]
Where Achilles is reckless and violent in his anger, Ulysses
is "valiant, with caution," "Bold with prudence."[28] He wins
his way not by frontal attack, but by disguise and resourcefulness. While Achilles rages almost mindlessly, Ulysses is
"upon all emergencies master of his passions" (*Odyssey*
XXIV.279n.), *"master of a great presence of mind"* (XIII.338n.).
In his own wars Pope could draw as well on Ulyssean
strengths. Prudence and a love of dissimulation are central
attributes in Johnson's famous analysis of Pope's character.[29] Whether or not he sensed the affinity as he translated
the *Odyssey*, the poet who made such skilled use of equivo-
cation and innuendo, who could appear all things to all
men, who won his way by yielding to the tide, was playing a
Ulyssean role.

If Achilles, Hector, and Ulysses represent attributes that
Pope admired and made use of himself, then Thersites
may embody not his ideals but his worst fears:

> Loquacious, loud, and turbulent of Tongue:
> Aw'd by no Shame, by no Respect controul'd,
> In Scandal busie, in Reproaches bold:
> With witty Malice, studious to defame,
> Scorn all his Joy, and Laughter all his Aim.
> But chief he glory'd with licentious Style
> To lash the Great, the Monarchs to revile.
> His Figure such as might his Soul proclaim;
> One Eye was blinking, and one Leg was lame:
> His Mountain-Shoulders half his Breast o'erspread,

---

[27] Pope, "A general view of the Epic Poem," *Poems*, IX, 22. Again, Pope
follows Le Bossu, who says that the union of prudence with dissimulation
"was necessary for the Goodness of *Ulysses*, for without that his *Dissimulation* might have degenerated into wickedness and knavery": *Treatise of the
Epick Poem*, p. 197.

[28] "Poetical Index." Pope often commented on the contrast between the
two: "*Achilles* has consummate valour, but wants the wisdom of *Ulysses*:
Ulysses has courage, but courage inclining to caution and stratagem, as
much as that of *Achilles* to rashness" (*Odyssey* XVI.70n.).

[29] "Life of Pope." See also below, pp. 270-72.

Thin Hairs bestrew'd his long mis-shapen Head.
Spleen to Mankind his envious Heart possest,
And much he hated All, but most the Best.

(Iliad 11.256-68)

Thersites, so Pope's note reads, is a "pernicious Creature of
Wit," moved by the desire of "promoting Laughter at any
rate" and "Contempt of his Superiors." An "ill-natur'd
Wit," he has gifts of the mind without virtue. Homer's
Thersites is an ugly and disorderly scold, quarrelsome and
vain, who deals in coarse abuse. Pope transforms this low
character into a maliciously witty satirist, whose vaunts are
properly understood as "manifest Strokes of Irony . . . an
infinite deal of Spirit, Humour, and Satyr" *(Iliad* 11.284n.).
Pope must have realized that these attributes of body and
mind would seem to the malicious a candid self-portrait.
Indeed, the passage contains little that was not found in the
printed attacks on Pope that began appearing in 1716. Furthermore, his enemies jumped at the chance to turn Pope's
lines against him. Burnet's *Homerides: Or, A Letter to Mr.
Pope* (1715), an attack on Pope's forthcoming *Iliad*, was
headed by an epigraph from Homer's portrait of Thersites
and originally entitled "The Hump Conference," cruelly
alluding to the deformities of Thersites and Pope.[30] But
one need not be malicious to see the affinity "to our poet."
Gilbert Wakefield notes in commenting upon *Dunciad* 1.6,
"we many well apply his character of Thersites."[31]

These correlations between Pope's character and career
and the character of Homer's warriors must remain conjec-
tural. Pope's interpretation of their characters is, after all,
largely traditional. Their situations and leading attributes
are perhaps generalized enough to be a part of any
reader's real or imagined life.[32] And Pope left no explicit

[30] *Pamphlet Attacks*, pp. 20-21.
[31] Wakefield, *Observations on Pope* (London, 1796), p. 286.
[32] The story of the *Odyssey*, says Pope, is "a series of calamities, which
concern every man, as every man may feel them. We can bring the suffering of *Ulysses* in some degree home to our selves, and make his condition
our own" *(Odyssey* 11.381n.).

declaration of affinity, as he did with Horace and Montaigne. During the protracted labors of translation, any poet might be expected to identify with his chief characters to some extent.[33] Whether the correlation amounts to something more, we cannot say. But the possibility of a deeper interpenetration is an intriguing one. In Homer's poems Pope could find a gallery of every kind of heroism,[34] and self-projection would accord with our sense, based on sounder evidence, that Pope in his early career tried on, in action or at least in imagination, a variety of traditional roles. And we can find Pope, particularly in the latter part of his career, acting or imagining in ways that accord strikingly with the paradigms embodied in Achilles, Hector, and Ulysses. But can one man combine qualities of all three heroes? Pope was ambivalent on the subject: "*Virgil* endeavour'd to form a compleat Heroe in *Aeneas*, by joining in his person the forward Courage of *Achilles* with the wisdom of *Ulysses*, and by this conduct gives us a perfect character" (*Odyssey* xvi.70n.). " 'Tis a meer Chimaera to imagine a Heroe that has the Valour of *Achilles*, the Piety of *Aeneas* and the Prudence of *Ulysses*, at one and the same time. This Vision might happen to an Author" (*Poems*, ix, 21). Only an author like Pope might attempt it—in a poem or in his life. Was the result in his case a perfect whole, or a clash of contraries?

"Incongruous Animal"

As he contemplated himself, the young Pope must have seen contraries. He must have been struck, as is any reader

[33] One might expect Pope to identify with the two poets in the *Odyssey*, Demodocus (Bk. viii) and Phemius (Bk. xxii). But as he remarks, "by these Poets Homer probably means only himself" (*Odyssey* xxii.371n.). Note, however, that like Pope, Phemius, "self-taught," sings "the moral lay" (xxii.383-92).

[34] "In reading Homer, the Odyssey is to be look'd upon as a sequel of the Iliad, and then [the reader] will find in the two Poems the perfection of human nature, Consummate courage join'd with consummate piety" (*Odyssey* xvi.70n.).

of his early correspondence with the variety and often the incongruity of his self-images—man of wit and man of sincerity, lover and "little man," rake and philosopher—images found not uncommonly in the same letter. His self-contradictions are already a matter for detached amusement in the *Farewell to London*, where Pope himself becomes an oxymoron, the "gayest Valetudinaire," the "most thinking Rake alive." He had begun to reflect on his inconsistency long before 1715: "we change our minds as often as [actors] can their Parts, & he who was yesterday Cesar, is to day Sir J. Daw" (*Corr.* I, 71). But about 1713-1714 Pope began to think of himself more frequently as an "incongruous animal":

> You can't wonder my thoughts are scarce consistent, when I tell you how much they are distracted! Every hour of my life, my mind is strangely divided. . . .
>
> Good God! what an Incongruous Animal is Man? how unsettled in his best part, his soul; and how changing and variable in his frame of body? The constancy of the one, shook by every notion, the temperament of the other, affected by every blast of wind. What an April Weather in the mind! In a word, what is Man altogether, but one mighty inconsistency.[35]

The metaphor of variable weather is a favorite one: "No fair day in the fancy is to be neglected, considering what a climate what a right English climate, there is in my head, where few days pass without being clouded, or feverish" (1715, *Corr.*, I, 292). Some years later he wrote to Swift: "If I liv'd in Ireland, I fear the wet climate wou'd indanger more than my life, my humour, and health, I am so Atmospherical a Creature" (*Corr.*, II, 522). The immediate context of each remark is probably the medical one—Pope's weak constitution and his susceptibility to colds—but he implies too that his mind, affected by the body, re-

[35] Pope to Caryll, 1713, but printed in 1735-1742 as to Addison: *Corr.*, I, 185, 185-86.

sponds acutely to the winds and pressures of both inner and outer weather, or simply to the moment: "Whatever I write will be the real Thought of that hour, and I know you'll no more expect it of me to persevere till Death in every Sentiment or notion I now sett down, than you would imagine a man's Face should never change after his picture was once drawn" (1716, *Corr.*, I, 353). He responds like a weathercock to his reading. When in 1717 Atterbury renewed efforts to convert him to the Anglican Church, Pope reported that he had long before read through Anglican-Catholic controversies and "found myself a Papist and a Protestant by turns, according to the last book I read" (*Corr.*, I, 453-54).

Inconstancy can be for Pope a matter of whimsical delight: he can "grow all to all" (*Imit. Hor. Ep.* I.i.32), that is, be all things to all men.[36] But inconstancy or incongruity, both internal—a vigorous mind in a crazy carcass, sharply conflicting impulses—and external—a man at odds with a world that refused him political and religious liberties, and with a literary world that, despite his success and fame, was already in 1715 pestering or attacking him—could also be a matter for distress and even anxiety: "the world and I agree as ill, as my soul and body, my appetites and constitution, my books and business."[37]

Pope's view of himself as a bundle of incongruities, a view which appears with some frequency about 1715,[38]

[36] See *Corr.*, I, 269: "Every one values Mr Pope, but every one for a different reason"—because he is Catholic, broad-minded, grave, whimsical, etc.

[37] *Corr.*, I, 322; see also ibid., 369.

[38] Just as Cibber made satiric use of Pope as spider/little man, so John Dennis, in his *The True Character of Mr. Pope* (1716), made cruel sport with Pope's "contradictions": "a very little but very comprehensive Creature, in whom all Contradictions meet, and all Contrarieties are reconcil'd; when at one and the same time, like the Ancient *Centaurs*, he is a Beast and a Man, a Whig and a Tory, a virulent *Papist* and yet forsooth, a Pillar of the Church of *England*, a Writer at one and the same time, of GUARDIANS and of EXAMINERS, an assertor of Liberty and of the Dispensing Power of Kings; a Rhimester without Judgment or Reason, and a Critick without Common Sense; a Jesuitical Professor of Truth, a base and a foul Pre-

coexists, as we have seen, with several other self-images. But while the other self-images often seem roles tried on, poses assumed with some strain, the inconstant Pope seems less an affectation, more suited to his mind and body. It is a view that, unlike many of the others, lasted into Pope's maturity. Long after he had stopped thinking of himself as rake, wit, or lover, Pope continued to reflect on the incongruity of his body and soul: "my life in thought and imagination is as much superior to my life in action and reality as the best soul can be to the vilest body" (1730, *Corr.*, III, 156). "Were not my own Carcase (very little suited to my Soul) my worst Enemy" (1736, *Corr.*, IV, 15). The inconstant self furthermore became one of Pope's favorite ways of describing himself in the *Horatian Imitations* of the 1730s,[39] where he picks up and reshapes some of the ideas and phrases about himself he was using about 1715: "Papist or Protestant, or both between" (*Imit. Hor. Sat.* II.i.65); "I, who at some times spend, at others spare, / Divided between Carelessness and Care" (*Ep.* II.ii.291-92);[40] "As drives the storm, at any door I knock" (*Ep.* I.i.25); "no Prelate's Lawn with Hair-Shirt lin'd, / Is half so incoherent as my Mind" (*Ep.* I.i.165-66).[41]

---

tender to Candour; a Barbarous Wretch, who is perpetually boasting of Humanity and Good Nature, a lurking way-laying Coward, and a Stabber in the Dark; who is always pretending to Magnanimity, and to sum up all Villains in one, a Traytor-Friend, one who has betrayed all Mankind" (pp. 4-5).

[39] See Chap. 6 below. However well it suited Pope, the inconstant self is no less a *role* than the wit or man of sincerity. Pope would have known discussions of human inconstancy in La Rochefoucauld and La Bruyère, and, most important, in Montaigne's "Of the Inconstancy of our Actions," an essay Pope called "the best of his whole book" (Spence, 1, 142). What made this essay of particular interest to Pope may have been its frankly autobiographical aspect. Pope owned and heavily annotated a copy of Montaigne's *Essays* in Charles Cotton's translation; see Maynard Mack, "Pope's Books: A Biographical Survey with a Finding List," in *English Literature in the Age of Disguise*, ed. Maximillian Novak (Berkeley, 1977), pp. 225, 274-81. An essay has yet to be written on the ways in which Pope may have modeled himself after Montaigne, and on the surprising affinities between the two writers.

[40] On his deathbed Pope again applied these lines to himself: Spence, 1, 266.

[41] The line has an unexpected application to Pope's own manner of

Man or Poet

Even if Pope felt that his basic impulses were out of harmony with one another, temperamental inconstancy could usually be looked on with amusement. But a want of harmony might be more vexing where it concerned a man's deliberate choices and responsibilities. Perhaps the most serious "incongruity" Pope identified and reflected upon was the conflict between the obligations he felt to live a moral life and to serve the muse.

Pope would *appear* to be a particularly clear example of a man who had made poetry his life. He himself speaks of the "unweary'd Mill / That turn'd ten thousand Verses" (*Imit. Hor. Ep.* II.ii.78-79). Mr. Pope, wrote Swift, "hath always some poetical scheme in his head."[42] Johnson's description may serve to summarize the views of many:

> He considered poetry as the business of his life, and, however he might seem to lament his occupation, he followed it with constancy: to make verses was his first labour, and to mend them was his last. From his attention to poetry he was never diverted. . . . He was one of those few whose labour is their pleasure; he was never elevated to negligence, nor wearied to impatience.[43]

Pope's own considered view is somewhat more ambivalent. It is true that from an early age he seems to think of himself as a professional author: "Every day with me is litterally Another To-morrow; for it is exactly the same with Yesterday: It has the same Business, which is Poetry; and the same Pleasure, which is Idleness" (*Corr.*, I, 42). Espe-

---

dressing. Johnson notes that Pope was "extremely sensible of cold, so that he wore a kind of fur doublet under a shirt of very coarse warm linen with fine sleeves": "Life of Pope," p. 197.

[42] Swift, *Correspondence*, ed. Harold Williams, 5 vols. (Oxford, 1963-1965), IV, 484.

[43] "Life of Pope," pp. 217-18. See also Norman Ault, *New Light on Pope* (London, 1949), p. 3, and E. R. Marks, who finds "a picture of a man almost obsessively dedicated to his art, scarcely more able to quit poetry than to quit breathing, and deeply convinced of its supreme importance" ("Pope on Poetry and the Poet," *Criticism*, 12 [1970], 273).

cially during the years when he set himself the daily task of translating Homer, he reflected on the exclusiveness of his task: "I will venture to say, no man ever rose to any degree of perfection in writing, but through obstinacy and an inveterate resolution against the stream of mankind (1714, *Corr.*, I, 239). He can speak amusedly of his absorption in Homer (*Corr.*, I, 240), or complain of his "poetical star" (both inclination and obligation), which fixes him to attend "the gingling of rymes and the measuring of syllables" (*Corr.*, I, 324). He can rail at that "old stale wife, . . . this jade of mine," his Muse, "whom every body think I love, as a Mistress, but whom in reality I hate as a Wife" (*Corr.*, I, 292, 293). But he can also take the metaphor of betrothal more seriously: "To follow Poetry as one ought, one must forget father and mother, and cleave to it alone" (*Corr.*, I, 243). Even after the translating tasks had become "easy," he retains a sense of the sacredness of his calling and of the sacrifices it entails:

> To write well, lastingly well, Immortally well, must one not leave Father and Mother and cleave unto the Muse? Must not one be prepared to endure the reproaches of Men, want and much Fasting, nay Martyrdom in its Cause. 'Tis such a Task as scarce leaves a Man time to be a good Neighbour, an useful friend, nay to plant a Tree, much less to save his Soul. (*Corr.*, II, 227)

This sober consideration, not just of suffering, but of other duties abandoned, should be given greater weight than most critics have granted.[44] It may remind us of the persistent appearance in the letters, especially in the decade or so after 1722,[45] of the claims of the man over against the claims of the poet that amount to more than conventional modesty or self-depreciation:

[44] Indeed, in context Pope's remarks suggest that the task is *not* worth the sacrifice.

[45] But the theme—happiness and virtue versus poetry—is sounded as early as 1713; see *Corr.*, I, 191.

whoever takes me for a Poet, or a Wit (as they call it) takes me for a creature of less value than I am. . . . you shall find me a Much better Man, that is, a much better friend, or at least a much less faulty one, than I am a Poet.

I am already arriv'd to an Age which more awakens my diligence to live Satisfactorily, than to write un-satisfactorily, to my self: more to consult my happi-ness, than my Fame; or (in defect of happiness) my Quiet.

I am very sensible, that my *Poetical* Talent is all that may make me *remember'd*: But it is my *Morality* only that must make me *Beloved*, or *Happy*.[46]

Running through these passages from a decade of letters (1722-1731) is a single theme: the claims of morality versus the claims of art. It seems not unreasonable to suspect that Pope's turn to moral poetry in the 1730s, often attributed to his attempt to polish a reputation tarnished by the *Dun-ciad*, may be in part an attempt to resolve some of the con-flict between his duty to art and his duty to morality. But the *Essay on Man* and the *Moral Essays* did not produce in Pope a lasting *discordia concors*. In the 1730s the conflict of impulses took a slightly different form: the claims of the private life and the claims of a larger world on a figure who came to think of himself as a "public man."

Pope's divided impulses are most clearly expressed in a letter to Caryll explaining the paradox of an "unbusied and independent man" who yet has no time for himself:

a man that will be busy in his friend's concerns, and feels a part in the general concerns of mankind cannot have much leisure. And whosoever is linked by one re-lation, or other of society to half the town, and is (in one sense) a public person, tho' his heart and constitu-tion both require him to be but a private one, such an

[46] *Corr.*, II, 137 (1722), 226 (1724), III, 172 (1731); see also II, 194-95, 274, 339, III, 486, IV, 102, 207.

one, I say, can hardly be an independent. (*Corr.*, III, 402)

Private life is commonly Pope's pleasure, public life a responsibility that he does not always bear without pain: "It is in private Life only that I hope for pleasure; for as to the Public, I see nothing but melancholy Prospects" (*Corr.*, IV, 363). He was not, however, always so despairing about his public role. Regularly swept up in the hurry of "Various business" (*Corr.*, IV, 165), Pope knew plainly that he lived "in the World" (*Corr.*, IV, 166), and no doubt derived pleasure from his tireless activity in the world of publishing. Other public duties probably seemed to him more solemn. Two won him particular praise, and no doubt offered particular gratification: his roles as public moralist and as patriot. In Pope's last years, when he had for the most part turned away from public responsibilities, men like his friend Lyttelton tried to call him back:

> [I] Exhort and Animate You not to bury your excellent Talents in a Philosophical Indolence, but to Employ them, as you have so often done, in the Service of Virtue. The Corruption, and Hardness of the present Age is no Excuse; for your Writings will Last to Ages to come, and may do Good a thousand Years hence, if they can't now; but I believe they wou'd be of great Present Benefit; some sparks of Publick Virtue are yet Alive, which such a Spirit as Your's might blow into a flame, among the Young men especially; and even granting an impossibility of Reforming the Publick, your Writings may be of Use to private Society. (*Corr.*, IV, 369)

But these roles were not simply assigned to Pope by his admirers. He himself had adopted them and had been performing them on a public stage for a decade.

In the early 1730s, for example, he presents himself in letters and poems as a kind of secular priest. He hopes, so he writes Caryll, "to contribute to some honest and moral purposes in writing on human life and manners, not exclusive of religious regards" (*Corr.*, III, 155). Several years later, after the publication of the *Epistle to Bathurst*, he again writes in this role: "I have some title to *sermons*. . . . I find the last I made had some good effect, and yet the preacher less railed at than usually those are who will be declaiming against popular or national vices."[47]

In later years, as Pope's politics were temporarily revived by Lyttelton and the "Boy Patriots" and by the letters and friendship of the Earl of Marchmont, he laid particular stress on his love of country, even though he knew little would come of it. In writing to Marchmont in 1740, for example, he quotes with pleasure a letter from Bolingbroke: "He [Marchmont], and you [Pope], & I, are, by different causes, in much the same situation; Lovers of our Country, grieved at her present state, & unable to help her." Pope then goes on: "I am so elevated in my own opinion by his adding me to the Triumvirate, that I am the better in my Heart for it, tho no way else. I feel an ardent desire to be worthy to be join'd to you, tho but an impotent Wish, nor any ability, to do good" (*Corr.*, IV, 272-73). The helplessness or "inability to do good" may only have heightened the purity and intensity of his patriotism into a passion for a lost cause. In September 1740 Pope set over the entrance to his grotto an inscription which emphasizes his conception of himself as a beleaguered patriot exiled within his own country. The passing traveler is bid to approach

Where, nobly-pensive, ST. JOHN sate and thought;
Where *British* Sighs from dying WYNDHAM stole,

[47] *Corr.*, III, 345. Cf. the letter contrasting Swift the "Satyrist," whose satires are called "Libels," and Pope the "Philosopher," whose satires are called "Epistles" consisting "more of morality than wit" (ibid., 366). Earl Wasserman notes that "during the years given to composing the *Essay on Man* and 'Bathurst,' Pope frequently thought of himself as a kind of lay theologian": Wasserman, *Pope's Epistle to Bathurst* (Baltimore, 1960), p. 13.

And the bright Flame was shot thro' MARCHMONT's Soul.
Let such, such only, tread this sacred Floor,
Who dare to love their Country, and be poor.[48]

Here, as not uncommonly in Pope's life (though the verse
is uncommonly flat and lifeless), the public self partially resolves (though here perhaps is forced) into a private one.
The patriot withdraws into a small circle of like-minded
friends, to keep alive as best he can the "Sacred Fires" of
political virtue.[49] Pope's intention is perhaps clear enough,
but he leaves the unsatisfactory impression (quite apart
from the inaptness of "poor") of a private scene in which
have been deposited political figures, still caught, almost
like statues, in public rhetorical poses. Contrast the fine
imagined vitality of the turn, in the epistle to Fortescue,
from the world's din to the grotto's peace, where the same
public characters, "Chiefs, out of War, and Statesmen, out
of Place," indulge innocently in the "Feast of Reason, and
the Flow of Soul."

Friend of Virtue

Whether or not Pope ever resolved to his own satisfaction
the conflict between man and poet, between lover of pri-
vacy and public man, we can perhaps never say. We should
hesitate to pronounce that he achieved a personal *discordia
concors* to mirror one of the favorite themes of his poetry.
Yet in some respects Pope may have achieved a measure of
self-integration. We can find suggestions in letters and in
poems that he at times found ways to unite conflicting impulses and responsibilities, not so much by constructing a
discordia concors as by adjusting one responsibility into
another, by reinterpreting a public duty into a private one,
as we have seen him seem to do in the "Verses" on the

[48] *Verses on a Grotto*, first enclosed in a letter in 1740 (*Corr.*, IV, 262) and
published in 1741 in the form I quote (*Poems*, VI, 383).
[49] The phrase comes from one of Lyttelton's letters (1738) praising the
efforts of Pope "and other Honest Men" to encourage a "Love of the Publick" in the Prince of Wales (*Corr.*, IV, 138).

shadowy cave. In most of the conflicts I have described—
morality versus poetry, service to self versus service to
others, private versus public man—there are suggestions
that this adjusting process is at work.[50]

The man-poet problem, as I have speculated may have
been in part resolved by Pope's turning to a more moral
poetry in the 1730s. It is perhaps not surprising to find him
writing to Caryll in 1733 about a poetic godson: "I would
rather see him a good man than a good poet; and yet a
good poet is no small thing, and (I believe) no small earnest
of his being a good man" (*Corr.*, III, 340). So too in the
exactly contemporaneous letter to Gay, Pope has "nothing
so much at heart, as to shew the silly world that men of Wit,
or even Poets, may be the most moral of mankind."[51] We
may trace more easily in the letters the tendency of self-
love to become social love, or rather, the interpretation of
self such that it *includes* a wider circle. Pope thought of
friendship as a virtual community of interest: "How entirely my own heart makes all your interests mine; and how
sensible a stroke to it everything must be, which affects
your quiet, or happiness in any kind" (*Corr.*, I, 323). As
early as 1713 he writes to Caryll: "I never return so much
into my self, as when I think of you, whose friendship is
one of the best comforts I have for the insignificancy of my
self" (*Corr.*, I, 186). The sole self, somehow "insignificant"
in its isolation, is strengthened and enlarged as friends are
brought into its being, as the "tottering Column" of the self
becomes a part of a larger "Fabrick of Friendship" (*Corr.*,

[50] He thereby arrived at a conception of self which bears some affinities
with the "perceiving active being" of Berkeley and Reid (see above, p.
60): it is fixed, permanent, and a moral agent.

[51] *Corr.*, III, 347. See also ibid., II, 138-39, where Pope states his
"maxime" that "the most Ingenious Natures" are "the most Sincere," "the
most distinguishd in Capacity, the most distinguishd in Morality." Similarly, in the 1717 Preface Pope suggests that "good writer" and "good
man" need not be in opposition. The idea that to be a good poet is to be a
good man—an idea Pope struggles to affirm—is a classical one; see S. H.
Butcher, *Aristotle's Theory of Poetry and Fine Art* (London, 1898), pp. 200-
202.

II, 253). It is perhaps a commonplace that one "lives in one's friends," or that our friends "live in us," but for Pope, chronic illness and (especially in the 1730s) the death of friends gives that commonplace new life: "I wish your health confirmed. Mine I fear never will be better; but if I cannot live long in myself, I would in my friends" (*Corr.*, II, 432). Let us preserve the memory of a dead friend, he writes, "by recollecting what his behaviour would have been, in every incident of our lives to come, and doing in each just as we think he would have done: so we shall have him always before our eyes, and in our minds, and (what is more) in our lives and manners." The letter closes, "faithfully at your service while I continue to love his memory," that is, he adds, "while I continue to be my self" (*Corr.*, II, 376). "I am so far of your Opinion that life is good for nothing otherwise than for the love we have to our Friends," Swift wrote to Pope, "that I think the easiest way of dying is so to Contrive Matters as not to have one Friend left in the World" (*Corr.*, II, 407).

Indeed, the death of friends affected Pope deeply.[52] At Congreve's death he wrote to Gay: "Every year carries away something dear with it, till we outlive all tenderness, and become wretched Individuals again as we begun" (*Corr.*, III, 3). Just as the self escapes individuality through friends, so it returns to that cursed state, losing part of *itself* with the death of each friend. At the death of Gay, Pope laments: "Good God! how often are we to die before we go quite off this stage? in every friend we lose a part of ourselves, and the best part. God keep those we have left! few are worth praying for, and one's self the least of all" (*Corr.*, III, 335). When at last he came to write "Years foll'wing

[52] "Nothing, says *Seneca*, is so melancholy a circumstance in human Life, or so soon reconciles us to the thought of our own death, as the reflection and prospect of one Friend after another dropping round us!": *Corr.*, II, 253. In his review of Sherburn's edition of the *Correspondence* (*Philological Quarterly*, 36 [1957], 398-99), Maynard Mack cites and comments briefly on three of the letters I quote on the death of friends (*Corr.*, II, 253, III, 3, 355).

Years, take something ev'ry day, / At last they steal us from our selves away" (*Imit. Hor. Ep.* II.ii.72-73), Pope had so internalized friends that they are included in his self.[53] For Pope, attention to self, one's highest duty, then readily included attention to friends. The narrowest sphere of loyalty thus merges insensibly with the next largest.[54]

At times, the widest spheres of Pope's concerns—love of country, service to virtue—may well have merged with the sphere of his enlarged self. Public virtue, he suggested, depended on the private: "I much better understand the Duties of Friendship & the Merits of Virtue in Private life, than those of Public: and should never love my Country if I did not love the Best Men in it" (*Corr.*, IV, 339). Put more succinctly, "the way to have a Publick Spirit, is first to have a Private one."[55] And as we have seen, love of country in turn sometimes resolved into a love of the "Best Men." So too, love of Virtue found its concrete embodiment for Pope in love of virtuous men. The friendships he sought most were those with men of merit. "The obtaining the love of valuable men," he told Swift, "is the happiest end I know of this life" (*Corr.*, II, 481). He does not regret that the unwarranted publication of his letters in 1736 "hath at least done him this service, to show he has constantly enjoy'd the friendship of worthy men" (*Corr.*, I, xxxviii). With increasing frequency in his last years, Pope declares such

[53] Losses of self lamented in the poem are not limited to friends. Pope names "Amusements," "a Mistress," "a Friend," and, most serious of all, "my Rhyme." See a 1736 letter, where friends are only part of the self: "Not our friends only, but so much of our selves is gone by the mere flux and course of years, that were the same Friends to be restored to us, we could not be restored to ourselves, to enjoy them" (*Corr.*, IV, 50).

[54] Pope seems to have associated "mending his soul" and friendship from an early age: "Friendship here is an emanation from the same source as Beatitude there [in the next world]: the same benevolence and grateful disposition that qualifies us for the one, if extended farther, makes us partakers of the other. The utmost point of my desires in my present state terminates in the society and good-will of worthy men, which I look upon as no ill earnest and fore-taste of the society and alliance of happy souls hereafter" (*Corr.*, I, 213). See also ibid., I, 236.

[55] *Corr.*, II, 333; see also I, 357.

friendships his highest goal. His first principles, he says, are "a General Benevolence, & fix'd Friendships wherever I have had the luck to know any honest or meritorious Men" (*Corr.*, IV, 208). He has "no other, or no equal merit to that of loving & pursuing Merit, in, & thro' others" (*Corr.*, IV, 250). Likewise, he himself as poet "has no other Merit than that of aiming by his Moral Strokes to merit some Regard from such men as advance Truth & Virtue in a more Effectual way."[56] Virtue and friends come then to be defined in terms of one another: "The friendship and society of good men does not only make us happier, but it makes us better" (*Corr.*, II, 375). The most concise and memorable expression of this view is, of course, a line translated from Horace in 1733: "TO VIRTUE ONLY and HER FRIENDS, A FRIEND" (*Imit. Hor. Sat.* II.i.121). It is significant perhaps that in Pope's version, *aequus virtuti* (*aequus* = "fair," "just," "kind") becomes the more active and impassioned "*Friend* to Virtue." If the role of Virtue's friend was first learned from Horace, it was recreated by Pope in his poems and letters for the next decade. If it was a public self, it was also a private self. On his deathbed Pope gave moving testimony to that image of himself. After receiving the last rites he was heard to utter, "There is nothing that is meritorious, but Virtue, & Friendship, and Friendship indeed is only a part of Virtue" (*Corr.*, IV, 526).

In this light, Pope's sending presentation copies of the deathbed edition of the *Moral Essays* to a group of friends, one of his last public acts, is the perfect close to such a life. Pope's own view of it shows how his self, his friends, and his love of virtue were as one: "I am like Socrates, distributing my Morality among my friends, just as I am dying" (*Corr.*, IV, 525). An enemy once had written of him: "You make a great ado with your *Virtue only*, and your *Uni aequus virtuti atque ejus amicis*. . . . I have sometimes thought, that you put *Virtue* for *Self*, and that *Virtue only* is *Self only*; and

[56] *Corr.*, IV, 370. Cf. his comfort "that good men have not been ashamed of me": ibid., IV, 364.

that *Uni aequus virtuti atque ejus amicis*, means only, *Uni mihi aequus, & mihi amicis*; To my self only and my Friends a Friend."[57] One can almost imagine Pope assenting to the adaptation. For him, a proper love of himself, of his friends, of his country, of Virtue itself, were different terms for the same thing.

A reading of Pope's poems and letters suggests that there may have been moments of complete integration, when conflicting impulses seemed in harmony, when he seemed to have become his "best self." There is little reason to doubt that, especially in his last years, Pope believed in this image. In Johnson's terms, he sallied out in the colors of the present moment. But an impartial reader may continue to see conflict. Pope's love of quiet and obscurity on the one hand, and his eager desire for literary fame on the other, remained to a great extent irreconcilable.[58] Even at the end of his life Pope seemed to want to enjoy undisturbed the fruits of a private life, and yet to speak his mind to the world.[59] A man who prized moderation, Pope was himself often flagrantly immoderate in his behavior as a man and as a poet.[60] And though he delighted to find and celebrate instances of *discordia concors*, Pope could also smile at the "incoherence" of his own mind. Furthermore, it appears that in some respects the incoherent self must be at odds with the best self. For, to use the terms of contemporary philosophers of personal identity, an unstable self

[57] *A Letter to Mr. Pope, Occasioned by Sober Advice from Horace* (1735), p. 12.

[58] On Pope's ambivalence toward fame, see Donald Fraser, "Pope and the Idea of Fame," in *Alexander Pope, Writers and Their Background*, ed. Peter Dixon (Athens, Ohio, 1972), pp. 286-310. See also Chaps. 3 and 5 below.

[59] As Cibber put it, "You seem in your *Dunciad* to have been angry at the rain for wetting you, why then would you go into it? You could not but know, that an Author, when he publishes a Work, exposes himself to all Weathers": *A Letter from Mr. Cibber to Mr. Pope* (1742), p. 13.

[60] Although Pope spoke more than once of moderation—"In Moderation placing all my glory" (*Imit. Hor. Ep.* 1.i.33)—even the most sympathetic critic may doubt that Pope was a moderate man. Johnson's Pope was a man of "so little moderation": "Life of Pope," p. 215.

cannot be the basis of a moral system.[61] Although Pope
seems to insist that his instability is an attribute of temperament rather than of moral imagination, one may question
whether Montaignian inconstancy and single-minded service to virtue can harmonize. Psychologically speaking, a
rigid personality—uncompromising, assertive, proud of
his conscious rectitude as aspiring idealist—coexists in him
with a fluid one—flexible, yielding, modest, amused at his
inconsistency, aware of limits. The former perhaps receives its fullest expression in the late *Epilogue to the Satires*
(1738), as Pope hardened in opposition to what he per-
ceived as political and cultural decay, but it is also present
throughout the poems of the 1730s. The latter is likewise
evident throughout Pope's career, even as late as the *Epistle
to Bolingbroke* (1737), though it finds an outlet most prominently in the early 1730s, in the *Epistle to Fortescue* (1733)
and the *Moral Essays* (1731-1735). Pope's wry amusement at
human inconsistency (his own included) was never so
strong as in the *Epistle to Cobham*:

> Our depths who fathoms, or our shallows finds,
> Quick whirls, and shifting eddies, of our minds?
> . . . .
> A bird of passage! gone as soon as found,
> Now in the Moon perhaps, now under ground.[62]
>
> (29-30, 156-57)

---

[61] In response to this problem, philosophers posited an innate moral
sense, or an intuited permanent self as moral agent. Cf. Shaftesbury,
Characteristics, II, 105, 276; Hume, *Enquiry Concerning Human Understanding* (1748), ed. L. A. Selby-Bigge (Oxford, 1941), p. 98; and Reid, *Essays on
the Intellectual Powers of Man*, ed. A. D. Woozley (London, 1941), pp. 214-
15.
[62] The best account of Pope's attitude toward human inconstancy in the
first and second *Moral Essays* is Benjamin Boyce's *The Character Sketches in
Pope's Poems* (Chapel Hill, N.C., 1962). A more recent account, Thomas A.
Stumpf's "Pope's *To Cobham, To a Lady*, and the Traditions of Inconstancy," *Studies in Philology*, 67 (1970), 339-58, adduces a tradition in
which inconstancy is viewed with "serious condemnation," but exagger-

And his celebration of the flexible personality, "with the best kind of contrarieties," reaches a peak in the famous portrait of Patty Blount at the end of the *Epistle to a Lady*:

> Heav'n, when it strives to polish all it can
> Its last best work, but forms a softer Man;
> Picks from each sex, to make its Fav'rite blest,
> Your love of Pleasure, our desire of Rest,
> Blends, in exception to all gen'ral rules,
> Your Taste of Follies, with our Scorn of Fools,
> Reserve with Frankness, Art with Truth ally'd,
> Courage with Softness, Modesty with Pride,
> Fix'd Principles, with Fancy ever new;
> Shakes all together, and produces—You.
>
> (271-80)

Could this not in fact be another idealized, oblique self-portrait by a poet who valued pleasure and fancy, even tenderness and an appreciation of folly?

From another angle, Pope's literary personality embraces two competing principles. One might be called Achilles. It is amoral, vengeful, driven to aggressive self-assertion; it appears most clearly in the *Dunciad* and less prominently in other poems. The other might be called Hector. It is moral, loving, moved to virtue and friendship; it appears, for example, in the Aeneas-like role Pope sometimes assumes in the Horatian poems. To what extent, in Pope's own mind, self-love and social love were really the same, or the Friend of Virtue consonant with the aggressive and abrasive wit, is perhaps impossible to say. But the reader of the *Horatian Imitations* and the *Dunciad* finds what seem almost like two different Popes. What we can say is that Pope made poetry out of the moments of integration and the moments of chaos or inconsistency. Indeed, his

---

ates Pope's disapproval. The range of Pope's feeling runs from delight to pained perplexity.

poetry often seems a dramatization of the conflict between harmony and inconstancy, between love of virtue and contempt of vice or dulness. If we approach Pope's poems from a study of his self, using that self as a lens, we may shed no new light, but we might discover that the available light, newly refracted, sets in new order a variety of familiar landmarks in Pope's poetic landscape.

···❦│II│❧···

STUDIES IN POPE'S POEMS

·•❧|3|❧•·
"Candidate for Praise": The 1717 Volume

Although Pope did not begin to take himself for an explicit subject until the *Horatian Imitations* of the 1730s, he figures as a significant presence in his poems from the beginning of his career. In the major poems of the 1717 volume—the *Pastorals, Windsor Forest*, the *Essay on Criticism, The Temple of Fame*, and *The Rape of the Lock*—we hear the voice of a poet we can recognize as the "early Pope" and can distinguish it from that of the later poems. What are the qualities of this voice? In the 1730s Pope looked back on the 1717 *Works* as a kind of poetry he claimed to have outgrown: "Soft were my numbers, who could take offence / When pure description held the place of Sense? . . . not in Fancy's maze he wander'd long, / But stoop'd to Truth, and moraliz'd his song" (*Epistle to Dr. Arbuthnot*, 147-48, 340-41). Pope here points to subject matter as one difference between his early and later styles; genre is perhaps another (descriptive poetry versus moral essay and satire). But equally important is the poet's attitude toward his material: "pure" descriptive poet versus man of sense, leisurely wanderer versus purposive hunter. We can recognize the difference between early and late Pope in the accents of the speaker's voice as well, the difference between

My humble Muse, in unambitious Strains
Paints the green Forests and the flow'ry Plains. . . .
Enough for me, that to the listning Swains
First in these Fields I sung the Sylvan Strains.
                    (*Windsor Forest*, 427-28, 433-34)

> This verse to *Caryll*, Muse! is due;
> This, ev'n *Belinda* may vouchsafe to view:
> Slight is the Subject, but not so the Praise,
> If She inspire, and He approve my Lays.
>
> > (*Rape of the Lock*, I, 3-6)

and

> Yes, I am proud, I must be proud to see
> Men not afraid of God afraid of me.
>
> > (*Epilogue to the Satires*, II, 208-9)

> Shut, shut the door; good *John*, fatigu'd I said,
> Tye up the knocker, say I'm sick, I'm dead.
>
> > (*Epistle to Dr. Arbuthnot*, 1-2)

The differences are clear: humble muse and proud satirist; yielding, "unambitious" retirement and assertive, heroic defiance. But the key difference may be that Pope is present in the early poems only as *poet*, the man who made the verse. In the later poems, on the other hand, the first-person voice is that of a poet who thinks of himself more widely as a public person with a personality, a history, a home territory, a circle of friends, and known political and social interests and connections. Self-reference in the early major poems is governed by general reticence and is limited to Pope's sense of his own capacities and limitations as poet, of the power of art to confer immortality on poet or subject, of the dangers of a writer's life, and of the costs of fame.

Although the range of self-reference is restricted, the poems nonetheless express important elements of Pope's literary personality. Among the contradictory qualities Pope displayed in the early part of his career were on the one hand a brisk self-assurance, and on the other a hesitant diffidence about his abilities and future as a poet. Thus the young Pope carried on a jaunty literary correspondence with men of reputation who were three times his age, and he boldly laid down a series of rules governing versification. But the same Pope trembled at the hostile reception the critics might give his as yet unpublished poems, and he remained acutely sensitive to criticism all his life. This paradox of self-confidence and doubt is clearly present in the early poems. They are manifestly successful and clearly demonstrate Pope's apparently effortless mastery of the neoclassical genres—pastoral, georgic, verse essay, mock-epic, heroical epistle—as well as his confident authority in discussing wit or criticism or the coquette's follies. Nonetheless, Pope's voice, when he pauses to reflect on his work, is sometimes diffident, modest, and self-deprecatory.

If the diffidence was sometimes genuine, Pope may occasionally have chosen to affect a "seeming Diffidence" (*Essay on Criticism*, 567) for reasons of prudence. Here too a deep strain in his personality is being expressed. A calculating and cautious strategist throughout his career, Pope may already in the early poems have developed an instinct for what Johnson, writing primarily about Pope's careful composition and uniform versification, called "poetical prudence": "he wrote in such a manner as might expose him to few hazards."[1] Among the prudential devices of his later career was innuendo, allowing him to hint and imply but affording grounds for plausible denial. In his early career a major self-protective device may have been an affected diffidence. As with many features of Pope's public image, we cannot easily distinguish between fact and artifice, between genuine and "seeming Diffidence." If, as Johnson notes, continued affectation may become habit, Pope himself may not have been able to distinguish.

Diffidence and humility predominate in Pope's first major poem, the *Pastorals* (1709). If the *Pastorals* have "any merit," noted Pope at the end of the prefatory Discourse, "it is to be attributed to some good old Authors, whose works as I had leisure to study, so I hope I have not wanted care to imitate." In the opening lines of his four poems Pope further acknowledges his debt by transparently imitating the openings of the eclogues of Virgil, Spenser, and

[1] "Life of Pope," p. 219.

Theocritus.[2] At the outset then, Pope modestly avows that he simply follows in the steps of his masters. He carves out no independent territory, has no poetic identity apart from his predecessors. We are reminded that Pope began his poetic career with juvenile imitations, translations, and paraphrases of classic and earlier English writers. But imitation, though it acknowledges the greatness of predecessors, was in Pope's age to some extent an imperative ("All that is left us is to recommend our productions by the imitation of the Ancients" [1717 Preface]), a recognized and respectable kind of poetry, and an opportunity to match or perhaps outdo the classics on their own ground. But a pastoral humility is largely preserved and emphasized in the body of the poems. In *Spring, Summer*, and *Autumn* he juxtaposes himself with his dedicatee, in each case a man represented as eminent in letters. Sir William Trumbull, in *Spring*, has retired from his post in the great world. A good and wise man, and once a great man, he deigns to return to the poetic shades of Windsor Forest, where Pope awaits him:

> O let my Muse her slender Reed inspire,
> 'Till in your Native Shades You tune the Lyre:
> So when the Nightingale to Rest removes,
> The Thrush may chant to the forsaken Groves,
> But, charm'd to Silence, listens while She sings,
> And all th' Aerial Audience clap their Wings.
>
> (11-16)

The apparent compliment to Trumbull requires that Pope be the thrush who will sing his "Sylvan Strains" in solitude and yield to the superior beauty of the much-applauded nightingale. In *Summer* Pope is Alexis, a modest "Shepherd's Boy" who "seeks no better Name"; his poems are but "early lays." The poem is dedicated to Dr. Samuel Garth, an established and successful author, deserving now

---

[2] In a note first added in 1736 Pope pointed out that his openings are "manifestly imitations."

of the critic's "ivy" (for acting as Pope's critic) as well as the poet's "Bays." But Alexis makes an implicit claim to merit too. His poetic father is Spenser:

> That Flute is mine which *Colin*'s tuneful Breath
> Inspir'd when living, and bequeath'd in Death;
> He said; *Alexis*, take this Pipe. . . .

$$(39\text{-}41)$$

Such descent both intimidates and ennobles. And in "Autumn" Pope contrasts his own "Rural Lays" with the celebrated comedies of Wycherley, praised for his sense, humor, judgment, and spirit. The lavish praise seems to set Wycherley above Pope, but it may imply that such a judge "skill'd in Nature" is required to estimate Pope's skill in representing the "Hearts of Swains."

These slight hints of nascent poetic mastery were all that Pope permitted himself at the first publication of the *Pastorals* in 1709, and even at their reprinting in 1717. But beginning with the 1736 collected edition, Pope looked back on the *Pastorals* with poetic assurance. In the new headnote to the poems Pope proudly cites the testimony of Walsh and Granville that he need not blush to be set beside Virgil:

> The Author seems to have a particular genius for this kind of Poetry, and a judgment that much exceeds his years. He has taken very freely from the Ancients. But what he has mixed of his own with theirs is no way inferior to what he has taken from them. It is not flattery at all to say that Virgil had written nothing so good at his Age. . . . if he goes on as he has begun in the Pastoral way, as Virgil first tried his strength, we may hope to see English poetry vie with the Roman.

The notice (and reminder) that the poems were written at age sixteen acts as a plea both for lenient judgment (these tepid things are but juvenilia) and greater admiration (these fine things were written by a mere boy). We are clearly encouraged to read the poems as highly contrived performances by a poet who quite consciously limited himself to certain effects. "The reason for his laboring them into so much softness," says Pope in the headnote, "was, doubtless, that this sort of poetry derives almost its whole beauty from a natural ease of thought and smoothness of verse; whereas that of most other kinds consists in the Strength and fulness of both." Not unwilling to boast, Pope adds that the "several Niceties of Versification" have perhaps "never been strictly observ'd in any English poem, except in these Pastorals." We are invited to read the poems—and so in fact they have been read—as virtuoso displays of a poet who could have done more if he had chosen. Some of this retrospective assurance, however, may possibly be discerned in the poems as first published, though it is carefully contained in a conventionally modest voice. "First in these Fields I try the Sylvan Strains, / Nor blush to sport on Windsor's blissful Plains." Thus the *Pastorals* begin, implying that they are only Pope's *first* step, that many others will follow. Quite conscious of what he is doing, he is not embarrassed to write in a humble genre. Likewise, at the close, Pope takes a poet's leave of his chosen ground:

Adieu ye *Vales*, ye *Mountains, Streams*, and *Groves*,
Adieu ye Shepherd's rural *Lays* and *Loves*,
Adieu my Flocks, farewell ye *Sylvan* Crew,
Daphne farewell, and all the World adieu!

Thyrsis concludes his song, and Pope concludes the sequence. We do not need his 1736 note to see that "these four last lines allude to the several Subjects of the four Pastorals, and to the several Scenes of them." Behind Thyrsis we hear perhaps the young, sophisticated, self-limiting poet, whose restraint intimates great reserves of maturing strength. Having demonstrated his skill in pastoral, he bids it a master's farewell.

Windsor Forest (1713) more clearly presents an apparently similar case: pastoral humility signals the confidence of the role player who could do more if he would. But Pope's consistent refusal of poetic loftiness might be an instance of "poetical prudence," whereby he writes in a manner "as might expose him to few hazards." The poem strains at the bounds of rural-descriptive verse to encompass prophecy of England's future greatness and celebration of Windsor's royal heroes. But the poet himself, curiously enough, shrinks from such grandeur and seeks retirement, "silent Shade," and "sequester'd Scenes." The generous decorum of the georgic kind, which binds mundane local description to national myth, is not enough to explain the poem's bifurcation. It would seem that Pope set out in 1704 to write a retirement poem and that he was half-reluctant to expand it in 1713 to include epic matter.

The 1704 portion (lines 1-290) in itself forms a coherent and nearly concluded poem. The poem, Pope says, is "invited" by Windsor's "forests" and "green Retreats" and "commanded" by the poet-statesman Granville. The humble pastoral singer, with an eye on Milton's description of the "Groves of Eden," obeys this double appeal and begins a celebration of the groves of Windsor. The allusion to Milton suggests both high ambition and humble hopes ("were my Breast inspir'd with equal Flame"), but it is noteworthy that Pope alludes not to the epic but to the pastoral parts of *Paradise Lost*. The poem then proceeds to a formal description of the forest's "order in variety" (lines 11-42), a historical survey of Windsor's Norman past (lines 43-92), an animated account of hunting scenes in the present (lines 93-164), and a mythological narrative of the metamorphosis of Lodona into a local stream (lines 165-218). For the most part, Pope restricts his gaze to the topography before him, as it was in the past, present, and in myth. Only occasionally does he widen his gaze to include a larger political order ruled by a benevolent queen:

Thy Forests, *Windsor*! and thy Green Retreats,
At once the Monarch's and the Muse's Seats.

(1-2)

Peace and Plenty tell, a STUART reigns.

(42)

Nor envy *Windsor*! since thy Shades have seen
As bright a Goddess, and as chast a Queen;
Whose Care, like [Diana's] protects the Sylvan Reign,
The Earth's fair Light, and Empress of the Main.[3]

(161-64)

After the Lodona passage, however, Pope is drawn toward that larger view. He turns from Lodona to address the Thames, "great Father of the British Floods." On its shores stand the "lofty Woods," the "tow'ring Oaks"—symbols of England's royal greatness and timber for her "future Navies." He glimpses the importance of the Thames to the commercial nation: "Not *Neptune*'s self from all his Streams receives / A wealthier Tribute, than to thine he gives. / No seas so rich, so gay no Banks appear." And he is led upstream to a vision of Windsor Castle ("the Mansion of our earthly Gods"), the Queen, and the "bright Beauties" of her court.

The next paragraph begins, "Happy the Man whom this bright Court approves, / His Sov'reign favours, and his Country loves" (235-36), and one expects Pope to continue the praise of the great world. Surprisingly, however, the poem turns away from the lofty theme and toward "humbler Joys":

Happy next him who to these Shades retires,
Whom Nature charms, and whom the Muse inspires,
Whom humbler Joys of home-felt Quiet please,
Successive Study, Exercise, and Ease.

(237-40)

[3] For the view that the entire poem is political at the core, see Earl Wasserman's essay in *The Subtler Language* (Baltimore, 1959). I think Wasserman overstates the case for the poem's unity.

He continues for eighteen lines more, describing the activities of the retired man. The drift toward lofty song
checked by an impulse to retirement may help to account
for an ambiguity readers have often noticed in these lines:
"Happy next him." Who is happier, the courtier or the retired poet? Most happy the courtier, and happy next to
him the poet? ("Happy next he . . ." would have made this
sense clearer.) Or, happy the courtier next after the poet?[4]
Perhaps Pope tries to have it both ways, to compliment
both Granville and himself. What is beyond dispute, however, is that Pope is more interested in the retired poet and
casts his lot with him:

> Ye sacred Nine! that all my Soul possess,
> Whose Raptures fire me, and whose Visions bless,
> Bear me, oh bear me to sequester'd Scenes.
> The Bow'ry Mazes and surrounding Greens.
>
> (259-62)

Pope's real affinity, as he defines it, is not with the political
and commercial greatness symbolized by the Thames, but
with the virgin simplicity of Lodona, who likewise seeks to
return to her "native Shades" (202). Just as she shrinks
from the dangerous glory of having strayed "beyond the
Forest's verdant Limits" (182), so Pope perhaps shrinks
from the imperial theme, preferring to keep a cool distance, to act the "musing Shepherd" who gazes at a "watry
Landskip" reflected in Lodona's glassy wave (211-13).

The poem might have ended here, with the poet roam-
ing "from Shade to Shade" (269) through walks conse-
crated to poetry. But Pope is led to think of the godlike
poets who once sang in these shades, though now their
voices have been stopped by fate. Perhaps reluctant to offer
himself as the obvious heir of Denham and Cowley, he

---

[4] The couplet on the courtier is not in Pope's original manuscript version; see Robert Schmitz, *Pope's Windsor Forest 1712: A Study of the Washing-
ton University Holograph* (St. Louis, 1952), p. 35. It was perhaps introduced
to smooth the transition from Queen Anne's "bright Beauties" to the
more attractive "Shades."

asks, "Who now shall charm the Shades where *Cowley*
strung / His living Harp?" (279-80), and answers with the
name of his dedicatee:

> But hark! the Groves rejoice, the Forest rings!
> Are these reviv'd? or is it *Granville* sings?
>   'Tis yours, my Lord, to bless our soft Retreats,
> And call the Muses to their ancient Seats,
> To paint anew the flow'ry Sylvan Scenes,
> To crown the Forests with Immortal Greens,
> Make *Windsor* Hills in lofty Numbers rise,
> And lift her Turrets nearer to the Skies;
> To sing those Honours you deserve to wear,
> And add new Lustre to her Silver *Star*.
>
> (281-90)

Here too the poem might have ended—and indeed was
ended in 1704. Pope lurks in the shadow of the greater
poet, Granville, who takes over the task Pope himself attempted as the poem began, to sing the glories of "the
Muse's Seats" (2), to make the groves of Windsor "Live in
Description and look green in Song" (8).

Why did Pope expand the poem by 144 lines in 1713?
Perhaps, as the epigraph hints, because he was again
"commanded": "Non injussa cano" ("Unbidden strains I
sing not").[5] That the bidding was again Granville's is
likewise there hinted: " 'tis of thee, Varus [to whom Virgil's
poem was dedicated], our tamarisk shall sing, of thee all
our groves. To Phoebus no page is more welcome than that
which bears on its front the name of Varus." Indeed, one
might fairly say that in the continuation of *Windsor Forest*
Pope does "sing Granville" and make Granville (rather
than himself) sing the glories of the peace.

The added lines pick up where Pope had left off. Granville, bidden earlier to paint Windsor's "Sylvan Scenes," is
now urged to sing of Windsor's heroes:

---

[5] Virgil, Eclogue VI.9 in Virgil, *Eclogues, Georgics, Aeneid (Bks. 1-6)*, trans.
H. R. Fairclough, 2 vols., Loeb Classical Library, nos. 63-64 (London,
1967), I, 43.

Oh wou'dst thou sing what Heroes *Windsor* bore,
What Kings first breath'd upon her winding Shore,
Or raise old Warriors whose ador'd Remains
In weeping Vaults her hallow'd Earth contains!

(299-302)

And Pope goes on to recall the glories of Windsor's kings and warriors from Edward III to Charles I as an appropriate subject for poetry—Granville's, not his own. Pope himself speaks not lofty poetry but instructions to a poet: "With *Edward*'s Acts adorn the shining Page . . . Make sacred *Charles*'s Tomb for ever known."

The subsequent introduction of Father Thames marks a return to the mythological mode of the first version: "In that blest Moment, from his Oozy Bed / Old Father *Thames* advanc'd his rev'rend Head." Thames appears with his "Sea-born Brothers" around his throne, and Pope luxuriates in a brief river catalogue (lines 340-48), but Thames's real function is to serve as a symbol of England's commercial and political glory. Significantly, however, Pope again refuses to sing those glories in his own voice. Instead—and his readers have long found this an awkward displacement—he has the river god himself sing: "Hail Sacred *Peace*! hail long-expected Days" (355). The vision of England's future imperial glories unfolds over the next sixty-five lines in one of the most rapturous celebrative passages Pope ever wrote.

"Return Alpheus, the dread voice is past, / That shrunk thy streams; Return Sicilian Muse." As if in answer to Milton's plea, Pope's own voice returns in the poem's final paragraph. "Here cease thy Flight" seems at first addressed to Thames, but as Pope goes on he makes clear that he speaks to himself, the presenter, after all, of Thames's words: "nor with unhallow'd Lays / Touch the fair Fame of *Albion*'s Golden Days." He dares not approach closer to this lofty subject. Let Granville take it up: "The Thoughts of Gods let *Granville*'s Verse recite, / And bring the Scenes of opening Fate to Light." As for Pope, he will remain in the shades and sing the kind of verse he set out to sing, the kind he originally urged Granville to sing:

My humble Muse, in unambitious Strains,
Paints the green Forests and the flow'ry Plains

(427-28)

The expanded version then concludes much as did the 1704 poem, with Pope yielding to Granville. But this time, Granville having stepped up to epic (and having urged Pope to write epic), Pope occupies alone the pastoral place he once shared with Granville (note the striking resemblance between line 427 and lines 285-86). It is as if Pope responds reluctantly to Granville's bidding: if you want a lofty poem, you must write it yourself; I will remain a pastoral singer. The call to celebrate the peace is both refused and in a way answered. However, it leaves Pope more sure of his chosen role and of his adequacy to fill it. He has moved from " 'Tis yours, my Lord, to bless our soft Retreats" to the confidence that the task is his own: "Enough for me, that to the listning Swains / First in these Fields I sung the Sylvan Strains." By alluding to the opening line of his *Pastorals* ("First in these Fields I *try* the Sylvan Strains") Pope also implies that the trial has been successful, the task has been completed: the sylvan strains have been sung. Both in the *Pastorals* and in *Windsor Forest* Pope has demonstrated his mastery of the pastoral mode. At the same time, the line refers to the poem just concluded: the celebration of Windsor Forest has in fact been "sung." Though Pope himself has remained within the safer shades of pastoral, he has managed, by calling on Granville and Father Thames at strategic moments, to appear the heir of Cowley and Denham and to associate himself with the glories of Windsor, "the Monarch's and the Muse's seat," to produce a lofty poem. It is a paradox that repeats itself in Pope's early verse: diffident poet and confident poem.

The *Essay on Criticism* contains this same paradox. Reuben Brower has well described its predominant tone: the poem, he says, "has the bounce and go of verse by a terribly bright young man who has recently acquired all the right ideas, which he gets off with dazzling verbal skill and cheerful superiority."[6] And yet, in the two passages where Pope openly refers to himself, his voice is diffident:

> Hail *Bards Triumphant*! born in *happier Days*;
> *Immortal* Heirs of *Universal* Praise! . . .
>
> Oh may some Spark of *your* Coelestial Fire
> The last, the meanest of your Sons inspire,
> (That on weak Wings, from far, pursues your Flights;
> *Glows* while he *reads*, but *trembles* as he *writes*).
>
> (189-90, 195-98)

Again, at the end of the poem, when Pope describes the revival of criticism in Britain and the restoration of "Wit's *Fundamental Laws*" by Sheffield, Roscommon, and his friend Walsh, he laments the death of the last, a "Judge" who gave Pope a true critic's help:

> The Muse, whose early Voice you taught to Sing,
> Prescrib'd her Heights, and prun'd her tender Wing,
> (Her Guide now lost) no more attempts to *rise*,
> But in low numbers short Excursions tries.
>
> (735-38)

Pope's modesty, Ripley Hotch has recently argued, simply enables him to avoid seeming pretentiousness and demonstrates that he is possessed of humility, a virtue belonging to the ideal poet-critic that Pope has just shown himself to be.[7] But Pope's diffidence is, I think, more than a rhetorical gesture, and the poem is less than an unequivocal proof of superiority.

---

[6] Brower, *Alexander Pope: The Poetry of Allusion* (Oxford, 1959), p. 196.
[7] Hotch, "Pope Surveys His Kingdom: *An Essay on Criticism*," *Studies in English Literature*, 13 (1973), 474-87.

The poem has rightly been read as a virtuoso display of Pope's youthful powers. The *Essay*, says Johnson, "displays such extent of comprehension, such nicety of distinction, such acquaintance with mankind, and such knowledge both of ancient and modern learning, as are not often attained by the maturest age and longest experience." He implies too that Pope saw the poem that way, that is, as an exhibition of powers early attained. Readers have always seen the poem as a performance. Already in Johnson's time the paragraph on versification ("ten low words," the wounded snake, swift Camilla) was "celebrated."[8] And, as a recent commentator notes, this section of the poem is "memorable for the brilliance of its display, not for its contribution to an argument. . . . what it tells most clearly is that Alexander Pope is a very skillful poet. That, in fact, is what much of the poem conveys more convincingly than anything else."[9]

Developing this traditional view, Hotch sees, rightly I think, that the poem is ultimately "not about criticism, but about the young poet writing the poem, his situation, and his claim to merit." But he simplifies the *Essay* when he goes on to argue that it is "a proof of the qualifications of the author to assume his place as head of the kingdom of wit he describes. Treating criticism as the interpreter of the law which governs the well-ordered kingdom of poetry, Pope vindicates his own qualities as law-giver and ruler, and therefore justifies his own role as heir-apparent to the crown of poetry."[10] What Hotch does not take into account is Pope's genuine diffidence about the "situation" of the modern poet-critic, even if he is successful. Literary eminence, Pope reflects anxiously, can be a "painful preheminence."

The successful writer's two greatest enemies are Time and Envy: "Short is the Date, alas, of *Modern Rhymes*" (476),

---

[8] "Life of Pope," pp. 94, 218, 219.

[9] Patricia M. Spacks, *An Argument of Images: The Poetry of Alexander Pope* (Cambridge, Mass., 1971), pp. 39-40.

[10] Hotch, "Pope Surveys His Kingdom," pp. 474-75.

Pope laments. Not only does fame soon die—"Now Length of *Fame* (our *second* Life) is lost, / And bare Threescore is all ev'n That can boast" (480-81)—but the impermanence of language itself means that the poet's "bright Creation" fades. Nor are the greatest exempt: "And such as *Chaucer* is, shall *Dryden* be" (483). More disturbing yet than time is the nature of man, his inevitable envy of his fellow's excellence:

> Unhappy *Wit*, like most mistaken Things,
> Attones not for that *Envy* which it brings.
> In *Youth* alone its empty Praise we boast,
> But soon the Short-liv'd Vanity is lost!
> Like some fair *Flow'r* the early *Spring* supplies,
> That gaily Blooms, but ev'n in blooming *Dies*.
> What is this *Wit* which must our Cares employ?
> The *Owner's Wife*, that *other Men* enjoy,
> Then most our *Trouble* still when most *admir'd*,
> And still the more we *give*, the more *requir'd*;
> Whose Fame with *Pains* we guard, but lose with *Ease*,
> Sure *some* to *vex*, but never *all* to *please*;
> 'Tis what the *Vicious fear*, the *Virtuous shun*;
> By *Fools* 'tis *hated*, and by *Knaves undone*!
>
> (494-507)

The second section of the *Essay* (lines 203-559), of which this passage is a part, is devoted to "causes hindering a true Judgment," and Pope presents most of these causes—pride, imperfect learning, judging by parts—as errors that can be avoided: "A perfect Judge will *read* each Work of Wit / With the same Spirit that its Author *writ* . . . Avoid extremes. . . ." But his tone of assurance here fails him; time and envy are not to be evaded.[11] It is the nature of wit

---

[11] Hotch must gloss over these passages (indeed, he says nothing of the latter) to maintain his view that Pope never loses his "serene confidence" that envy and transience are but "temporary faults, a result of not knowing the universal scheme . . . temporary distortions of the proper order of nature's court" (ibid., 482). This makes Pope (and Hotch) sound perilously like the philosopher in Johnson's *Rasselas*, Chap. 22.

to draw envy, to isolate the writer, and to burden him with "care" and "trouble." The pronouns "we" and "our" emphasize the urgency and suggest that Pope feels personally threatened.

Worse still, the successful writer himself may become corrupted. Having reached Parnassus's lofty crown, he may now employ his pains "to spurn some others down" (515). Ruled by "Self-Love" and urged by the "Sacred Lust of Praise," he is in danger of losing his humanity: "Nor in the Critick let the Man be lost" (523). Pope here adumbrates a theme that was to preoccupy him in his later poetry and in his constant reflections about his own career in the letters: the good writer must be a good man; "Good-Nature and Good-Sense must ever join" (524). Judging by Pope's subsequent preoccupation with this theme, he hardly considered the problem settled by his terse warning here. Although the poem recovers its predominant brio in the third section, which concerns rules for good critical conduct and the history of criticism and concludes with its restoration in the Renaissance, it never loses this undercurrent of concern: bad critics still abound, criticism itself was once enslaved to superstition and dulness.

Plainly, however, Pope in this section is more confident about the possibilities of criticism and of his own abilities. But where he is forthright about the dangers of success, he is hesitant (though perhaps with only "seeming Diffidence" [567]) to advance claims of his own merit. "Where's the Man," Pope asks in introducing the portrait of the ideal critic,

> who Counsel can bestow,
> Still pleas'd to teach, and yet not proud to know?
> Unbiass'd, or by Favour or by Spite;
> Not dully prepossest, nor blindly right;
> Tho' Learn'd, well-bred; and tho' well-bred, sincere;
> Modestly bold, and Humanly severe?
> Who to a Friend his Faults can freely show,
> And gladly praise the Merit of a Foe?

Blest with a *Taste* exact, yet unconfin'd;
A *Knowledge* both of *Books* and *Humankind*;
Gen'rous Converse; a *Soul* exempt from *Pride*;
And *Love to Praise*, with *Reason* on his Side?

(631-42)

Clearly, this is an idealized portrait of the man he sought to be.[12] Although Pope hesitates to answer that *he* is the man, he lets the reader know that he has apprenticed himself for the office. In the closing lines the youthful poet who attempts more than "short Excursions" quietly characterizes himself as critic:

Content, if hence th' Unlearn'd their Wants may view,
The Learn'd reflect on what before they knew:
Careless of *Censure*, nor too fond of *Fame*,
Still pleas'd to *praise*, yet not afraid to *blame*,
Averse alike to *Flatter*, or *Offend*,
Not *free* from Faults, nor yet too vain to *mend*.

(739-44)

Oblique echoes and syntactic parallels (compare lines 637-38 and 742, 634 and 744, 632 and 742) ask that we superimpose the modest self-description on the idealized portrait and see the resemblance. If Pope does not yet deserve the perfect critic's ivy, he has made a start. But the description by negatives (*not* too fond of fame, *not* afraid, *not* vain) limits the self-assertiveness. Pope may be genuinely reluctant, and not just falsely modest, to advance boldly into the limelight. And yet, after all, the poem does focus on Pope at the close. Protected by his customary caution and "poetical prudence," expressing itself here as in other early poems in the form of diffidence, even if only a "seeming Diffidence," Pope exposes himself to less risk, perhaps guarding himself against the perils of success he already so acutely perceives.

[12] Cf. the lines on Voiture, another model and projected self-image: "Still with Esteem no less convers'd than read; / With Wit well-natur'd, and with Books well-bred" (*Epistle to Miss Blount, with the Works of Voiture*, 7-8).

Clearly a troublesome, if not a central, concern in the *Essay on Criticism*, fame becomes the subject in *The Temple of Fame*, which was published in 1715 but written in 1711, the year the *Essay* was published. Pope was no doubt drawn to modernize Chaucer's *House of Fame* for a variety of reasons. Among those reasons, however, must have been that his lifelong obsession with fame—its attainability, its value, its usefulness in dissuading bad men and encouraging good, its cost—had already begun.[13]

Pope's initial description of the temple establishes that this self-confessed "Candidate for Praise" (500) approaches the goddess with ambivalence. A "glorious pile" that shines like Parian marble, the temple nevertheless is built "High on a Rock of Ice": "Steep its Ascent, and slipp'ry was the Way" (27-28). The famous lines comparing the rock's summit to "*Zembla*'s Rocks," rising white and glittering and ageless, emphasize the lifelessness as well as the immortality of fame: "Pale Suns, unfelt, at distance roll away, / And on th' impassive Ice the Lightnings play" (55-56). We need only remember the opening lines of the poem—"In that soft Season when descending Showers / Call forth the Greens, and wake the rising Flowers; / When opening Buds salute the welcome Day, / And Earth relenting feels the Genial Ray"—to realize that pursuing and winning fame means losing the warmth and openness of life. The "Train of Phantoms" (9) and the "wild promiscuous Sound" like billows on a "hollow Shoar" (24) suggest furthermore that fame is somehow illusory. The hostile force of time (lines 31-44) implies too that most fame is transient. Scenes within the temple confirm this fundamental ambivalence. Some true heroes are found—Homer, Virgil, Horace, Pindar, Aristotle, and Tully—but most of the petitioners are rewarded indiscriminately: "Some she disgrac'd, and some with Honours crown'd; / Unlike Successes equal Merits

---

[13] For a survey of Pope's interest in fame throughout his career, see Donald Fraser, "Pope and the Idea of Fame," in *Alexander Pope, Writers and Their Background*, ed. Peter Dixon (Athens, Ohio, 1972), pp. 286-310.

found. / Thus her blind Sister, fickle *Fortune* reigns, / And undiscerning, scatters Crowns and Chains" (294-97).

Chaucer's framework gave Pope ample opportunity to explore the uncertainty of fame ("So hard to gain, so easy to be lost" [504]) and its insubstantiality. But it did not allow him to reflect on the cost of fame (the lines on Zembla's Rocks are essentially Pope's invention). Hence he adds an epilogue to Chaucer's unfinished poem in order to provide a natural conclusion and "a Moral to the whole" (Pope's note to line 497). There Pope gives a frankly personal focus to the problem of fame. Asked why he has come to the temple, he speaks about his own literary career and shows that for him the more serious fear is not to fail to win fame, but to win it and then lose himself:

'Tis true, said I, not void of Hopes I came,
For who so fond as youthful Bards of Fame?
But few, alas! the casual Blessing boast,
So hard to gain, so easy to be lost:
How vain that second Life in others' Breath,
Th' Estate which Wits inherit after Death!

(501-6)

Thus far Pope laments only the uncertainty of fame. But he goes on to specify the price:

Ease, Health, and Life, for this they must resign,
(Unsure the Tenure, but how vast the Fine!)
The Great Man's Curse without the Gains endure,
Be envy'd, wretched, and be flatter'd, poor;
All luckless Wits their Enemies profest,
And all successful, jealous Friends at best.

(507-12)

He concludes not by forswearing fame, but by cautiously specifying the terms on which he would seek and accept it:

Nor Fame I slight, nor for her Favours call;
She comes unlook'd for, if she comes at all:
But if the Purchase costs so dear a Price,

As soothing Folly, or exalting Vice:
Oh! if the Muse must flatter lawless Sway,
And follow still where Fortune leads the way;
Or if no Basis bear my rising Name,
But the fall'n Ruins of Another's Fame:
Then teach me, Heaven! to scorn the guilty Bays;
Drive from my Breast that wretched Lust of Praise;
Unblemish'd let me live, or die unknown,
Oh grant an honest Fame, or grant me none!

(513-24)

The final refusal of fame is only conditional, but the cumulative pressure built up by the repeated "if" suggests that fame almost inevitably corrupts.

Fame is likewise a central concern of Pope's only indisputably great early poem, *The Rape of the Lock*, though here the subject is the poet's ability to confer fame through praise. The close of the poem, in which the poet addresses Belinda directly and offers immortal fame as compensation for the loss of her lock, seems one of Pope's most confident and assertive moments:

Then cease, bright Nymph! to mourn thy ravish'd Hair
Which adds new Glory to the shining Sphere!
Not all the Tresses that fair Head can boast
Shall draw such Envy as the Lock you lost. . . .
This Lock, the Muse shall consecrate to Fame,
And mid'st the Stars inscribe *Belinda*'s Name!

Whether or not we read *"This Lock"* as referring to Pope's poem, it is his own power as poet that he celebrates as much as Belinda's name. But such self-confidence paradoxically grows out of an initial poetic diffidence and a decision to limit himself to an ostensibly "slight" subject.

The mock-epic form, I suspect, licenses a kind of loftiness that Pope in his early verse does not ordinarily attempt.[14] He is enabled to sing of ironically "mighty Con-

---

[14] *Messiah* (1712) and the *Ode for Musick* (1713) are exceptions.

tests" *because* they appear to "rise from trivial Things," and in any event he claims little credit for himself. The poem is "due" to Caryll, who asked Pope to write it, and will succeed in conferring "Praise" if Belinda inspire and Caryll approve it. More surreptitiously, Pope may also confess another kind of limit on his power. His complicity with the attenuated masculine world of the poem (airy sylphs, beaus and witlings, barren-Baron, husbands-monkeys-lap dogs) is suggested in the opening line: "In Tasks so bold, can Little Men engage?" (i.11). The tasks are those of both the Baron and the little poet, at once assaulting the gentle belle and exploring the "mighty rage" that dwells in such soft bosoms. Pope may even see himself in the poem's lap pets. In a contemporary letter (1712) Pope ironically sees himself as a lady's pet monkey: "pray acquaint me, that I may wear her Chain forthwith; I fancy my Size and Abilities may qualify me to Match her Monkey very well."[15] Ariel too may be an oblique image of Pope, who was a favorite of women—permitted a sylph's "intimate Familiarities," yet not taken seriously as a male; admitted to ladies' closets (so a later attack put it) as a "harmless creature"; consulted in the choice of garments and servants.[16] He himself vowed that were he Lady Mary's "Guardian Spirit, your Happiness would be my whole 'Care'" (*Corr.*, 1, 471). In the course of the poem, however, the little poet overmasters the "mighty rage," reduces the women (and the men) by witty mockery, and, a protector after all, graciously grants Belinda at the poem's end the promise of eternal fame.[17]

[15] The letter was published for the first time by Maynard Mack in the *Scriblerian*, 9 (1976), 1-7. As Mack notes, however, the apparent admission of inadequacy is contrasted with a kind of sexual boast two lines earlier, where Pope says that he requires "two Dozen" nymphs for his "ordinary Occasions."

[16] *Memoirs of the Court of Lilliput* (1727), in *Pamphlet Attacks*, p. 99. In *The Progress of Wit; a Caveat* (1730), Aaron Hill describes "Alexis" (i.e., Pope) as "The ladies plaything": Hill, *Works*, 4 vols. (London, 1753), iii, 371.

[17] In fact, the proffered fame is subtly undermined: the stellified lock will be misinterpreted by the "Beau monde," pining lovers, and astrologers; only "quick poetic eyes" will see its rise; and when last seen in the poem, Belinda was still raving. Would she care to be famous for foolish spleen?

The blend of confidence and polished ease on the one hand and of diffidence, humility, and even mild anxiety on the other—a mixture so characteristic of Pope's early verse—finds its fullest expression in the Preface to the first collected edition of these poems, the *Works* of 1717. In it the "youthful bard," who knows he has written well, has won fame and material reward (the Homer subscription had been a success), constructs an elaborate apology for himself and his poems that manages at once to boast of his triumph and to excuse or beg leniency for his failure. Although his poems, particularly the *Essay on Criticism* and *The Rape of the Lock*, had received some adverse criticism, and although his own person had been attacked in the shrill *Character of Mr. Pope* (1716), the assertive-defensive Preface is not to be accounted for, I believe, as an *answer* to Pope's critics. Sensitive as he was to criticism, nowhere in this Preface (the longest he wrote to any volume of his original works) does he respond to a specific critic or charge. Rather, we should see the *Preface* as a manifestation of his self-protective impulse, the need to reduce his vulnerability, and as a reflection of the same state of mind informing the *Essay on Criticism* and the *Temple of Fame*. Even more than those poems, the Preface is a meditation on the condition of the young modern writer, who is faced with demanding readers and hostile critics, intimidated by the ancients, forced to work in a perishing medium, and, for the sake of an elusive fame, to "give up all reasonable aims of life."

The first part of the *Preface* is dominated by the idea that a poet must regard his audience from a suspicious distance. Instead of being the poet's natural ally, sympathetic, receptive, and grateful, the audience unreasonably *expects* the writer to spend his "whole time and care" in providing entertainment and watches closely to catch the poor poet out in any failing or folly. The writer and critic likewise view each other with suspicion, reserve, or open hostility. Ideally, both are committed to the pursuit and admiration of excellence, but in practice a critic conceives his part to consist in proving a writer to have failed. Consequently, poets "are resolv'd not to own themselves in any error."

But if an aspiring poet suspects, as Pope did, that he has a genius for poetry, he has no way to "discover" it except by "appealing to the judgment of others." If he writes badly while endeavoring only to please (no sin, Pope notes), he is ridiculed or allowed to think well of his work until the bookseller tells him the unpalatable truth. By then he has wasted his time and spoiled himself for any other profession, for he is judged by "the first steps he makes in the world" and has been marked a failure. If he writes well, he loses just the same: "a good Poet no sooner communicates his works with the same desire of information, but it is imagin'd he is a vain young creature given up to the ambition of fame; when perhaps the poor man is all the while trembling with the fear of being ridiculous." If not scorned, he falls under another "very unlucky circumstance; for from the moment he prints he must expect to hear no more truth, than if he were a Prince, or a Beauty." Flattery will either make him a coxcomb, or make him diffident and suspicious of all praise. Success will also win him the envy and ill-will of the "worst and most ignorant" of his readers. All the rest, even the honest and innocent, will "hate, or suspect him" for a dreaded wit or "satyrist."[18]

As Pope paints it, there is scarcely a more perilous life than the life of writing. His response to this peril can be sober and deliberate, weighing the cost and withholding commitment:

> I believe, if any one, early in his life should contemplate the dangerous fate of authors, he would scarce be of their number on any consideration. The

[18] See the 1714 letter in which Pope worries about the cost of fame: "The utmost fame they [the "human sciences"] are capable of bestowing is never worth the pains they cost us, and the time they lose us. If you attain the top of your desires that way, all those who envy you will do you harm, and of those who admire you, few will do you good. All unsuccessful writers are your declared enemies, and probably some successful ones your secret enemies; for those hate no more to be excelled than these to be rivalled" (*Corr.*, I, 236).

life of a Wit is a warfare upon earth; and the present spirit of the world is such, that to attempt to serve it (any way) one must have the constancy of a martyr, and a resolution to suffer for its sake.[19]

The literary life, even if one takes it up on these conditions, is a life of solitary combat, without the solidarity of either audience or fellow writers.

It is all the more curious then that Pope can take quite the contrary view of poetry in the same Preface, indeed, in the same paragraphs. In part, perhaps, Pope is retreating into pretended indifference. Poetry after all is just a diversion, "only the affair of idle men who write in their closets, and of idle men who read there." In the metaphor Pope himself frequently used in letters from these years, poetry is like the jingling of a horse's bells: it enables one "to jogg on a little more merrily" on one's way.[20] The perils of poetry have vanished; writing is effortless, carefree, even a means of pleasing "the best and most knowing." A genius for poetry brings advantages: "the agreeable power of self-amusement when a man is idle or alone; the privilege of being admitted into the best company, and the freedom of saying as many careless things as other people, without being so severely remark'd upon." It might be protested that Pope is merely being facetious. This is likely enough in the two instances I have cited. But when the same idea occurs a third time, it is presented in a straightforward, confessional manner:

I confess it was want of consideration that made me an author; I writ because it amused me; I corrected because it was as pleasant to me to correct as to write; and I publish'd because I was told I might please such as it was a credit to please. To what degree I have done this, I am really ignorant; I had too much fondness for

[19] I follow here Pope's 1717 text, without the revisions added in subsequent editions. For one revision, see n.21 below.

[20] *Corr.*, I, 330; see also I, 191, 236, 324, II, 176, 209.

my productions to judge of them at first, and too much judgment to be pleas'd with them at last. But I have reason to think they can have no reputation which will continue long, or which deserves to do so: for they have always fallen short not only of what I read of others, but even of my own Ideas of Poetry.

This show of imperturbability is all the more surprising when we note that in 1717 these words immediately followed the passage on the wit's warfaring life. The original rhetorical connection accentuates the contrast: the idea that no reflective man would be a poet "on any consideration" leads directly to Pope's claim that it was "want of consideration" that made him an author. Not surprisingly, Pope suspects his readers may not believe such calm professions of unconcern ("If any one should imagine I am not in earnest . . .") after the harrowing view of poetry as martyrdom.[21] The contradiction may of course reflect Pope's ambivalence as a young writer publishing his *Works* (presumptuous title) at the precocious age of twenty-nine. At a deeper level, the ideas that the life of a wit is a constant struggle and that it is a pleasant way to amuse oneself may serve Pope in the same way: each permits him to protect himself from the potential attacks of a hostile audience, to reduce his vulnerability, and, at the same time, to claim a single-handed triumph.

Paradoxically, the warfaring wit is well insulated. Having anticipated all perilous circumstances, he cannot be ambushed. Furthermore, most attacks incriminate themselves

[21] In later editions of the Preface Pope, more secure in his fame, inserted two sentences just after the "life of a wit" sentence. He claims disingenuously that he has been "less concern'd about Fame than I durst declare till this occasion [i.e., in 1717, though this was written in 1736], when methinks I should find more credit than I could heretofore: since my writings have had their fate already, and 'tis too late to think of prepossessing the reader in their favour." Pope rewrites his own history. The poet who knew he had succeeded exaggerates the modesty and indifference he felt as a young man. But even so, he suspects a reader's disbelief: "I could wish people would believe what I am pretty certain they will not. . . ."

as envy or ignorance. As a martyr Pope is in a peculiarly advantaged position: his defeat is his victory. Likewise, as a self-pleasing amateur Pope is well-nigh invulnerable. If poetry is essentially a private activity, then critics have no reason to comment. Apparently removing himself from the ranks of serious littérateurs, Pope in fact reinstates himself at their head. He has been told he might please the best judges (themselves superior to the common critics), but manages, with modesty, to imply that his own standards are higher than theirs.

Over the central section of the Preface falls the long shadow cast by the ancients. Laboring in their shade, the "modern" writer of Pope's day could only hope to imitate their works.[22] But just as Pope turns the hostility of critics to his advantage, so too he converts the disability of being a modern into a kind of virtue. Though unable to excel the ancients as a "good writer," Pope implies that he has done less on that score than he might, that he has chosen instead to be remembered as a "good man."

While granting the ancients their traditional eminence, Pope in fact neatly cuts them down to size. "To say the least of them," he begins, they had "*as much* Genius as We." The irony works two ways: dry understatement of the genius of the ancients, and sly hint that moderns may be their equal. The ancients of course had the advantage of coming first. They had the good fortune, furthermore (and no credit to them), to write "in languages that became universal and everlasting," while a modern's, through no fault of his own, must be "limited both in extent, and in duration." Finally, the ancients took great pains: "They constantly apply'd themselves . . . to that single branch of an art, to which their talent was most powerfully bent; and it was the business of their lives to correct and finish their works for posterity." To take more pains, Pope notes, "cannot fail to produce more complete pieces." Thus, if moderns "can pretend to

[22] For a recent discussion of this theme, see W. J. Bate, *The Burden of the Past* (Cambridge, 1970).

have used the same industry, let us expect the same immortality." But is it worth such pains, such industry? In letters from the period Pope often wonders: "after a life of perpetual application, to reflect that you have been doing nothing for yourself, and that the same or less industry might have gained you a friendship that can never deceive or end, a satisfaction which praise cannot bestow, nor vanity feel, and a glory which . . . yet shall be felt and enjoyed to eternity."[23]

In the Preface Pope implies on the one hand that life has other higher claims on a man than writing and correcting: "One may be ashamed to consume half one's days in bringing sense and rhyme together; and what Critic can be so unreasonable as not to leave a man time enough for any more serious employment, or more agreeable amusement." On the other hand, he in fact devotes himself to correction, but as an amusement, not a "business": "I corrected because it was as pleasant to me to correct as to write."[24] Pope thus has it both ways: he has met the rigorous demands of art, but at the same time he has served another ideal, the serious employment and agreeable amusement of the good man.

The Preface concludes with more artful self-pleading: "In this office of collecting my pieces, I am altogether uncertain, whether to look upon my self as a man building a monument, or burying the dead?" This is disingenuous. What reader can doubt that Pope is here consciously laying the foundation of the monument that he would spend the rest of his life building?[25] And yet the professed diffidence gives Pope plausible protection from charges of boasting:

[23] *Corr.*, I, 236. "That man makes a mean figure in eyes of reason who is measuring of syllables and coupling rhimes, when he should be mending his own soul and securing his own immortality": ibid.; see also I, 324.

[24] Johnson, for one, did not believe him. Does he half-remember this phrase in his description of Pope: "He considered poetry as the business of his life" ("Life of Pope," p. 217).

[25] On Pope's continuing concern with "monuments" as "testimony" to his character, see below, Chaps. 6 and 7.

may these Poems (as long as they last) remain as a testimony, that their Author never made his talents sub-
servient to the mean and unworthy ends of Party or
self-interest; the gratification of publick prejudices, or
private passions; the flattery of the undeserving, or the
insult of the unfortunate. If I have written well, let it
be consider'd that 'tis what no man can do without
good sense, a quality that not only renders one capable
of being a good writer, but a good man. And if I have
made any acquisition in the opinion of any one under
the notion of the former, let it be continued to me
under no title than that of the latter.

Self-effacing and assertive at once, Pope both disowns and
claims the title of "good writer." He likewise contrives to
make anticipated failure an occasion to declare his own
worth. At first, the usual apologies are offered: if the
poems should perish, let the reader consider the poet was
young, never sought to vindicate his work, never bribed,
insulted, or slandered to advance his career. But the final
excuse becomes ingenious apologia: "To conclude, if this
volume perish, let it serve as . . . a *Memento mori* to some of
my vain co-temporaries the Poets, to teach them that when
real merit is wanting, it avails nothing to have been en-
courag'd by the great, commended by the eminent, and
favour'd by the publick in general." Pope agrees that his
poems may one day be judged to lack "real merit." But he
also implies that he has met with critical and popular success. And by shifting our attention to his contemporaries,
Pope turns the lines against them: if *they* lack merit, their
temporary success will be of no avail. Somewhat illogi-
cally,[26] but no less effectively I think, the lines may also hint
that, in contrast with the vain poets, Pope himself has "real
merit."

[26] Insertion of "my vain co-temporaries" helps to weaken the logical
and syntactical connection between "if my volume perish" and "it must
have lacked real merit," and implies that it is Pope's contemporaries who
want real merit.

From such lengthy and (necessarily) close analysis, Pope's Preface emerges as a masterful piece of poetic apology (in both senses of the word), an assertion of merit disguised as an apologetic plea for lenient judgment. Its most remarkable feature is just this blend of confidence and diffidence, neither of which, I think, is feigned. A poet wholly confident of himself and his work, as Pope was in his later work, would not need to go to such elaborate lengths to pretend modesty or reduce his vulnerability. And no poet overwhelmed by diffidence would presume to publish his collected *Works* at twenty-nine. As often in the 1717 volume, so in the Preface Pope finds strength in lowliness, can speak most powerfully when most prudently protected—by irony, by self-limitation, by seeming diffidence. Like his own Martha Blount, Pope uses his strength when least he seems to, and though he rules, never shows he rules.

··❧4❧··
Poetry and Friendship:
The Familiar Epistles

In the major poems of the 1717 *Works* Pope enters as the self-consciously "youthful bard," reflecting on the writer's situation, his capacities and limits, but silent about his wider life as a man. Only in the Preface to the 1717 volume does he hint at other values, other claims. But in another group of early poems, a sequence of familiar epistles written from 1710 to 1721, Pope begins to extend the range and depth of self-reference. Although in these poems he still focuses on himself as poet, the poet is both artist and friend; he speaks intimately, usually to a close friend, about some matter that, whatever its public or social implications, is first of all intensely personal: friendship or love, the poet's anxious concern for his power to grant permanence to the persons he loves and celebrates, the poet's weakness, after all, in the face of decay and death. If Pope's poetic career may be described as his gradual discovery that he was his own best subject, the familiar epistles form a transitional stage between his early triumphs during the period 1709-1713 and the autobiographical Horatian satires and epistles of the 1730s.

These six poems—the epistle *To Mr. Addison, Occasioned by his Dialogue on Medals* (1720; written c. 1713), the *Epistle to Miss Blount, on her leaving the Town, after the Coronation* (1714), the *Epistle to Mr. Jervas, with Dryden's Translation of Fresnoy's Art of Painting* (1715), the *Epistle to James Craggs* (1718), the *Epistle to Robert Earl of Oxford* (1721), together with the earlier *Epistle to a Young Lady, with the Works of Voiture* (1710)—share a number of common features. No doubt sensing their similarity, Pope in 1735 published these poems as a group, gathered together with the *Epistle to Dr. Arbuthnot* and the four *Moral Essays*, under the general title, *Epistles to Several Persons*.[1] In each poem the occasion—the gift of a book, the publication of Addison's *Dialogue* or of Pope's edition of Parnell's poems, the departure of a friend from town—gives rise to brief reflections, usually of an ethical nature. But the occasion and its attendant reflections yield to a quiet, sober, intimate close, where in the context of transience, loss, death, art's failure, and separation of friends Pope focuses on the mutual efforts of himself and his correspondent to establish communion or combat decay. In each, the commonplace elegiac theme is, so to speak, revalidated by Pope's personal witness. He in effect testifies that his advice, celebration, compliment, satirical thrust, even the moral "matter" of the poems, grows out of personal conviction. Whatever his belief in traditional standards, for him these standards, as a recent critic has rightly argued, "only come alive when the individual rediscovers them for himself, and then re-embodies them." The poet must stand witness to truth, and "for Pope the basis of this witness must always be the individual sensibility of the poet."[2] But in these early poems the individual sensibility is not solitary; rather, it joins with another, a friend, or fellow artist.

Structurally, each poem moves toward a moment of imaginative communication between Pope and his addressee. The moment of communion, however, is not marked by direct declaration of affection or of imagined reunion.

[1] In the initial 1735 quarto edition of Vol. II of his *Works*, the epistles to Addison and Oxford were grouped with the *Epistle to Dr. Arbuthnot* and the *Moral Essays* as the second book of the "Ethic Epistles," the first book being the *Essay on Man*. But in the subsequent small octavo edition Pope grouped the four *Moral Essays* as the second book and the six familiar epistles, together with the *Epistle to Dr. Arbuthnot*, as "Epistles, the Third Book. To Several Persons." See *Pope Bibliography*, I, pt. 2, 310-12.

[2] G. K. Hunter, "The 'Romanticism' of Pope's Horace," *Essays in Criticism*, 10 (1960), reprinted in *Essential Articles: Alexander Pope*, ed. Maynard Mack, rev. ed. (Hamden, Conn., 1968), pp. 605-6. Hunter's interest centers on the *Horatian Imitations* and *To Fortescue*.

Usually, in fact, no literal reunion is foreseen. Rather, Pope and his friend are united, at a distance, in imagination, by some mediating occasion or object: a book, a shared effort, a snatch of melody. Finally, the language of these poems is "the language of the heart," a phrase that recurs in Pope's poems and letters, always associated in his mind with honest feeling, with "sincerity," as opposed to the conceited "wit" of the *head*. The voice is soft, retiring, particularly attuned to the tears of things. Although we can hear this voice throughout Pope's career, it is especially frequent in the years just before and after his volume of 1717. The elegiac language and mood serve to link this group of poems to the rest of Pope's early verse, where, as critics have noted, an elegiac current often flows beneath the glittering surface.[3] Each of the poems, though an address to a close friend and thus a personal utterance, was designed (even when the poem is an epistle actually sent to a friend) to be read by thousands of strangers. For those strangers—his readers then and now—such utterance has a special effect. We are made privy to a semiprivate moment between Pope and a friend, enabled to share without embarrassment in their intimacy. Equally, one may suspect that, from Pope's point of view, the poems may have seemed both private and public. On the one hand, they are more intimate or "familiar" than the *Horatian Imitations* of the 1730s or the *Epistles to Several Persons*, which were also addressed to friends by a man who had in effect become a self-consciously public personality.[4] On the other hand, these early epistles, however much they focus on Pope himself, in fact tell us little about him, except that he responded ardently to transience or loss and valued the compensating comforts of friendship. It is true that Pope appears in one poem as a man of wit; in several others we

---

[3] See particularly Thomas Edwards, *This Dark Estate: A Reading of Pope* (Berkeley, 1963) (hereafter cited as *This Dark Estate*).

[4] The *Epistles to Several Persons* are longer, weightier poems, as their more common name, *Moral Essays*, suggests.

get hints of Pope as a melancholy lover (but always distanced from the object of his love); over most of the poems plays a mood we might associate with the man of heartfelt sincerity. But these epistles do not make significant use of Pope's rich and varied self-images in the way that the *Imitations* so prominently do, neither developing a single image nor playing off one image against another. In the period 1713-1720 Pope was still learning how to explore and speak out in his own person. The Pope of the familiar epistles is still a relatively undifferentiated self. We appreciate less the quality of that self than the simple fact of its presence.

To argue that Pope's familiar epistles draw on the poet's sensibility is not to ignore that such poems have a rhetorical dimension and a literary history. Familiar epistles had been written since Horace's day by numerous Latin and English writers; conventions governing the writing of an epistle had developed in time: the easy familiar manner, the profession of sincerity, the pose of the worldly gentleman discoursing casually on some commonplace topic. Pope's immediate model may well have been Dryden, whose late familiar epistles to Godfrey Kneller, to his "dear friend Mr. Congreve," and to his kinsman John Driden antedate Pope's own efforts by less than twenty years. It seems probable that Pope set out quite consciously to master this poetic genre inherited from antiquity, as he had earlier demonstrated his skill in pastoral. However, it is no more an error to read Pope's poems as if their forms had no history than it is to assume, even if Pope's own contemporaries took a conventional view of such poems, that the "status" of the form, its generic features and rhetorical dimension, fully determines its meaning.[5] The former approach is

[5] For a recent example of the rhetorical-generic approach to verse epistles, see two articles by J. A. Levine: "The Status of the Verse Epistle before Pope," *Studies in Philology*, 59 (1962), 658-84; and "John Dryden's Epistle to John Driden," *Journal of English and Germanic Philology*, 63 (1964), 450-74.

naive, but the latter ignores the individual reinterpreting that every great poet undertakes to perform. Conventional familiar epistles of the early eighteenth century are for the most part forgotten. We remember and still read Pope's, in part because his reputation for greatness was established on other, greater poems, but also because he found that the conventional form "hit his case," that he could turn the form to his particular and personal ends. The thematic and structural features of Pope's familiar epistles, as I have sketched them, do not derive from models. Individual elements can perhaps be discovered in earlier poems, but Pope's particular combination and emphasis are his own.

Furthermore, his epistolary style was not achieved without some trials and false starts. As early as 1707-1708 Pope sent to his friend Henry Cromwell two verse letters in comic octosyllabic couplets, but he never thought enough of these somewhat rollicking performances to publish them (they were later published piratically). His first major poem in this genre, the *Epistle to a Young Lady, with the Works of Voiture*, likewise differs from the manner of his later epistles. Together with the *Epistle to Belinda, with The Rape of the Lock* (1713), it is still a gay and witty, "conceited" compliment, and by no means an intimate, familiar expression of friendship. As has been pointed out, there is in fact some uncertainty about Pope's original correspondent. When the poem first appeared in 1712, it was entitled "To a Young Lady. . . ." Only in 1735 was the title altered to "To Miss Blount. . . ." Although in 1735 the poem was no doubt intended to compliment Martha Blount, it may have been originally addressed to an imaginary lady.[6] What may at first have been in effect a poetic exercise, and not at all a poem to accompany a gift, seems to have struck Pope some twenty-five years later as an appropriate compliment to the good humor of the still unmarried "Patty" Blount.

It is perhaps not surprising then to discover in the poem

[6] Or perhaps even to Teresa. See Norman Ault, *New Light on Pope* (London, 1949), pp. 49-56, and *Poems*, vi, 65.

the rather impersonal voice of a moralist, who compliments Voiture for the "easie Art" of his published correspondence, offers his own advice on the proper way to make of one's life "A long, exact, and serious Comedy" (which can at once both please and preach), urges his own correspondent to avoid the errors of her sex (excessive trust in the resistless charms of her early beauty), and closes with a compliment to the lady's charmingly bright eyes. The only explicit self-reference comes early in the poem, when Pope offers advice about living and then describes how he himself hopes to live:

Let mine [my life], an innocent gay Farce appear,
And more Diverting still than Regular,
Have Humour, Wit, and native Ease and Grace;
Tho' not too strictly bound to Time and Place:
Criticks in Wit, or Life, are hard to please,
Few write to those, and none can live to these.

(25-30)

Deft transposition of terms from a context of dramatic criticism to one of ethics and facetious self-deprecation keeps this passage light. The bright epigrammatic wit and the wish for the aristocratic amateur's "native ease and grace" suggests an early self—Pope as man of wit—that was later to be abandoned.

At the end of the poem, when he shifts into a somewhat more personal mode, Pope still remains distant. Instead of Pope-the-poet, the ghost of the dead Voiture establishes a kind of communion with the addressed lady. Pope imagines that Voiture in Elysium is pleased to have his letters read by the lady and, though dead, retains a kind of life both in his own capacity for pleasure and in his capacity "Still to charm those [eyes] who charm the World beside." In a curious way, however, Pope tends to merge with Voiture, so that he too is present at the poem's end, though in a reticent and mediated fashion. The process begins in the opening couplet: "In these gay Thoughts the Loves and

Graces shine, / And all the Writer lives in ev'ry Line."
These "Thoughts" are both the enclosed "Works of Voiture" and the attached poem; the living writer is at once
Voiture and Pope. Pope then compliments Voiture and offers a description of the way he himself would like to be
seen—an elegant poet whose "easie Art" can charm and
please, who gains an entree for his breeding and conversation as well as his wit:

> Pleas'd while with Smiles his happy Lines you view,
> And finds a fairer *Ramboüillet* in you,
> The brightest eyes of *France* inspir'd his Muse,
> The brightest Eyes of *Britain* now peruse,
> And dead as living, 'tis our Author's Pride,
> Still to charm those who charm the World beside.[7]
>
> (75-80)

Inspired by Voiture's letters, as Voiture himself was inspired by his correspondents, Pope now is pleased to have
the happy lines of his own letter read by his correspondent.
"Our Author" refers primarily to Voiture, but Pope too, a
living author, takes pride in charming the eyes of a lady
with his graceful epistle. Whatever communion between
poet and correspondent may be hinted at, however, it remains a formal compliment. The lady could be any young
lady of beauty, the poet any lively and graceful wit. There
is no evidence yet of what Pope would later call "the language of the heart." Perhaps as a consequence, the poem
remains "minor," "charming," and "bright" (like its somewhat stiffly elegant diction), without much resonance.
Pope's verse of this kind is in fact almost always richer and
more resonant when informed with his own presence and
marked by recognizably sincere feeling.

The epistle *To Mr. Addison, Occasioned by his Dialogue on*

---

[7] Pope's friend Cromwell may have recognized Pope's effort to emphasize similarities between himself and Voiture. In a 1710 letter he
writes: "Your poem shows you to be, what you say of Voiture, *with books
well bred*" (*Corr.*, 1, 109). For a full discussion of Voiture as one of Pope's
models, see E. Audra, *L'Influence française dans l'oeuvre de Pope* (Paris,
1931), pp. 315-46.

Medals conveys a compliment more obviously and specifically suited to its correspondent than the Voiture poem. Even so, it is unclear whether the poem was ever actually sent to Addison or was ever read by him. Not published until after Addison's death, it was apparently revised in 1719 and intended for publication in the posthumous edition of Addison's *Works* (1721).[8] In this epistle Pope keeps self-reference to a bare minimum. Generalized reflections on the ruins of Rome, whose imperial triumphs have now shrunk "into a coin," give way to a compliment to Addison's learned numismatics and a prophecy of future British medals which will commemorate patriots, warriors, "laurell'd Bards" like Addison, and statesmen like Addison's friend Craggs.[9] The only explicit self-reference comes with the introduction of Craggs:

> Then shall thy CRAGS (and let me call him mine)
> On the cast ore, another Pollio, shine.
>
> (63-64)

Craggs was a close friend of both Addison and Pope, and the recipient of Pope's contemporary *Epistle to James Craggs*. In this light, the final lines of the Addison poem seem to refer equally to Craggs's relations with Addison and with Pope:

> Statesman, yet friend to Truth! of soul sincere,
> In action faithful, and in honour clear;
> Who broke no promise, serv'd no private end,
> Who gain'd no title, and who lost no friend,
> Ennobled by himself, by all approv'd,
> And prais'd, unenvy'd, by the Muse he lov'd.
>
> (67-72)

---

[8] See *Poems*, VI, 205, on the disputed question of date of composition.

[9] The Twickenham editors believe the concluding lines on Craggs (63-72) to have been written after Addison's death, "when Pope learned that Addison had bequeathed to Craggs the edition of his works then in preparation" (*Poems*, VI, 206): hence "thy CRAGS" (63). I see no reason, however, why the phrase might not simply refer to Addison's well-known friendship for Craggs.

The Muse whom Craggs loved, and who praised him in return, is at the same time Addison and Pope, much as the letter writer who charms the lady is at once Voiture and Pope. Self-revelation is clearly not in the forefront of Pope's motives. A discreet and reticent self-concealment protects him and keeps Pope's presence in the poem from growing into that of a warm friend and intimate communicant. At the same time, there is a marked difference in tone between the Voiture and Addison poems. In the former, graceful compliment and light satire dominate the elegiac strain heard briefly in "Love, rais'd on Beauty, will like that decay." But in the latter the celebrative and commemorative power of medals (and implicitly, of all art) barely overcomes the deep sense of loss and decay of all human splendor, and of the vanity and ironic weakness of all efforts to withstand decay, that pervades the first half of the poem.

Art's battle against decay is perhaps the deepest subject of another poem, *To Mr. Jervas, with Dryden's Translation of Fresnoy's Art of Painting*, the first unreservedly personal of Pope's familiar epistles. Admiration for Jervas and the theme of art's limited powers gain strength from Pope's frequent reference to their friendship and mutual labors. Through Pope's own experience, offered as relevant material in the poem, the conventional theme is revalidated. The opening of the poem is dominated by the friendship and mutual labors of two practitioners of the sister arts.

> This verse be thine, my friend, nor thou refuse
> This, from no venal or ungrateful Muse. . . .
>
> (1-2)

> Read these instructive leaves, in which conspire
> *Fresnoy*'s close art, and *Dryden*'s native fire:
> And reading wish, like theirs, our fate and fame,
> So mix'd our studies, and so join'd our name,
> Like them to shine thro' long succeeding age,
> So just thy skill, so regular my rage.
>
> (7-12)

With fine economy Pope makes the Fresnoy-Dryden poem, sent as a gift to Jervas, a model for their own cooperation. "This verse be thine" refers both to Fresnoy's poem and to Pope's epistle, and it links Pope to the earlier artists even before that connection is explicitly spelled out. Details of their joint studies then follow: the fruitful exchange of ideas—"images reflect from art to art"—and criticism— "each finding like a friend / Something to blame, and something to commend." Pope finds in this friendship between fellow artists a source of "strength and light." Time itself seems to weigh less heavily on them: "How oft' in pleasing tasks we wear the day, / While summer suns roll unperceiv'd away." As the poem continues, however, time's relentless rolling becomes not only perceptible, but also destructive. Imaginary excursions to Italy bring to mind the grace, warmth, and strength of Renaissance painters whose fate and fame Pope and Jervas would imitate, but also a reminder of the death of Raphael, Virgil, and Cicero. Art too has the power to "live," to "build imaginary *Rome* a-new," but art itself, like the "vanish'd piles" and "fading Frescoes," is transient.

This double sense of art's power and art's weakness is then focused in Pope's own work. Though the beautiful countess of Bridgewater is dead, she can survive in Pope's verse as a model for every "sister, daughter, friend and wife," and in Jervas's "breathing paint" as a beautiful woman. But beauty blooms " a thousand years" only "in thy colours" (that is, in the painter's pigment), in a picture which, for all its "living image," is simply not the same thing as a living and breathing woman. The conclusion to the poem carries on this mixed sense of decay and permanence. Even in the midst of a celebration of art's highest possibilities, Pope makes clear how limited in power art is:

Yet should the Graces all thy figures place,
And breathe an air divine on ev'ry face;
Yet should the Muses bid my numbers roll,
Strong as their charms, and gentle as their soul;

With *Zeuxis' Helen* thy *Bridgewater* vie,
And these be sung 'till *Granville*'s *Myra* die;
Alas! how little from the grave we claim?
Thou but preserv'st a Face and I a Name.

(71-78)

The traditional notion that art commemorates and preserves, outlasts death and perpetuates fame, is tested in the
poet's own experience and carefully qualified. A poet preserves a name, but his readers, forced to consider all that
descends irrevocably to the grave, reflect further with
Pope: to preserve a name may indeed be something, but it
is not everything.

The note of melancholy is gentle, almost sweet, a mark
of the early Pope (compare the larks in *Windsor Forest* that
fall dead and "leave their little lives in air" [134]). As a reminder of the relative thinness of the verse's texture and
elegiac sentiment, we may contrast Johnson's sterner use of
the same "Yet should . . . should . . ." figure in the harrowing account of the scholar's life in *The Vanity of Human
Wishes*: "Yet should thy soul indulge the gen'rous heat; . . .
Should Reason guide thee; . . . Should no disease thy tor-
pid veins invade. . . ." In Johnson, of course, the stakes are
higher. The eager scholar will suffer far more directly and
painfully than the commemorating artist. Johnson also
brings more dense weight of impinging circumstance to
bear on the scholar's quest, even as he magically wards off
one threat after another. By comparison, Pope's gentler,
much less economical lines invoke or recapitulate relatively
little of the steadily effacing pressure of time.

The slightest of the six familiar epistles is the poem addressed to "James Craggs, Esq; Secretary of State." It is a
brief, seventeen-line tribute to Craggs's virtues as he succeeds to the post formerly held by Addison. Pope praises
him for the worthy soul and unfeigning face he has already
displayed as a "Man" and urges that he proceed in the
same path now that he has become a "Minister":

All this thou wert; and being this before,
Know, Kings and Fortune cannot make thee more,
Then scorn to gain a Friend by servile ways,
Nor wish to lose a Foe these Virtues raise;
But candid, free, sincere, as you began,
Proceed—a Minister, but still a Man.

(8-13)

Although the poem lacks the elegiac mood of the other epistles, it shares with them the movement at the close toward a personal context. Pope asks that Craggs not forget or be ashamed of his old friends, including "ev'n . . . Me." More important, the dignified praise and advice already accorded are given a particularly personal focus:

Be not (exalted to whate'er degree)
Asham'd of any Friend, not ev'n of Me.
The Patriot's plain, but untrod path pursue;
If not, 'tis I must be asham'd of You.

(14-17)

The moral standards are thus embodied in Pope himself. Their violation would in effect be a personal affront and would call forth Pope's own "shame" on behalf of his friend.

The two remaining epistles, the *Epistle to Miss Blount, on her leaving the Town, after the Coronation* and the *Epistle to Robert Earl of Oxford*, are more personal, and perhaps as a consequence better, poems than the previous ones. The true subject of both is friendship. In each Pope himself is quite consciously presented as a poet, acting not as commemorator or celebrant but as a companion who effects an imaginative union with a distant friend in distress—Miss Blount's comic-pathetic enforced retirement into the country after the coronation of George I, and Oxford's enforced retirement after his fall from power. The poems differ in one important respect. The latter was actually sent to Oxford "with Dr. Parnell's Poems published by our Authour, after the said Earl's Imprisonment in the Tower and Retreat into the Country, in the year 1721."[10] The poem's biographical import—for contemporary readers and for posterity—as a document of Pope's friendship with the disgraced Harley is unquestioned.

The biographical status of the *Epistle to Miss Blount* is more difficult to determine; there is no direct correlation between art and life. The poem was first printed in the 1717 *Works*, where it followed the *Epistle to a Young Lady, with the Works of Voiture* and was simply entitled, *To the same, on her leaving the Town after the Coronation*. Evidence from early manuscripts and from Pope's 1714 letters to the Blount sisters indicates that the poem was first addressed to Teresa.[11] But when Pope in 1735 retitled the "Voiture" poem as *Epistle to Miss Blount*, he left the impression— without actually saying so—that both it and the "Coronation" poem were addressed not to the estranged Teresa but to Martha. There may in fact be a kind of psychological truth in Pope's transformation of the original event into art. Friendship with Teresa did not last, but the poem continued to be reprinted, and Martha remained his lifelong friend.[12] This was not the only transformation of actual events. An attempt to tie the poem closely to Pope's own movements in 1714 uncovers significant disparity between art and life.[13] Nonetheless, although false to the surface

[10] Pope's own note, first published in 1740. The poem was sent in a letter accompanying the edition of Parnell: *Corr.*, II, 90.

[11] Zephalinda was Teresa's pet name, Parthenissa Martha's. At the time of the coronation Martha was ill with smallpox: *Corr.*, I, 264; Ault, *New Light on Pope*, pp. 56-59.

[12] Since Pope in 1714 seems to have treated the Blount sisters virtually as one, what was originally a tribute to one sister may without strain have been transferred many years later to the other.

[13] In the poem Pope represents himself as "still in town" after the lady has retired to the country. This fits neither Teresa nor Martha. At the time of the coronation (October 20), all three were in town. Both Teresa and Pope are presumed to have taken part in the attendant revelry, while Martha was ill at home. Pope left town shortly afterwards, returning in early November: *Corr.*, I, 264-65. The Blount sisters left shortly after him because of Martha's health, and were still away when Pope wrote to Martha on November 24. None of this is mentioned in the poem.

texture of events, the poem may remain true to their depths. To admit that there is no one-to-one correlation is not to dismiss the strongly personal quality of a poem. If the epistle centers, as I shall argue, on Pope's imaginative communion with an absent friend, then Martha may well have seemed in 1735 to be that friend.[14]

The "Coronation" epistle displays what we often find in a great poet: conventional materials reimagined and made to bear surprising emotional weight. It is far from being a merely light-verse compliment, "Full of grace and charm, . . . conceived in the vein of exquisite and well-bred pleasantry which characterises the Rape of the Lock."[15] The poem may perhaps begin in this vein, but by the close turns into something warmer and more plaintive. It is built on the stock contrast between the gay, worldly town and the dull country, where, from the point of view of a hundred Restoration comedy witty virgins, all beyond Hyde Park is a desert. It also employs the common device of a "letter from town to a friend in the country," a favorite form of familiar epistle in which Restoration poets and their successors passed on the latest news of politics or social gossip.[16] Indeed, the poem begins as if Pope were quite aware of the conventionality, almost the theatricality, of the situation:

> As some fond virgin, whom her mother's care
> Drags from the town to wholsome country air,
> Just when she learns to roll a melting eye,
> And hear a spark, yet think no danger nigh;

[14] See a letter from Pope to Teresa about Martha's smallpox: "Whatever Ravages a merciless Distemper may commit, I dare promise boldly what few (if any) of her Makers of Visits & Complements dare to do; she shall have one man as much her Admirer as ever" (*Corr.*, I, 265).

[15] Courthope, in *Works of Pope*, III, 223.

[16] The so-called "Lines suppressed at the End of the Epistle" (printed in *Poems*, VI, 232) clearly belong to this tradition. They describe, in Ruffhead's words, how "The beau Esprits spent their time in town." Their manner is licentious, the tone coarsely bawdy ("If poor *Pope* is cl-pt, the Fault is yours"). They seem discordant additions to the poem, either Pope's own (in a facetious moment) or a later "editor's." Cf. Rochester's "Letter from Artemisia to Chloe."

From the dear man unwilling she must sever,
Yet takes one kiss before she parts for ever:
Thus from the world fair *Zephalinda* flew. . . .

The "fond virgin," "spark," and "dear man" derive from the world of Restoration comedy, the "melting eye" and "fair Zephalinda" from the fantasy world of rococo love lyric. Pope suggests by such *literary* language and by the exaggeration of "drags" the falseness of the conventional situation and implies an ironic attitude toward the excessive emotion of the girl who must suffer a fate worse than death: "she parts for ever," and for the country! At the same time, he begins to discover in the stock situation the glimmer of a genuine emotion. The artless simplicity of "She sigh'd not that They stayed, but that She went" and the quiet repetition of "She went" hint at a pathos that Pope will later develop.

Pope then pursues the lady into the country, giving first the stock comic version of dull rural pleasures:

She went, to plain-work, and to purling brooks,
Old-fashion'd halls, dull aunts, and croaking rooks.

This is again the country world of stage comedy as Harriett describes it to Dorimant: " a great, rambling house that looks as if it were not inhabited, the family's so small. There you'll find my mother, an old lame aunt, and myself, sir, perched up on chairs at a distance in a large parlor, sitting moping like three or four melancholy birds in a spacious volary" (*The Man of Mode*, v). The whirling town world of "Op'ra, park, assembly, play" makes a sharp and comic contrast with "morning walks, and pray'rs three hours a day . . . reading and Bohea." But as the description continues, and as Pope puts greater emphasis on the young lady's isolation and arrested motion, the tone shifts slightly toward pathos:

To muse, and spill her solitary Tea,
Or o'er cold coffee trifle with the Spoon,

Count the slow clock, and dine exact at noon;
Divert her eyes with pictures in the fire,
Hum half a tune. . . .

(16-20)

The pathos is not allowed to gather, however, for Pope
quickly dissipates it with comic exaggeration—"Up to her
godly garret after sev'n, / There starve and pray, for that's
the way to heav'n"—and the deftly visualized scene of the
wooing visit by the hunting squire, another stock figure
drawn from Restoration wit comedy (compare Congreve's
Sir Wilful Witwoud).

The young lady, however, is plainly out of her native
element, and she dreams on her elbow of the town she has
left. The coarse squire, with his gun, dogs, and toast in
sack, yields in her imagination to "Lords, and Earls, and
Dukes, and garter'd Knights," "sceptres, coronets, and
balls."[17] Again Pope mixes comedy with pathos; he smiles
at the commonplace substance of her dream, but when the
"vision flies," Pope's emphasis falls for a moment on deprivation and desolation: "And leave you in lone woods, or
empty walls." We may even sense a diminished echo of the
prophetess or sibyl who drops from the bright glory of her
"vision" into the darkness of common day.

The scene then shifts to town and to the writer of the
epistle, plainly Pope himself, the friend of John Gay (line
47), the poet plagued as Pope no doubt sometimes was with
"want of rhyme" and with an aching head (line 42). What
begins as a stock comic situation is transformed into a ten-

[17] Pope's emphasis on the lady's imagined vision of the coronation
night, in a sense, apply to Martha as well as to Teresa. The point of the
poem does not lie in "the effect the Coronation had on the 'Young Lady'
who saw it" (Ault, *New Light on Pope*, p. 59), but in the effort, by her and by
Pope, to imagine what is not present: "imaginary sights," "vision," even
"recall the fancy'd scene," as if the scene were *first fancied not seen*—and
subsequently recalled. Martha never saw the coronation, but no doubt
imagined it. But see a letter from Pope to Martha: "That Face must needs
be irresistible which was adorned with Smiles even when it could not see
the Coronation" (*Corr.*, 1, 268). In the actual event, Martha retained her
good humor, while the "Miss Blount" in the poem was melancholy.

der expression of friendship by the poet who intrudes into the poem. The conventional town-country polarity is also transformed or reimagined, and its falsity is exposed. The country may be dull, but the "green" and "rural shade" is also a place for dreaming. The town is gay and lively from a distance, but also a place filled with "streets, chairs, and coxcombs." By disparaging the town, Pope may even be offering his friend a gentle hint that place in itself has no value. She dreams of town; he dreams not of the country, but of her. Perhaps, however, Pope is here simply being discreet. He does not presume to say that she thinks of him (the unidentified "dear man" she leaves may or may not be the same as "your slave"). But discretion does not prevent intimacy, as a look at the personal pronouns will show. The lady begins as "fond virgin" (1), "Zephalinda" (7), "she" (10), but at line 22 becomes "you." So too Pope begins as "your slave" (41), "he" (44), and becomes "I." Indeed, much of the effect of intimate I-you communion in the last lines depends simply on the pronouns—"*Gay* pats my shoulder, and you vanish quite. . . . I knit my brow, . . . as you may now."

By the close, we are made to realize fully, perhaps for the first time, that the description of the young lady in the country was a product of the poet-correspondent's imagination.[18] Though still in town, he is in fact "abstracted from the crew," withdrawn in thought if not in body. He thinks of the distant lady, rendering her vividly present to himself and his reader. The closing lines of the poem suggest more strongly this communion in imagination. As the introductory "So when your slave . . ." indicates, the situations of the lady and the poet are parallel: each is stranded in an inhospitable scene; each longs to escape (Pope is "vext to be still in town"); he dreams of the country as she dreams of the town, and his vision, like hers, "van-

[18] The only previous hint that the country scene is the product of invention or speculation is the "perhaps" in "Some Squire, perhaps, you take delight to rack" (23).

ishes" when interrupted by a sudden, trivial movement. She hums "half a tune" (20), Pope likewise hums a tune (50) and imagines that the lady at that very moment may be doing the same ("as you may now").[19] Even after the vision has vanished, the moment of intimate communion persists, as Pope again imagines his distant friend. This little poem, perhaps Pope's best short piece, is richer still when we recall the full personal context, the poet's lifelong affection for Martha Blount, ever dear, ever inaccessible.[20] The importation of biography is legitimized by Pope himself, who so clearly identifies himself as the poem's distant lover.

Imaginative communion with a distant friend is the deepest subject too of Pope's last major familiar epistle, the *Epistle to Robert Earl of Oxford*. As with the "Coronation" epistle, the ostensible subject—in one the town-country polarity, in the other the death of Parnell and Pope's dedication of the edition of his poems to Oxford—gives way to Pope's own declaration, as absent friend and attendant muse, of loyalty to the fallen statesman. As with the epistles to Jervas and to Miss Blount "with the works of Voiture," the immediate occasion, the gift of a book written not by Pope but by a kindred spirit, serves to awaken reflections on art and friendship which Pope affirms by his own experience and in his own person.

The poem takes up, as it were, where Parnell's poems leave off: "Such were the Notes, thy once-lov'd Poet sung, / 'Till Death untimely stop'd his tuneful Tongue." Pope's efforts have perpetuated Parnell's songs—extended his breath, he might have said—in two respects. Oxford, by means of the presented edition, may "Still hear thy *Parnell* in his living Lays" (16). More important, perhaps, is that Pope himself, the living poet, maintains the friendship of

[19] The implication even arises, I think, that together they hum a single tune, she one half, he the other.

[20] Teresa too, while she remained a friend, was both dear and inaccessible. Cf. the *Verses sent to Mrs. T. B. with his Works*, and the *Hymn Written in Windsor Forest*: "And love the brightest eyes, but love in vain!"

poet and statesman that marked the Scriblerus Club, whose short-lived meetings in 1714 included Oxford, Parnell, Swift, and Pope (all but Pope are specifically named in the poem). The poem looks back to the days just before Oxford's fall in the summer of 1714, reaffirming that their spirit has not been shattered by intervening events—the dispersal of the Scriblerians, Parnell's death, Oxford's imprisonment and retreat.

Parnell himself receives relatively little attention in Pope's poem. Thoughts on the dead, lamented in the opening lines, quickly lead to thoughts of the mourner. Parnell was "Dear to the Muse" (to Poetry and, probably, to Pope), "to Harley dear—in vain!" The following lines and subsequent paragraphs deal with Oxford, to whom this poem is dedicated, recalling how "for him" (that is, for Parnell) Oxford "despis'd the Farce of State," was "pleas'd to 'scape from Flattery to Wit." Now, however, Oxford's poetical friends are "Absent or dead." The dead friend claims a tear, and now among the immortals (Pope speculates), "perhaps forgets that Oxford e'er was Great," and from the "Seats Divine," "Beholds thee glorious only in thy Fall."[21] The living but "absent friend" (Pope so calls himself) likewise pays tribute to Oxford from a distance. He claims from Oxford "a sigh," and urges that, like Parnell, he too may remain "dear." In the poem's final paragraph attention shifts wholly to Oxford and to Pope, the absent friend, the living poet:

> In vain to Desarts thy Retreat is made;
> The Muse attends thee to the silent Shade:
> 'Tis hers, the brave Man's latest Steps to trace, .
> Re-judge his Acts, and dignify Disgrace.
>
> (27-30)

Again Pope avoids directly naming himself, but it is plain

[21] This is perhaps a secular parody of the Christian idea of the fortunate fall. Like Adam, Oxford in his fall proved himself superior "in each hard instance try'd," conquering "all Pain, all Passion, and all Pride, . . . and the Dread of Death."

that the "Muse" is Pope as poet. In the original autograph version the line reads, "My Muse attending. . . ." Though the revised version is more indirect or oblique, it is no less personal. "The Muse attends" both conceals and reveals Pope. It emphasizes his role as recording-dignifying poet and thus dignifies his attendance. As one by one the worldly desert the disgraced statesman, the Muse attends "to the Scaffold, or the Cell" (Pope visited Oxford in the Tower) and accompanies him, "ev'n now," in the "Evening Walk" of his life's "Various Day." Just as Parnell from his perspective could see Oxford "glorious only in thy Fall," so Pope from an earthly vantage "Thro' Fortune's Cloud One truly Great can see, / Nor fears to tell, that MORTIMER is He."[22]

The poem, which opens with a retrospective glimpse of a fondly remembered past (the Scriblerus Club) and attains a timeless view of Oxford's "Soul supreme" (the judgment *sub specie aeternitatis*), closes firmly in the present ("Ev'n now . . . Ev'n now . . .") and in a personal context, with Pope and Oxford. As we have seen him do before, Pope concludes the poem with an affirmation of continued loyalty and friendship and establishes an imaginative communion that bridges the physical distance between them. Oxford himself seems to have received the poem in this way; he responded to Pope's letter enclosing the epistle: "I received your Packet by the Carrier, which could not but give me great Pleasure, to see you preserve an Old Friend in Memory; for it must needs be very agreeable to be Remembred by those we highly Value." He objects that he comes far short of what "your great friendship and delicate Pen would partially describe me," and he looks back "to those Evenings I have usefully & pleasantly spent, with Mr Pope, Mr Parnel, Dean Swift, the Doctor, &c. I should be glad the world knew You admitted me to your Friendship" (*Corr.*, II, 91). Parnell is mentioned but once in Oxford's letter;

[22] In the letter enclosing the epistle, Pope wrote to Oxford that "I will not bow the knee to a Less Man than my Lord Oxford, & I expect to see no Greater in My Time" (*Corr.*, II, 90).

emphasis falls almost wholly on Pope's friendship for Oxford. Although Pope neither names himself nor makes use of the first person pronoun (perhaps he hesitates to obtrude because the poem dedicates a volume of Parnell), his presence in the poem is vivid.

The *Epistle to Oxford* (1721) is Pope's last familiar epistle of major consequence. The brief epistle *To Mr. Gay* (1720) is of some interest because it concentrates so squarely on the poet himself. Gay had written a "congratulatory letter on the finishing his house" at Twickenham. Pope responds, however, with a lament:

> In vain my structures rise, my gardens grow,
> In vain fair Thames reflects the double scenes
> Of hanging mountains, and of sloping greens. . . .
>
> (2-4)

For Lady Mary is not there; all joy has fled to dwell with her. In this poem Pope is *not* able to communicate with his dear absent friend (he is "unseen" by her, his sighs "unheard") and thus turns for some small relief to the sympathetic Gay: "Ah friend, 'tis true—this truth you lovers know" (1). However, Pope does not develop the theme of consolation or communion; he prefers to focus on his own loneliness. The exterior landscape becomes a psychological one: parterre and shade, bower and colonnade are but "soft recesses of uneasy minds / To sigh unheard in, to the passing winds" (9-10). In the final four lines the love-woe is clearly exaggerated, made melodramatic by the simile of the "struck deer," who

> in some sequester'd part
> Lies down to die, the arrow at his heart;
> There, stretch'd unseen in coverts hid from day,
> Bleeds drop by drop, and pants his life away.

The poem breaks off there in a distinctly literary, even histrionic, pose, in contrast with the much finer "Coronation" epistle, where the stock situation and language serve only as preamble to a more fully imagined scene and a more finely balanced tone. The epistle to Gay is perhaps of greater psychological than artistic interest.[23]

The lines *To Mrs. M[artha] B[lount] on her Birthday* (1724) are by contrast more personally reticent, more emotionally convincing, and more successful as art. Pope appears only discreetly masked, as the last of heaven's blessings—"Long Health, long Youth, long Pleasure, and a Friend" (2). The tone is witty, especially in the first verse paragraph: the birthday of a vain woman is but "the fun'ral of the former year" (10); for such women life is only a sieve that lets blessings slip through. Yet Pope achieves considerable intimacy, particularly in the closing lines. For Martha, Joy and Ease will calm and inspirit (contrast the vexing riches and tiring vanities of line 4). Far from losing blessings, she will find day "improve on day, and year on year." Death itself will come not as funereal gloom, but as a lover:

> Till Death unfelt that tender Frame destroy,
> In some soft Dream, or Extasy of Joy:
> Peaceful sleep out the Sabbath of the Tomb,
> And wake to Raptures in a Life to come.

This is finely and tenderly imagined, a delicate and discreetly fervent wish on the part of a devoted admirer to a spinster of thirty-three, for both of whom such ecstasy or rapture in marriage was denied. Only in imagination, perhaps, could it be permitted them. And in some sense they here share that rapture.

One can find evidence of Pope's private sensibility at work elsewhere in the poems from the 1710s. The voice attuned to loss and pathos, the voice that stresses an elegiac theme by reference to personal experience, appears in

---

[23] The poem was probably not designed for publication. Its personal opening lines did not appear until 1803. The more generalized lines 7-14 appeared in 1737.

some of Pope's other poems from that period: for example, *Eloisa to Abelard* and the *Elegy to the Memory of an Unfortunate Lady*.

Eloisa and the *Elegy* are chiefly of concern here as poems of passion and pathos, but they close, as do the epistles, with an intimate communion between Pope and the lady he describes. Although he makes little self-reference in the body of the poems, Pope ends each with a kind of "personal coda"[24] in which he emphasizes that a sympathetic poet-narrator must understand and speak the "language of the heart." As Eloisa concludes her epistle, she imagines some "future bard" remembering her story:

> And sure if fate some future Bard shall join
> In sad similitude of griefs to mine,
> Condemn'd whole years in absence to deplore,
> And image charms he must behold no more,
> Such if there be, who loves so long, so well;
> Let him our sad, our tender story tell;
> The well-sung woes will sooth my pensive ghost;
> He best can paint 'em, who shall feel 'em most.

Self-reference or self-revelation remains veiled, although it is fairly certain that Pope alludes in lines 361-62 to his own sorrow at Lady Mary's absence in 1716-1717.[25] Pope, who may have originally been inspired not by Lady Mary but by Martha Blount,[26] seems in any case to have been more interested in writing a passionate poem than in hinting at his love woe (he did not hesitate to express love woe *directly* in letters addressed to the absent Lady Mary).[27] He did write to Martha Blount while working on the poem, noting that the "Epistle of Eloise grows warm, and begins to have some Breathings of the Heart in it, which may

[24] Geoffrey Tillotson's term, in *Poems*, II, 357. Cf. *The Temple of Fame*, 497-524.
[25] See *Corr.*, I, 389-90, where Pope laments her "loss," thinks he will never see her again unless at the Day of Judgment, and compares himself to an Enthusiast or Solitaire who falls in love with saints.
[26] See Tillotson's introduction to the poem, in *Poems*, II, 310-12.
[27] See *Corr.*, I, 353, 364, 369, 389, 406, 469.

make posterity think I was in love."[28] Whether or not Pope
sought to create the impression that he too was in love with
an absent woman—the letter to Martha Blount ingenu-
ously seeks to discount such a suspicion—he declares his
empathy and intimates private suffering.[29]

Although both *Eloisa to Abelard* and the *Elegy* seem to
have been inspired in part by Pope's love for Lady Mary,[30]
in neither poem does he openly present himself as the historical Alexander Pope. Perhaps this obliquity allows the
poems, particularly *Eloisa to Abelard*, to become self-
expressive in a different and deeper way.[31] As it is, Pope
has Eloisa establish a kind of communion with the "Bard"
who will one day tell her story, both through the shared
suffering ("sad similitude of griefs") and the memorial
power of art. The thought that her woes will be well sung
brings Eloisa some comfort, but the memorializing and
celebrative power of art is counterbalanced by the poet's
own grief.

[28] *Corr.*, I, 338. A letter to Lady Mary (ibid., 407) hints that *Eloisa* may
allude to her.

[29] The last lines, "added by the Poet in allusion to his own case, and the
state of his own mind," had such an effect on Joseph Warton: "I am well
informed that what determined him in the choice of this epistle, was the
retreat of that lady into a nunnery, whose death he had lately so patheti-
cally lamented, in a foregoing Elegy, and for whom he had conceived a
violent passion. . . . The recollection of this circumstance will add a beauty
and pathos to many passages in the poem" (*Essay on the Genius and Writings
of Pope*, 4th ed., 2 vols. [London, 1782], I, 345-46). Though Warton was
probably wrong about the origin of the poem, he suggests how
eighteenth-century readers viewed it, and, probably, the impression Pope
sought to create.

[30] Tillotson, "Lady Mary Wortley Montagu and Pope's *Elegy to the Memory of an Unfortunate Lady*," *Review of English Studies*, 12 (1936), 401-12.

[31] See above, p. xvi. In his letters to Lady Mary during her absence
(1716-1718) Pope frequently speaks of her departure and absence as a
"death"; see, for example, *Corr.*, I, 345, 354, 357, 381. Eloisa's frustrated
passion for Abelard seems in some ways a reflection of Pope's own for
Lady Mary. Like Eloisa, Pope prominently praises his lover's eyes (*Corr.*, I,
369; *Eloisa*, 63, 122, 245, 283, 295). He thinks of Lady Mary as a saint or
angel (*Corr.*, I, 390, 406, 469), and he imagines meeting her again at the
Day of Judgment (ibid., 369, 384). The delicate eroticism of Pope's
letters—the near-idolatry, the attraction now to the naked soul and now to
the body—suggestively resembles Eloisa's.

In the case of the *Elegy*, viewed from the vantage of the poet, art's power is even weaker:

> Poets themselves must fall, like those they sung;
> Deaf the prais'd ear, and mute the tuneful tongue,
> Ev'n he, whose soul now melts in mournful lays,
> Shall shortly want the gen'rous tear he pays;
> Then from his closing eyes thy form shall part,
> And the last pang shall tear thee from his heart,
> Life's idle business at one gasp be o'er,
> The Muse forgot, and thou belov'd no more!

The lady will be remembered and "beloved" so long as the poet survives. But when his eyes close, her fame too will die. Unlike many conventional elegies, which offer the consolation of earthly fame and perpetuation through mortal memory and through art, Pope's *Elegy* offers only temporary aid, the fidelity of a single sensibility. He cannot promise for the hearts of other readers. The tribute remains a private communion between the dead lady and the poet himself.

After the early 1720s Pope rarely made use of this kind of intimate address. Even in epistles addressed to friends (the *Moral Essays*, the *Imitations of Horace*), the real audience is Pope's wider reading public. But in one instance he retained that favorite device from his early poems. The *Epistle to a Lady* moves from a survey of the characters of women to a celebration of Martha Blount's good humor, which makes her a model for all women. But here too the "moral essay" is focused, at the close, on the poet's personal relationship to the lady he praises. "Ah Friend!" begins the poem's final section, and Pope goes on to contrast Martha Blount, a spinster of forty-four, with the toasts and queens of the world—vain dazzlers, soon to meet their fate as the world's veterans. The "Friend" (249), later "You" (280), is without question Martha Blount. Warburton argued that by endowing the "Friend" (called "She" in lines 259-68) with a daughter, husband, and loved sister, Pope was making plain that he intended to present "an encomium on an imaginary lady."[32] For, as Pope plainly indicates in several places—"Virgin Modesty" (255); the lack of "pelf" to purchase a "tyrant," that is, a husband (287-88)—Martha was unmarried. But the passage easily admits of another interpretation. Pope is illustrating the effects of "Temper" in hypothetical situations, and he perhaps also confronts the sad fact that the best women in his world, no less than the worst, live incomplete or unfulfilled lives. To speak of husbands is to recall that Martha lacks one. Pope puts a good face on her spinsterhood in the closing lines but does not pretend that her fortune is unmixed. He implies that she never married only because she had no dowry. As compensation (if indeed she needs compensation for having escaped the state which Pope discreetly presents as domestic tyranny and the wealth which he dismisses with contempt as drossy pelf), Phoebus, who "kept dross for duchesses . . . To you gave Sense, Good-humour, *and a poet*." Pope presents himself as her "servant," but the declaration of devotion, though indirect, is nonetheless warm and sincere. Not only does Pope bring her just fame—it is through his doing that "the world shall know" her virtues and her superiority to a whole sex of wealthy duchesses—but he also brings loyalty and love. Just as fame compensates for the lack of money, so the friendship of a poet compensates in part for the lack of a husband. But the poem has made it abundantly clear that in such a world a woman has no life except in marriage. As in *The Rape of the Lock*, the compensation is qualified by our lingering elegiac awareness. Yet Pope's final complaint is all the more moving for acknowledging what has been lost.

Such intimacy, as I have suggested, is rare in Pope's later poetry. But the late poems are no less personal, though in a

[32] Quoted in *Poems*, III, pt. 2, 46, 72. As Maynard Mack reminds me, Warburton disliked Martha and may have been trying to divert glory from her.

different manner. What he retains from his early epistles is his habit of drawing on his personal sensibility, of focusing a moral issue in terms of his own personal experience, and of validating the truth of a moral commonplace by the testimony of his own conscience.

·‥·◦[5]◦·‥·
"Ourselves to Know":
The Poet in
An Essay on Man

To seek out self-expressive elements in *An Essay on Man*
might at first appear to be a futile, or even perverse, misdi-
rection of critical energy. Is the *Essay* not a preeminently
"impersonal" poem, discursive-didactic in a familiar
eighteenth-century manner, an essay whose versified ideas
are so traditional, so commonplace that one can hardly
imagine Pope to be expressing anything significant about
himself? In fact, however, the very commonplace quality of
Pope's ideas might well make the reader shift his critical attention elsewhere, from the content of the poem to the
shaping and self-reflecting imagination of the poet. And
indeed, the best critics of the poem, from Johnson to the
present day, have done just that. The *Essay*, says Johnson,
is "an egregious instance of the predominance of genius,
the dazzling splendour of imagery, and the seductive powers of eloquence":

> Surely a man of no very comprehensive search may
> venture to say that he has heard all this before, but it
> was never till now recommended by such a blaze of
> embellishment, or such sweetness of melody. The vig-
> orous contraction of some thoughts, the luxuriant
> amplification of others, the incidental illustrations,
> and sometimes the dignity, sometimes the softness, of
> the verses, enchain philosophy, suspend criticism, and
> oppress judgment by overpowering pleasure.[1]

[1] "Life of Pope," pp. 243-44.

In our own day, Reuben Brower has also drawn attention to the "energy and controlling hand of the poet," the witty Horatian conversationalist, whose expert modulations of movement, feeling, and tone give "poetic life" to what would otherwise be little more than dull, expertly rhymed, popular "philosophy."[2] Even the author of a recent background study of the "context" of Pope's ideas concludes that "the fun in the *Essay on Man* is with Pope's performance, not with the validity of the philosophy. It is with watching an agile mind at work playing with ideas as with the pieces on a chess board."[3] And Thomas Edwards, in the most suggestive of current studies of the poem, argues that " 'philosophy' as doctrinal product matters less than the activity of trying to produce it, the continual redefining and shifting of emphasis required to think seriously about the case."[4] Although these critics disagree about Pope's implied stake in his performance (is he detachedly playing or seriously straining?), they agree that a reader is interested in the implied rhetorical and imaginative powers of the poet, in the "mind at work."

I take this consensus as my starting point for a further exploration of the ways in which we can say that Pope is felt to be present in the poem, of the ways in which the poem may usefully be called self-expressive. Pope makes little use in the *Essay* of the explicitly *self-referential* mode. What little there is, however, is significant. The poem opens and closes with the kind of obtrusive self-reference that characterizes Pope's Horatian epistles:

> Awake, my st. john! leave all meaner things
> To low ambition, and the pride of Kings.
> Let us (since Life can little more supply
> Than just to look about us and to die)

[2] Brower, *Alexander Pope: The Poetry of Allusion* (Oxford, 1959), p. 237.

[3] Douglas White, *Pope and the Context of Controversy* (Chicago, 1970), p. 193. Significantly, White's book is subtitled *The Manipulation of Ideas in An Essay on Man*.

[4] Edwards, "Visible Poetry: Pope and Modern Criticism," in Reuben Brower, ed., *Twentieth Century Literature in Retrospect*, Harvard English Studies, 2 (Cambridge, Mass., 1971), p. 317.

Expatiate free o'er all this scene of Man . . .
Together let us beat this ample field. . . .

Come then, my Friend, my Genius, come along,
Oh master of the poet, and the song! . . .
Teach me, like thee, in various nature wise,
To fall with dignity, with temper rise. . . .

These passages are an important index of the kind of discourse Pope is writing—easy, casual, conversational—and
of the kind of man he wants to portray himself as being—
witty gentleman, modest friend of famous men. His ultimate frame of reference is personal: we begin and end
with the figure of the inquiring poet. (The poem is only
tactically anonymous. Pope concealed his name at its first
publication only to secure an impartial reception. Once the
poem was a success, Pope was delighted to own it.) With the
exception of these two key passages, however, Pope does
not call on the reader to think of the historical Alexander
Pope.[5]

But the *Essay on Man* may of course be self-expressive
without being openly self-referential. I argue that it is
self-expressive in two loosely related ways. First, it perva-
sively reflects Pope's recurrent personal concerns (for
example, with disease and imperfection) and attitudes (toward his own mercurial temperament, toward the value of
self-love rightly understood). The personal import of these
ideas, unemphasized in the poem, is clear only to a reader
familiar with Pope's other poems and letters. Second, as
Edwards and others have already pointed out, the life of
the poem may lie in Pope's very self-consciousness as
rhetorician and philosopher. His shifting stance in relation
to his subject and his audience constitutes, at least from one
perspective, the poem's excitement and drama. The obtrusively personal passages at the opening and close of the
poem may in fact be indicators of this more pervasive self-
expressiveness.

[5] There is one other exception: in Epistle iv Pope asks "why so long (in
life if long can be) / Lent Heav'n a parent to the poor and me?" (109-10).

Readers familiar with Pope will have no difficulty recognizing the personal dimension of Pope's description of Virtue's prize as "the soul's calm sun-shine" (iv.168).[6] The poet whose own mind seemed filled with April weather, and who paid tribute to the sunny disposition and even temperament of Patty Blount, surely has in mind more than the happiness of mankind in general. To take another example, who but Pope might better describe man as a "Chaos of thought and passion, all confused"? The poem then is in some sense a metaphor for Pope's self, an attempt by an acutely self-conscious, self-centered poet to work out, in relatively impersonalized terms, a coherent view of some aspects of his life and nature that most disturbed him.

This is not to suggest, however, that the *Essay* is confessional, or even that it is an accurate and comprehensive register of Pope's deepest personal preoccupations in the years before and after 1730. We would not know, from reading the *Essay* alone, that Pope's personal troubles in the period 1730-1733 were particularly severe. Though his mother was not to die until 1734, she had been for some years in what he called "a constant and regular Decay," so often "on her last Bed" that Pope frequently confined himself to care for her (*Corr.*, III, 226). And yet, in the midst of such private pain, Pope casually mentions that he has been "busy in the Moral Book [apparently the *Essay on Man*] I told you of" (*Corr.*, III, 227). Pope's own health too was unusually bad in 1731: headaches, fevers, and rheumatism left him weak and sleepless. One long bout of illness is dryly summarized: "in the whole, nine weeks pain, confinement, and sickness; from all which I am just now free, whilst God pleases. I know to tell you This, is the chief thing you would hear from me, and next time that I am not utterly unresigned to bear them again, if it must be so"

---

[6] Cf. I.151-54: "As much that end [human happiness] a constant course requires / Of show'rs and sun-shine, as of Man's desires; / As much eternal springs and cloudless skies, / As Men for ever temp'rate, calm, and wise."

(*Corr.*, III, 189-90). These were the personal circumstances of a constantly suffering poet who set out jauntily to celebrate providence. Plainly, much of Pope's personal pain in those years is kept out of the *Essay*. Yet one might reasonably suppose (without being able to demonstrate it) that his resignation—"not utterly unresigned"—to bear pain "if it must be so" or if it please God might be one of the motive forces leading him to attempt to vindicate the ways of God to men.

If we look in the *Essay* not for undisguised personal detail but for the recurrent concerns of Pope's imagination, we can see the discussions of "partial evil, universal good," of man's divided state, of the ruling passion, of the struggles between reason and passion, of the progress of self-love into social love, of true happiness in virtue and benevolence as ancient moral commonplaces confirmed once again by Pope's own experience. To discern principles of natural and moral order in an apparently chaotic universe and riddlingly divided human nature might serve also as a means of justifying the ways of God to Pope, a man dizzied by the mercury of his own personality and the pervasive incongruity of his life, plagued by a mismatched mind and body, rewarded with more than his share of the world's success, and burdened by more than his share of the world's ills.

As we have seen, Pope through the 1720s often reflected on his divided, inconsistent nature, particularly on his apparently conflicting responsibilities as man and as poet. It was not until the 1730s that he began to work out, in letters and in poems, a satisfactory image of himself—as Virtue's friend—that combined several diverse impulses.[7] It is perhaps not mere coincidence that in the *Essay on Man*, which occupied much of his poetic energies in the early

---

[7] The *Epistle to Fortescue*, in which appears the line "TO VIRTUE ONLY and HER FRIENDS, A FRIEND," was published in February 1733. Pope was at work on the *Essay on Man* from 1730, and began publishing it in February 1733.

1730s, we find essentially two different conceptions of human personality: in Epistles I and II, an anxious, skeptical view of man as divided against himself, or united only by means of a disturbing mental "disease" or "principle of death," his ruling passion, and isolated from his fellows in his own private fantasy; and in Epistles III and IV a more reassuring view of man as reintegrated, reunited with his fellows in social and political order by means of the natural progress of self-love into social love, and the workings of virtue manifesting itself in benevolence. Viewed from this perspective, the *Essay on Man* is at once a compendium of familiar moral generalizations and a poem richly self-expressive both of Pope's worst fears about himself and his most idealized self-image.

Pope's subject in Epistle II is the "Nature and State of Man, with respect to himself, as an Individual." His basic theme, here as throughout the *Essay*, is the providential order underlying apparent disorder: "the Ends of Providence and general Good are answered in our Passions and Imperfections" ("Argument"). What is remarkable, however, is how darkly Pope treats the commonplaces about man's divided nature, how much emphasis he places on man's limited comprehension, his self-delusion, his "folly." The famous opening lines, for example, reduce man, that favored creature *paulo minus ab angelis*,[8] to chaos and riddle:

> Plac'd on this isthmus of a middle state,
> A being darkly wise, and rudely great:
>
> .   .   .   .
>
> in doubt to act, or rest,
> In doubt to deem himself a God, or Beast;
> In doubt his Mind or Body to prefer,
> Born but to die, and reas'ning but to err;
> Alike in ignorance, his reason such,
> Whether he thinks too little, or too much:

[8] Psalm 8:5, in the Vulgate Bible (Ps. 8:6 in the King James version). Pope quotes the phrase in a letter (*Corr.*, II, 320).

Chaos of Thought and Passion, all confus'd;
Still by himself abus'd, or disabus'd;
Created half to rise, and half to fall;
Great lord of all things, yet a prey to all;
Sole judge of Truth, in endless Error hurl'd:
The glory, jest, and riddle of the world!

Man's "middle state" is of course an ancient topic of moral philosophers, a way of defining man's special place in the creation, his special powers and capacities, "higher than the beasts, but lower than the angels." But Pope gives more emphasis to "Frailties" and "Limits" than to "Powers."[9] Instead of a productive middle, he sees the disabling clash of extremes: too much knowledge, too much weakness, wisdom obscured by darkness, greatness held back by rudeness, too much or too little thought, a chaos of thought and passion. Ultimately, he is reduced to moral paralysis:

With too much knowledge for the Sceptic side,
With too much weakness for the Stoic's pride,
He *hangs between*. . . .[10]

There he hangs, doubting (the word "doubt" recurs three times),[11] as Pope rhetorically drives the extremes farther apart. Man's disability prevents him from taking any single direction; one aspect of his nature cancels out another, just as the second half of Pope's line tends to cancel the first.

The epistle thus begins with an image of human chaos.

[9] Pope's gloss, added in 1735, refers to man's "Middle-Nature, his Powers, Frailties, and the Limits of his Capacity." The origin of the note may suggest the direction of Pope's thought. It stands in the Morgan manuscript at the beginning of Epistle ii, at the head of some canceled lines. The marginal note first read "His Capacity and Faculties" and is altered to "His Capacity how limited." See the facsimile edition, *An Essay on Man: Reproductions of the Manuscripts in the Pierpont Morgan Library and the Houghton Library*, with an introduction by Maynard Mack, published for the Roxburge Club (Oxford, 1962).

[10] Compare how much more comfortably Pope treats such a position in the exactly contemporary *Epistle to Fortescue*: "Papist or Protestant, or both between, / Like good Erasmus in an honest Mean, / In Moderation placing all my Glory."

[11] In the first edition, "in doubt" appears only twice.

Despite subsequent argument that the discordances of human nature—reason and self-love or the passions—cooperate and resolve into a *discordia concors*, that initial image of chaos or discord survives. Though reason is the card and passion the gale (lines 107-8), in fact, passion, and particularly the ruling passion, easily dominates reason, a "weak queen," a "sharp accuser, but a helpless friend" (150-54). And the ruling passion, though it seems to permit Pope to perceive a pattern in human personality beneath the apparent chaos, to fix "the Mercury of Man," turns out a mixed blessing. For like Aaron's serpent, it "swallows up" the other passions, and like a cancerous tumor, it grows to dominate and ultimately to destroy them:

> As Man, perhaps, the moment of his breath,
> Receives the lurking principle of death;
> The young disease, that must subdue at length,
> Grows with his growth, and strengthens with his
>   strength:
> So, cast and mingled with his very frame,
> The Mind's disease, its ruling Passion came;
> Each vital humour which should feed the whole,
> Soon flows to this, in body and in soul.
> Whatever warms the heart, or fills the head,
> As the mind opens, and its functions spread,
> Imagination plies her dang'rous art,
> And pours it all upon the peccant part.

(133-44)

Strictly speaking (note the elaborate "As . . . so" construction), Pope here describes the ruling passion's gradual domination of the mind. This is in itself perhaps alarming enough, but the analogy with the "lurking principle of death" and the ultimately mortal "disease" implies that the ruling passion finally destroys the man himself, degrades him to an obsessed automaton. And Pope's final vision of man in the epistle bears this out. Ruled by his predominant passion, whether "knowledge, fame, or pelf,"

The learn'd is happy nature to explore,
The fool is happy that he knows no more;
The rich is happy in the plenty giv'n,
The poor contents him with the care of Heav'n.

(263-66)

More darkly,

See the blind begger dance, the cripple sing,
The sot a hero, lunatic a king;
The starving chemist in his golden views
Supremely blest, the poet in his muse.

(267-70)

If this epistle has some direct or indirect bearing on
Pope's own nature, what then is his ruling passion? Judging by the letters of the 1720s and early 30s, Pope might
have wondered whether he had a ruling passion. If
pressed, he might have hesitated to decide between Poetry
and Friendship. Perhaps we may take as hints the disturbing lines at the end of Epistle II about the singing cripple
and the imparadised poet, who is no less entrapped in his
private vision than the starving alchemist. These lines may
imply that Pope fears that his own attachment to art and to
poetic fame might be a disabling, self-deluding, and ultimately isolating obsession.

Restoration, as Maynard Mack has noted, is the theme
of the last two epistles—restoration of man's union with
his fellows and the world, and restoration of a surely
grounded happiness.[12] The focus of Epistle III is social—
"the Nature and State of Man, with respect to Society"—
that is, societies of men rather than individual men, but
even here we can find reflections of Pope's view of himself.
For man's reunion with his kind is accomplished by the
progress of self-love into social love. In Pope's letters we
have already traced a similar movement: the intense concern with the moral health and aesthetic achievement of

[12] Mack, in *Poems*, Vol. III, pt. 1, *An Essay on Man*, ed. Mack, lxi.

the self; the rival claims of private and public life in the
1730s; and the gradual resolution of the rivalry as the private self is redefined to include a wider realm—friends
and, ultimately, the political community. "The way to have
a Publick Spirit, is first to have a Private one" (*Corr.*, II,
333). The private-spirited, self-loving man can at the same
time be the public-spirited political man: "Self-love forsook
the path it first pursu'd, / And found the private in the public good" (III. 281-82). In the third epistle Pope traces this
"spreading" of private interest: men are urged to society in
part by instinctual love of mates and children. But some
principle more enduring is required to maintain "more
lasting bands":

> Reflection, Reason, still the ties improve,
> At once extend the int'rest, and the love;
> With choice we fix, with sympathy we burn;
> Each Virtue in each Passion takes its turn;
> And still new needs, new helps, new habits rise,
> That graft benevolence on charities.
> Still as one brood, and as another rose,
> These nat'ral love maintain'd, habitual those:
> The last, scarce ripen'd into perfect Man,
> Saw helpless him from whom their life began:
> Mem'ry and fore-cast just returns engage,
> That pointed back to youth, this on to age;
> While pleasure, gratitude, and hope, combin'd,
> Still spread the int'rest, and preserv'd the kind.
>
> (133-46)

Although Pope's subject here is the evolution of societies,
he makes it plain that the same interests and passions drive
individual man and social man. The same self-love that
drives "To one Man's pow'r, ambition, lucre, lust," when
operating in all men, "becomes the cause / Of what re-
strains him, Government and Laws" (269-72).

Epistle IV makes clearer how, from the point of view of
individual men, self-love is "push'd" to social love and benevolence. As a recent commentator has put it, "Pope's po-

sition is that men do all out of self-love, but self-love is so bound up with benevolence that self-love and social love are the same; in doing good for themselves men do good for their fellow men."[13] The converse is also true: in doing good for others, men do good for themselves. Pope's analysis corresponds closely with his own view of himself in his correspondence.

The central argument of Epistle IV is that virtue, manifesting itself in benevolence, is the true ground of human happiness. Much of the epistle is taken up with the "false scale of Happiness" (288), the vanity of foolish human wishes for riches, honors, nobility, greatness. It is perhaps significant that Pope reserved for last two false goods— fame and "Superior Talents"—that particularly tempted him.

From the time of his *Temple of Fame* (1713), as we have seen, Pope had been ambivalent about poetic fame, its value, and its proper grounds. The *Essay on Man* is one of several declarations in the 1730s (the *Epilogue to the Satires* is another) that Pope is coming more and more to think of the truest fame as a man's own conscious rectitude:

What's Fame? a fancy'd life in others breath,
A thing beyond us, ev'n before our death.
Just what you hear, you have, and what's unknown
The same (my Lord) if Tully's or your own.
All that we feel of it begins and ends
In the small circle of our foes and friends;
. . . .
A Wit's a feather, and a Chief a rod;
An honest Man's the noblest work of God.
. . . .
All fame is foreign, but of true desert,
Plays round the head, but comes not to the heart:
One self-approving hour whole years out-weighs
Of stupid starers, and of loud huzzas;

[13] White, *Pope and the Context of Controversy*, p. 180.

And more true joy Marcellus exil'd feels,
Than Caesar with a senate at his heels.

(237-58; italics added)

"Parts superior" are no surer a foundation of happiness
than is vulgar fame. Lines 259-68 are addressed to Bolingbroke—"Tell (for You can) what is it to be wise?"—but
Pope had reason to apply them to himself as well. If he did
not suffer the loneliness of genius ("Condemn'd in business
or in arts to drudge / Without a second, or without a judge"
and "none aid you" hardly fit the cotranslator of Homer),
he would have shared with Bolingbroke the "Painful preheminence": all fear him, few understand, "Above life's
weakness, and its comforts too." Pope was of course preeminent for wit, and as early as the *Essay on Criticism* had reflected on the price a wit had to pay.[14] In the early 1730s
Pope was vulnerably preeminent for the wittily malicious
Dunciad, and since 1728 he had been the target of frequent
attacks. The *Essay on Man* may in part have been an attempt by Pope to shift to less dangerous ground, to turn
from lampoon to moral poetry, to celebrate not wit but benevolence.

When Pope at the end of Epistle IV locates the true
ground of worldly happiness in virtue and defines virtue
ultimately as "Love of Man," he is formulating a general
view of man that, however traditional, corresponds precisely with the man of wide friendship, benevolence, and
virtue that emerges from his own letters and the Horatian
poems of the 1730s: "TO VIRTUE ONLY and HER FRIENDS, A
FRIEND."

Know then this truth (enough for Man to know)
"Virtue alone is Happiness below."
The only point where human bliss stands still,
And tastes the good without the fall to ill;
· ·
Without satiety, tho' e'er so blest,
And but more relish'd as the more distress'd:

14 See above Chap. 3.

The broadest mirth unfeeling Folly wears,
Less pleasing far than Virtue's very tears.
. . . .
Never elated, while one man's oppress'd;
Never dejected, while another's bless'd;
And where no wants, no wishes can remain,
Since but to wish more Virtue, is to gain.

(309-26)

Virtue here is not so much conscious rectitude, the purity
of the "honest man" whose greatest concern is finally his
own integrity. Pope has shifted ground from the earlier
passage on "self-approval." Rather, virtue consists of an
out-reaching benevolence and fellow feeling, a sympathetic
act that makes a neighbor's blessings and ills one's own (line
354). Human society thus becomes "one close system of
benevolence":

" Self-love but serves the virtuous mind to wake,
  As the small pebble stirs the peaceful lake;
  The centre mov'd, a circle strait succeeds,
  Another still, and still another spreads,
  Friend, parent, neighbour, first it will embrace,
  His country next, and next all human race.

(363-68)

The self is redefined to include one's friends and, ultimately, humanity at large. Self-fulfillment is attained by
the widest benevolence; self-love and social love are one.
"There is nothing meritorious," as Pope said on his
deathbed, "but Virtue, & Friendship, and Friendship is
only a part of Virtue."

If this vision of virtuous benevolence at the end of the
Essay on Man corresponds to Pope's own idealized view of
himself, it may have been one of the last moments in his
career when his fellow feeling was so widely diffused, when
"height of Bliss" was "height of Charity," extending even to
one's enemies (line 356). Already in Epistle IV we can see
signs of a more rigorous Pope, concerned more with rectitude than sympathy. Increasingly in the 1730s, Pope's

poems sound the note of the one "honest man," for whom one "self-approving hour" counts more than to share in the blessings and oppressions of other men. As in his imagination he becomes more alienated from the moral and political worlds around him, he constricts his fellow feeling, narrows his self to the few friends of Virtue, and, if necessary, to himself alone. Martyrlike, he will willingly reascend the "painful preheminence" and defend against the world the high ground of Truth.

Such correlation as I have sketched between Pope's vision of mankind and his view of himself is but one aspect of the self-expressiveness of the *Essay on Man*. It does not so much provide an account of significant internal features of the poem as it integrates the poem with Pope's developing conception of himself, as reflected in his correspondence and the poems of the 1730s. The reader familiar with the life of Pope's mind will see, I think, that the poem has a personal dimension, and he will see links between the relatively reticent *Essay on Man* and the more obtrusively self-presentational *Horatian Imitations* published in the years immediately following. But the reader might justifiably object at this point that the general correlations between the ideas in the *Essay* and the private concerns of Pope the man do not finally *demonstrate* the poem's personal import. Either or both of two conclusions might be drawn. First, the *Essay* shows that a study of the self-expressiveness of Pope's poems must confess to some limits. Some of the poems respond less well than others to this kind of analysis. Second, the *Essay*, long felt by various readers to be unsatisfactory because it seems little more than embellished commonplaces, because it seems too glib, too reliant on an undeniable ability at clever (facile?) generalization, may disappoint them *because* it is not more personal, because it does not seem deeply felt, because they do not find more of Pope in the poem.

But it may be that such readers are looking in the wrong

place. True, personal experience does not consistently inform Pope's abstractions; concrete particulars do not always substantiate the generalizations. Johnson's *Vanity of Human Wishes* is usually judged better on these counts than Pope's *Essay*, but it would be very difficult to demonstrate this.[15] And the two didactic poems are, after all, quite different. Pope's poem is a performance, a display piece. Paradoxically, we can fairly say that as such it expresses something powerful in Pope, a delight in synthesizing, in comprehending "all" in a single, ordered pattern. The pattern is God's, but it requires the ordering genius of the poet to recreate it. To recreate and identify himself with a perfect "whole," furthermore, would be particularly gratifying to Pope, who felt himself alienated from his countrymen because of his religion and politics, from marriage and parenthood because of his deformity, from that very body itself that he often thought of as an "imperfect frame" (*Corr.*, III, 250).

If we seek largely in vain for concrete evidence of Pope-the-man in the *Essay*, we cannot fail to find Pope-the-poet. Although by no means as remarkably intrusive as Milton in *Paradise Lost*, the poet-expositor is hardly a mere transparent medium. He steadily, though implicitly, draws attention either to himself or to his poetic object (the attempt from a limited human perspective to "vindicate the ways of God to Man") and dramatizes, through his own role as expositor, man's special position and his special dilemma in the universe.

This aspect of the poem, as I have suggested, has been noticed occasionally, although it is perhaps only Thomas Edwards who has placed the poem's self-conscious rhetoric, its "visible poetry," in the center of his attention. It is Edwards's view that the poem dramatizes or makes visible a

[15] Donald Davie expresses a consensus in claiming that in the *Vanity* personal experience is "pressed up close behind every abstraction": Davie, *The Late Augustans* (London, 1958), p. xxiii.

failure in comprehension, an inability to "resolve . . . ideas into coherent unity": "Not the substance of a doctrine, but the activity of trying to formulate it satisfactorily—and only partly succeeding, and knowing that the success is only partial—is what Pope most powerfully expresses."[16] Edwards draws the subtle and acute distinction between mere failure or confusion—bad philosophy—and knowing failure, in fact a kind of success—"the making of poetry out of resistances to one's own doctrinal impulses." It is difficult to improve on Edwards's formulation of the tension that gives the *Essay* its poetic and philosophic life. He admirably charts the divided tendencies toward the assertion of order and the acknowledgment of chaos in Epistle II, the part of the poem he chooses for analysis. But to focus closely on Epistle II may not account adequately for the whole poem. I think it possible that Edwards is too close to the paragraph-to-paragraph movement of the epistle, alert to the "mighty maze" whose turns he traces, but perhaps not sufficiently to the larger "plan."[17] In my view, the poem is not a dramatization of partial failure, but the fully achieved expression of man's special perspective, his partial or intermittent comprehension, his capacity for limited vision. As one critic has recently noted, the *Essay* displays an "almost obsessive concern with 'seeing,' as both fact and metaphor."[18] But, as Pope insists, man only sees "a part"

[16] Edwards, "Visible Poetry," pp. 316-17. The roots of Edwards's argument seem to lie in his earlier book, *This Dark Estate*, where he says that although Pope "yearns for an imaginative myth of cosmic immutability to sustain and console him, . . . the myth does not work perfectly." Pope, he notes, " was not wholly convinced by his own vision of order" (pp. 44-45).

[17] In a subsequent edition, "Corrected by the Author" in 1733, Pope himself gave increased attention to the "plan." Epistle 1.6 first read "A mighty Maze! of walks without a Plan," putting the emphasis, as Mack (*Poems*, III, pt. 1, 12n.) notes, "on man's not having a chart of the maze" (*plan* as drawing). The revised reading emphasizes the "order in the maze (*plan* as scheme of arrangement) even though . . . man can obtain only glimmerings of its nature." William Empson comments ingeniously on the ways in which a maze "at once has and has not got a plan": Empson, *Seven Types of Ambiguity*, 3d ed. (London, 1953), pp. 204-5.

[18] Particia M. Spacks, *An Argument of Images: The Poetry of Alexander Pope* (Cambridge, Mass., 1971), p. 41.

with any clarity. The rest of the world remains to him a riddle. In effect, he always sees double, both the "maze" and the "plan," both the puzzle and the pattern. Man knows both that "Man's a fool" and that "GOD IS WISE," and he can be both chastened and consoled by that knowledge. The life of the poem, its excitement and drama, lie in the juxtaposition of "plan" and "maze," in maintaining two ways of seeing, that is, man's way and, insofar as we can attain it by imagination or faith, God's way.[19] But where Edwards finds the poem consistently less interesting and successful when it reaches beyond "natural experience," I find the juxtaposition of "experience" and "speculation" crucial. This divided vision Pope expresses most effectively through his own role as narrator-expositor and through his exploration of the narrator's relation to his task—his adequacy to undertake it, his stance or point of vantage, and the extent and limit of his knowledge.

Pope's first recorded remark about the *Essay on Man* suggests that he had some sense of the self-conscious role he would play in the poem. In 1725 he wrote to Swift, then at work on *Gulliver*: "Your Travels I hear much of; my own I promise you shall never more be in a strange land, but a diligent, I hope useful, investigation of my own Territories. I mean no more Translations, but something domestic, fit for my own country, and for my own time."[20] Already Pope sees himself as a philosophic explorer who travels not to strange lands but investigates at home (something English? contemporary? personal?) and will report the findings to his countrymen. When the four epistles were first published together in 1734, Pope again drew attention to the project he had undertaken. In "The Design," prefixed to Epistle 1, he takes the reader into his study and

[19] Herein I agree with Edwards's remark (*This Dark Estate*, p. 44) that the *Essay* "finally seems most interesting when read not as philosophy but as an expression of a conflict between views of reality as excitingly terrible and as ultimately orderly and peaceful."

[20] *Corr.*, II, 321-22. Warburton in 1751 identified this poetic project as the *Essay*; see *Poems*, IV, 327n.

shares with him the writer's view of the poem—what he set out to do, what problems he encountered, what solutions he contrived, what he thinks he has achieved: "a *temperate* yet not *inconsistent*, and a *short* yet not *imperfect* system of Ethics," and a "*general Map* of MAN" (the explorer again?). Not only the ends but also the means are brought to the reader's attention. Pope chose rhyme, he says, because he found he could express his principles "more shortly this way than in prose itself." The project required the utmost care: "I was unable to treat this part of my subject more in detail, without becoming dry and tedious; or more *poetically*, without sacrificing perspicuity to ornament, without wandring from the precision, or breaking the chain of reasoning." Alerted by such a preface, which, unlike most "advertisements," prefaces, and dedications by Pope and his contemporaries, draws unusual attention to the process of writing, a reader is prepared to listen for a self-conscious narrator, to attend to the process of the poem, and to judge Pope's success in accomplishing his announced goals.

The opening lines of Epistle I immediately begin to satisfy these expectations. The opening paragraph, addressed to Bolingbroke, expresses above all Pope's sense of his own adequacy to his task. He exudes the casual confidence of the gentleman-philosopher who can "expatiate" as easily over the "scene of Man" as he can wander, equipped with gun and dogs, through the park of a country house. The business is a worthy way to spend one's time (better than politics) but nothing to be solemn or strenuous about: "Let us (since Life can little more supply / Than just to look about us and to die) / Expatiate free. . . ." Life hardly holds any puzzles for such worldly men; its measure is easily taken by a quick "look about"; one knows not to expect too much ("Life can little more supply") or to be anxious about life's brevity. Though his time is but "a moment" and his space but "a point," he fully dominates that span of life.[21] The threat of death is easily contained in a

---

[21] Contrast the sense of human insignificance in a later formulation of the same idea: "All forms that perish other forms supply, / (By turns we

parenthesis tucked in between "Let us" and "expatiate," a wonderfully leisurely verb that betokens Pope's refusal to be hurried into anything simply because life is short. Though about to "die," he will nonetheless "expatiate" with a fine disregard and a negligent grace. His assurance is suggested too by the string of verbs implying a forceful and decisive mind: "awake," "leave," the almost impudent "expatiate." Then comes the analogy with hunting—"beat," "eye," "shoot," "catch"—and the seemingly effortless "laugh," "be candid," and finally, "vindicate." Again Pope uses a Latinate polysyllabic word, perhaps mock-pompous like "expatiate," after a series of plainer terms, in order to imply the grand aim of this leisurely project, but to suggest also that such vindication will fall in place rather easily. The same free flow of mind (hardly an effort) that manifests itself in laughter and candor will, in the natural course of things, vindicate the ways of God to man!

The audacity, underlined by Pope's allusion to Milton, is surely intended. Brower catches well the tone of the line and the difference from Milton's "justify":

> To "justifie" in Milton's context is to demonstrate largely the divine order and justice; but such meanings taken with Milton's prayerful tone have a very different effect from Pope's "vindicate." Though "vindicate" refers to similar kinds of justification, the word reeks with the atmosphere of debate and points scored. As qualified by Pope's tone the meaning becomes positively hearty and jaunty, an assertion of divine justice in the voice of a man ready to take on all comers.[22]

"*But* vindicate" may imply, as Brower suggests, that "justification seems to come in almost as an afterthought to other concerns." Yet, in the secular context of Pope's paragraph as much might have been implied by a simple "*And* vindicate," as if to say "and, by the way, vindicate. . . ." "But"

---

catch the vital breath, and die) / Like bubbles on the sea of Matter born, They rise, they break, and to that sea return" (III.17-20).

[22] Brower, *Alexander Pope*, p. 208.

seems more curious in its effect than that. It implies a kind of teasing distinction between man's concern and God's, man's work and God's. Whatever else it does, "but" prevents the final line from being the paragraph's rhetorical climax, the end point toward which everything moves. By contrast, Milton's grand paragraph expands phrase by pulsing phrase in a single sentence, building tension as it swells, until all is resolved in the final declaration: "I may assert Eternal Providence, / And justify the ways of God to men." Just as Milton's paragraph is a single, seamless whole, so Milton as poet acts simply as an instrument of God, inspired by Him to do His will. Only because he is so inspired is Milton able to attempt a task so presumptuous as to "justify the ways of God to men." By contrast, Pope first establishes his own worldly identity quite apart from God, and he emphatically sets God at a distance. How, in such a world, a poet might presume to "vindicate the ways of God to man" is thus presented as problematic. How, with merely human powers of observation and reflection, without appeal to Revelation, can a man justify God? And if only a man, what qualifies him to speak with such special authority to other men? These are problems that Milton disposes of immediately by declaring that he is inspired, but Pope keeps them alive as part of the subject of his poem.

The comparison with the opening lines of *Paradise Lost* might be extended to remark that Bolingbroke corresponds to Milton's "Heav'nly Muse": both are directly addressed, both bid to "say first." But where Milton humbly petitions his all-powerful muse for instruction and light ("Instruct me . . . what in me is dark / Illumine"), Pope clearly sets himself on a par with "my st. john." Where Milton's prayer gives all the credit to the muse who will alone make it possible for him to succeed, Pope's "vindicate" lies clearly within his and Bolingbroke's own power. At the same time, Pope's lines, with their many suggestions that the project is a modest one, an occupation for the left

hand, an amateur's cursory survey, a trial ("essay") or experiment ("*Try* what the open, what the covert yield") in
which Pope will simply do what he must or can ("Laugh
where we must, be candid where we can"), make Milton's
"advent'rous song" seem vast and ponderous. Pope's will
be a "middle flight," detached, polite, nonchalant.[23] His
aim, so he wrote to Swift while the poem was still in progress, in words that seem to accord with the temper of these
opening lines, was "to make mankind look upon this life
with comfort and pleasure, and put morality in good
humour" (*Corr.*, III, 117).

Inducted so cordially into the *Essay*, the reader expects to
overhear a good-natured Horatian conversation between
Pope and his muse, Bolingbroke; perhaps, if he is lucky, he
will be invited to join it, his opinions anticipated, his good
sense assumed. And indeed, so the second verse paragraph
begins: "Say first, of God above, or Man below, / What can
we reason but from what we know?" (17-18). Nominally
addressed to Bolingbroke, the question readily includes
the reader. The "we" assumes that the reader and Pope occupy the same ground. Yet every reader must be surprised
to find that the friendly collaboration rapidly evolves into a
quite different relationship. The first-person pronouns in
the lines immediately following—"Of man what see we . . .
'Tis ours to trace him" (19-22)—signal our equality and invite or assume our assent. The introduction of a third-
person exemplum of aspiring speculative reason—"He,
who thro' vast immensity can pierce . . . may tell us" (23-
28)—assures us that *someone else* is being talked about. The
next lines begin to contrast the soaring reasoner's knowl-

---

[23] Empson catches as well as anyone the tone of these lines with an
offhand remark: "I remember some critic saying that the whole attitude to
life which crystallized out round Pope, all that jaunty defiance against
mystery and disorder, all that sense of personal rectitude, in that it is virtue enough to have been sensible, all that faith in the ultimate rationality,
even the ultimate crudity, of the world, were summed up in the lines
which introduce the Essay on Man": Empson, *Seven Types of Ambiguity*,
p. 203.

edge with, so we presume, our own more limited knowledge:

> But of this frame the bearings, and the ties,
> The strong connections, nice dependencies,
> Gradations just. . . .
>
> (1.29-31)

What surprise and disorientation that the couplet concludes, "has *thy* pervading soul / Looked thro'? or can a part contain the whole?"

> Is the great chain, that draws all to agree,
> And drawn supports, upheld by God, or *thee*?
>
> (1.33-34)

Who is now being addressed? It cannot be the coventurer, Bolingbroke, who in any case drops out of the poem until Epistle IV. It must then be the proud reasoner, first referred to as "he," who now becomes the rhetorical adversary in a two-party colloquy whose character has suddenly changed from Horatian *sermo* to sharp rebuke. In such a rhetorical situation the reader has no choice but to assume that the poet is addressing him too. Pope has installed himself in the office of moral instructor. At intervals throughout the first epistle, and occasionally in the remaining three epistles, this instructor chastises our presumption, our folly:

> Go, wiser thou! and in thy scale of sense
> Weigh thy Opinion against Providence. . . .
>
> (1.113-14)

> All this dread ORDER break — for whom? for thee?
> Vile worm! — oh Madness, Pride, Impiety!
>
> (1.257-58)

> Go, wond'rous creature! mount where Science
>   guides. . . .
> Go, teach Eternal Wisdom how to rule —
> Then drop into thyself, and be a fool!
>
> (II.19, 29-30)

> Has God, thou fool! work'd solely for thy good,
> Thy joy, thy pastime, thy attire, thy food?
>
> (III.27-28)

This is a tone of voice we readily associate with the *Essay*: the steady satirical pressure Pope exerts against human pride, the judgmental voice of a satirist who presumably exempts himself from the condition he attacks, who assumes a position of authority over his audience.[24]

Yet this is not the only tone of voice in the *Essay*, nor is it the only relationship Pope sets up with his reader. Often in Epistle I, and especially in Epistle II, Pope indicates, both by a sweetly reasonable or modest tone of voice and by means of first-person pronouns, that as interpreter or expositor he shares all the limits of the human condition with the reader. Thus,

> Man, who here seems principal alone,
> Perhaps acts second to some sphere unknown,
> Touches some wheel, or verges to some goal;
> 'Tis but a part we see, and not a whole.[25]
>
> (I.57-60)

In Epistle II, in fact, the first-person pronoun is standard. Only once does Pope stand apart and ridicule the foolish reader. Ordinarily, he assumes a common humanity:

> On life's vast ocean diversely we sail.
>
> (107)

> Pleasures are ever in our hands or eyes.
>
> (123)

> We, wretched subjects. . . .
>
> (149)

> Thus Nature gives us (let it check our pride).
>
> (195)

---

[24] For an analysis of Pope's voice as antagonistic, almost bullying, see F. M. Keener, *An Essay on Pope* (New York, 1974), pp. 59-69. Miriam Leranbaum has plausibly argued that this voice is modeled on the hortatory and magisterial tone in Lucretius's *De Rerum Natura*: Leranbaum, *Alexander Pope's "Opus Magnum," 1729-1744* (Oxford, 1977, pp. 40-48.

[25] See also I.123, 241-42, 282-83.

This light and darkness in our chaos join'd.

(203)

'Tis but by parts we follow good or ill.[26]

(235)

In the third epistle, a primarily continuous exposition with few interruptive exclamations or addresses, Pope's relation with the reader is not an issue. Epistle IV, however, as Brower notes, becomes more "dramatic in the Horatian way": "We are more continuously aware that Pope is talking to a friend or a friendly enemy as he dexterously shifts his approach from the distinctly personal . . . to editorial "we's," to the publicly genial, "I'll tell you, friend!" to the most sharply satirical addresses and imperatives. . . ."[27] In particular, Pope reassumes the mantle of moral authority, castigating the fools and their false dreams of happiness:

Oh sons of earth! attempt ye still to rise,
By mountains pil'd on mountains, to the skies?

(73-74)

Excited to sharper and richer poetry by opposition (enemies, fools, adversaries), Pope draws lines sharply between "me"—the privileged satirist—and "you"—the fools, with whom the reader too is herded:

Yet sigh'st thou now for apples and for cakes?

(176)

Go! if your ancient, but ignoble blood
Has crept thro' scoundrels ever since the flood,
Go! and pretend your family is young;
Nor own, your fathers have been fools so long.

(211-14)

Yet, when Pope turns from the false grounds of happiness to the true, he exemplifies the benevolence he preaches by displaying it toward his reader:

[26] See also II.93, 109, 156, 193, 220, 255, 274, 289.
[27] Brower, *Alexander Pope*, p. 230.

Self-love thus push'd to social, to divine,
Gives thee to make thy neighbor's blessing thine.
Is this too little for the boundless heart?
Extend it, let thy enemies have part:
Grasp the whole worlds of Reason, Life, and Sense,
In one close system of Benevolence.

(353-58)

Here it is assumed that the reader, humane and decent and reasonable, need not be browbeaten into virtue but simply invited. Pope's final words too—"all our Knowledge is, OURSELVES TO KNOW" (contrast the earlier "Know then thyself" [II.1])—imply that, at the close, both reader and poet stand as equals in knowledge and morals.

Despite the resolution of differences between Pope and his reader at the end of the poem, we cannot say that the relationship steadily evolves from instructor-student to fellow reasoners. As we have seen, Pope alternates his chastiser's and his Horatian voice. In Epistle IV he can be both sharply satirical and sweetly reasonable. The situation is complicated, furthermore, by the fact that there are actually two personal relationships in the poem: one between Pope and his reader, and one between Pope and Bolingbroke. At the end of Epistle IV the latter relationship is suddenly and curiously reestablished:

Come then, my Friend, my Genius, come along,
Oh master of the poet, and the song! . . .

(373-74)

Teach me, like thee, in various nature wise,
To fall with dignity, with temper rise . . .

(377-78)

Oh! while along the stream of Time thy name
Expanded flies, and gathers all its fame,
Say, shall my little bark attendant sail,
Pursue the triumph, and partake the gale?

(383-86)

Can any reader have expected such a display of modesty and self-deprecation? Pope began the poem by showing himself the friend and *equal* of Bolingbroke, easily adequate to his rhetorical task, in need of no particular instruction from Bolingbroke or anyone else. He carried on the poem with authority, through masterly exposition of the order of things and firm rebuke of those proud fools who would violate that order. Yet now *he* has a "master," a "guide," and is himself but a "little bark." The note of modesty seems almost excessive, false to what has gone before—a saving penitential gesture, perhaps, after such a display of authority or presumption? The descent into humility *may* be a sign too that Pope has not fully resolved a problem he in effect posed at the beginning of the poem: what is the basis of his authority? on what grounds can he presume to urge man to "submit?"

We have seen the shifting relationship between Pope and his reader as revealed, for example, through the personal pronouns. Perhaps Pope never fully decided whether the *Essay* was to be an "I-you" poem (moral instruction) or a "we" poem (implied conversation between equals). Even in one of the poem's most famous lines—"Know then thyself, presume not God to scan"—we can perhaps find traces of that indecision. For in the Morgan Library manuscript version, which represents a late stage in the composition of the poem, Pope had, "Learn then thyself, not God presume to scan," changing it later to, "Learn we ourselves, not God presume to scan." In the Houghton Library manuscript, which apparently began as a fair copy of the Morgan manuscript but then was in turn revised, Pope first had, "Learn we ourselves, not God presume to scan," and revised it to, "Know we ourselves. . . ." In the printed version, of course, he rejected the "we ourselves" and returned to an earlier "thyself."[28]

[28] Other evidence from the manuscripts suggests too that at a late stage Pope was changing his mind about the proper nature of his narrative relationship with the reader. For example, in the Houghton manuscript, at

But the modest conclusion has another explanation, one consistent with the view that Pope is in full control of the poem.[29] The descent to humility serves to reconfirm the sense of human limits that has throughout been central to Pope's argument, to balance the easy mastery displayed in the overall conduct of the poem, and especially at the opening of Epistle I.

That Pope hesitated between "Know then thyself" and "Know we ourselves" may in fact suggest not so much indecision as that he saw the phrases as essentially equivalent, and it may hint that "you" is an oblique way of addressing himself. Might we then suppose that the "you" in the poem (when it is not Bolingbroke) refers to the presumptuous proud fool *in* Pope himself, the tendencies in him (as in every man) to resist, to complain, to assert the claims of self? In this view, "I" and "you," virtuous teacher and erring student, are warring impulses within Pope, and the poem a kind of psychomachia. To locate the proud "you" within Pope both focuses our attention on the figure of the poet and sharpens our sense that in the *Essay* Pope is self-consciously exploring the difficulty of his vindicatory enterprise, difficult because he is both rebellious and resigned, both mired in humanity and able to rise free from it.

The problem of Pope's authority in the poem manifests itself in relation not only to the proud antagonist in himself

---

II.35, Pope first refers to man in the third person ("Can he who tell'st each Planet where to roll") and then revised to direct address ("then thou who tell'st . . ."). In the first printed edition he returned to the third person ("Could he who taught each Planet . . ."). Similar shifts, from third to second back to third person, occur at II.38, 39, 41. George Sherburn drew attention to the revision and the improvement of the famous "Know then thyself" in "Pope at Work," in *Essays on the Eighteenth Century Presented to David Nichol Smith* (Oxford, 1945).

[29] This is especially true in the light of the concluding lines; see below, p. 164. An early version of the address to Bolingbroke first stood at the beginning of Epistle II. Twelve lines (which became the present IV.373-82) were added to the Morgan manuscript and remain in the later Houghton version. The "little bark" (385), accentuating Pope's modesty, first appears in the printed versions.

or in his reader, but also in relation to his subject matter. Has *his* "pervading soul" seen more of God's providential plan than his reader has? Does Pope have special access or allow himself special access to divine knowledge in order to enforce his argument? Again, one possible explanation is that Pope may not have fully resolved in his own mind the degree of authority and knowledge he would assume in the poem.[30] His central intention was to limit himself to the deductions of philosophy, to that which all reasonable human beings can observe or reflect, and to exclude Revelation. For the most part, Pope does so limit himself, but on several crucial occasions he seems to overstep those self-imposed limits. The problem is best focused in Epistle I, "Of the Nature of Man, with respect to the Universe." In the succeeding epistles the subject—man's own nature, government, happiness—rarely tempts Pope to rise beyond human philosophy.

The first epistle's modest beginning is reflected in the limited knowledge Pope claims: "Say first, of God above, or Man below, / What can we reason, but from what we know? ... 'Tis but a part we see, and not a whole" (17-18, 60). Yet, imperceptibly, that small "part" expands to include man's knowledge of the entire natural world in its amplitude and hierarchy:

> Nature to these, without profusion kind,
> The proper organs, proper pow'rs assign'd;
> Each seeming want compensated of course,
> Here with degrees of swiftness, there of force;
> All in exact proportion to the state;
> Nothing to add, and nothing to abate.
> Each beast, each insect, happy in its own;
> Is Heav'n unkind to Man, and Man alone?

> (179-86)

[30] At 1.235 in the Morgan manuscript Pope first had, "Above, how high progressive life must go," and revised it to the more cautious "may go." At 1.242, "inferior must on ours" is revised to "may on ours." In the Morgan manuscript, 1.21 ("thro' worlds unnumber'd tho' the God be known") first read more assertively, "Thro' endless worlds His endless works are known."

Although only one part of creation, man, as embodied in Pope-the-expositor, is able to rise above creation and attain a philosopher's perspective of Nature's "vast chain of being," its "thin partitions" and "Gradations just." From a mount of natural vision Pope bids his fellow men to *see* the scale of nature before them:

> Far as Creation's ample range extends,
> The scale of sensual, mental pow'rs ascends:
> Mark how it mounts, to Man's imperial race,
> From the green myriads in the peopled grass. . . .
>
> (207-10)

> See, thro' this air, this ocean, and this earth,
> All matter quick, and bursting into birth.
> Above, how high progressive life may go!
> Around, how wide! how deep extend below!
> Vast chain of being, which from God began,
> Natures aethereal, human, angel, man,
> Beast, bird, fish, insect! what no eye can see,
> No glass can reach! from Infinite to thee,
> From thee to Nothing!
>
> (233-41)

Despite the concession of human limits implied in "may" and "no eye can see," Pope here, and often in the *Essay*, conveys the sense of pattern one has in looking down on life's "mighty maze" from above rather than the perplexing puzzle or "riddle" that meets the mind caught in that maze. If Pope and his reader here keep to human limits, then they represent humanity at the extreme limit of its knowledge.

At other moments in the *Essay*, the moments when Pope most sardonically rebukes his proud and foolish reader, he again verges on, but fails to reach, a knowledge beyond the powers of man. Here, however, he stands not as one who can see what all reasonable men can see, but as one who can see more clearly than his readers. An instance of such special eminence comes early in Epistle 1. As he pivots from the proud aspiring reasoner—"He, who thro' vast immensity can pierce . . ."—to face his proud reader, Pope asks:

> But of this frame the bearings, and the ties,
> The strong connections, nice dependencies,
> Gradations just, has thy pervading soul
> Look'd thro'? or can a part contain the whole?
>
> (29-32)

Here the reader is ridiculed for pretending to a knowledge of the cosmic "frame" that Pope himself in these very lines claims. For how can Pope know that the world is one great architectural frame, with bearings, ties, dependencies, and gradations, unless his pervading soul has looked through it carefully? The poet, a mere "part" of creation, does in fact "contain the whole" in masterfully compressed couplets. Another instance comes at the end of the first epistle. Pope's hortatory ardor leads him to the rhetorical and moral climax of his argument of submission to the will of God:

> Cease then, nor ORDER Imperfection name:
> Our proper bliss depends on what we blame.
> Know thy own point: This kind, this due degree
> Of blindness, weakness, Heav'n bestows on thee.
> Submit — In this, or any other sphere,
> Secure to be as blest as thou canst bear:
> Safe in the hand of one disposing Pow'r,
> Or in the natal, or the mortal hour.
> All Nature is but Art, unknown to thee;
> All Chance, Direction, which thou canst not see;
> All Discord, Harmony, not understood;
> All partial Evil, universal Good:
> And, spite of Pride, in erring Reason's spite,
> One truth is clear, "Whatever is, is RIGHT."
>
> (281-94)

No doubt it is difficult for the would-be moralist to preach submission without claiming his own special status of more knowledge of God's plan, more virtue perhaps, even exemption from the general order to submit? Pope seems sensitive to the problem and makes a half-hearted attempt to include himself in his own charge by using first-person pronouns ("*Our* proper bliss . . . what *we* blame"). But the insistent "thee" and "thou" in the rest of the passage (he might have used we/us, or man/he) removes Pope again to a position of authority. The reader may be weak and blind, may not see or understand, but Pope the expositor *can* see that "All Nature is but Art," can hear the harmony, and, exempt from pride and the error of reason, can assert the one clear truth. The charge to the reader becomes not only "cease your rebellion and submit to the will of God," but also "cease your resistance to my argument and submit to me and my view of the world."

In asserting that "Whatever is, is RIGHT," Pope has employed his expositor's and rhetorician's powers to fulfill his announced intention of vindicating the ways of God to man. Strictly speaking, he has remained within human limits: as philosopher or natural religionist a man might claim that all chance is direction, all partial evil universal good. Pope's scheme did not allow him to introduce Milton's principal justification of God, the propitiatory sacrifice of Christ.[31] But more than once, as he himself realized, Pope seems to have exceeded his self-imposed limit to natural science and introduced knowledge available only through Revelation and explicated through the queen of sciences, theology.[32] "Nothing is so plain," Pope writes in 1733 to Caryll of the still-anonymous author of the *Essay*, "as that he quits his proper subject, *this present world*, to insert his belief of *a future state*" (*Corr.*, III, 354). The passage in question is probably,

[31] He had in fact written "an address to our Saviour, imitated from Lucretius' compliment to Epicurus," but he omitted it on the advice of Berkeley: Spence, I, 135.

[32] Both the fall of man and the immortality of the soul were omitted, Pope said, because they "lay out of my subject, which was only to consider man as he is, in his present state, not in his past or future": quoted in Spence, I, 136.

> If to be perfect in a certain sphere [the after-life],
> What matter, soon or late, or here or there?
> The blest today is as completely so,
> As who began a thousand years ago.
>
> (1.73-76)

Despite the "if," the passage is plainly *meant* to imply belief in immortal bliss.[33] Likewise, the lines on the hopeful soul—"The soul, uneasy and confin'd from home, / Rests and expatiates in a life to come" (1.97-98)—are plainly meant to imply belief in immortality. The soul's "home" is with God in heaven.[34] More explicitly, in the fourth epistle Pope extends his view of man's happiness to include the "prospect" of eternal bliss:

> For him alone, Hope leads from goal to goal,
> And opens still, and opens on his soul,
> 'Till lengthen'd on to Faith, and unconfin'd,
> It pours the bliss that fills up all the mind.
> He sees, why Nature plants in Man alone
> Hope of known bliss, and Faith in bliss unknown.
>
> (341-46)

Despite Pope's attempt to blur the distinction between the world of "nature" and the world of "faith," it is clear that he wishes at this point to introduce what an early commentator called "the promises of Revelation."[35]

[33] In the letter to Caryll, Pope worries that the author, though "quite Christian," may have his sense turned, because of inaccurate expressions, "a little unorthodoxically." And yet, Pope insists, "nothing is so plain" as his belief in immortality. But cause for worry remains. He instances the lines I have quoted: "and yet there is an *If* instead of a *Since* that would overthrow his meaning." He is concerned that his "if," in the sense "given or granted that" (*OED*, 1.1), might be misinterpreted as introducing a mere hypothesis (*OED*, 1.31). Pope was worried enough that the lines might be *mis*interpreted to imply that immortality was a mere hypothesis that he omitted them from all editions of the poem between its first appearance in 1733 and the 1743 Pope-Warburton edition, by which time Warburton had successfully defended Pope's orthodoxy.

[34] When Pope realized that his original reading, "confin'd *at* home," seemed to imply that the soul's true home was the earthly body, he altered the preposition to bring the line into harmony with the following one ("a life to come"). See Mack's note in *Poems*, III, pt. 1, 27.

[35] Mack argues that Pope is rather *reminding* his reader of Revelation

Pope adopts this essentially theological perspective at two key points in Epistle I, again tacitly violating his poem's original limits and thus implicitly raising the question: how much can man, with his unaided reason, know of the "order" of the world? The first instance comes early, when Pope, as many modern readers feel, assumes as true virtually all of the case his poem tries to make:

> Of Systems possible, if 'tis confest
> That Wisdom infinite must form the best,
> Where all must full or not coherent be,
> And all that rises, rise in due degree;
> Then, in the scale of reas'ning life, 'tis plain
> There must be, somewhere, such a rank as Man;
> And all the question (wrangle e'er so long)
> Is only this, if God has plac'd him wrong?
>
> (43-50)

The function of this passage, Mack remarks, "is evidently to summarize a set of propositions common to theodicean thinking and thence narrow the argument to the single question": has God placed man wrong? In another view, the function is to overwhelm the reader with propositions to which he now gives vague assent, and to suppress further inquiry into our grounds for holding them, particularly our grounds for knowing them by natural means. The reader, his consent thus painlessly secured, is hurried along to the safer ground on which Pope constructs his narrower argument. What masterful rhetorical strategy! Yet, as Johnson was to show in his attack on Soame Jenyns, belief in a hierarchical plenum, a chain of being from nothing to infinity, can be held only on faith.[36]

Pope of course would have had no interest in debating

---

than basing his argument upon it: *Poems*, III, pt. 1, 161. But given the preeminent status of Scripture, how can an argument be "cognizant" of Revelation without being "based" in part on it?

[36] See Johnson's review (1756) of *A Free Inquiry into the Nature and Origin of Evil*, in Johnson, *Works*, VIII (London, 1810), 23-61. See also Mack, in *Poems*, III, pt. 1, 18.

with Johnson. His passage, as I have suggested, is designed to suppress Johnson's kind of painstaking analysis, but not out of philosophical dishonesty. Rather, it is Pope's aim, I think, to show his reader, by inducing his belief in God's perfect system, how in practice we readily assent to the view that the world is not without a plan. Later, it will be Pope's own plan to offer a critique of that ready assent, not by demolishing it, as Johnson does, but by *juxtaposing* it with the equally human sense that the world is indeed a "maze."

At the end of the first epistle Pope stretches his terms to include knowledge born of revelation. He has been describing the "scale of nature" or the "chain of being." These traditional metaphors, distinctly hierarchical and even mechanical, imply a fixed order of ascending links or steps—only one of them occupied by relatively insignificant man—leading up to a final term, infinity or God. Pope now turns to an equally traditional metaphor, one particularly effective at this point because it by contrast implies an organic universe, a single "body" in which man, though "vile," is "informed" and "filled" by God. Pope's stance is not that of the philosopher on a figurative prospect, but of a mystic enraptured by an invading sense of the omnipresence of the Deity:

> All are but parts of one stupendous whole,
> Whose body Nature is, and God the soul;
> That, chang'd thro' all, and yet in all the same,
> Great in the earth, as in th' aethereal frame,
> Warms in the sun, refreshes in the breeze,
> Glows in the stars, and blossoms in the trees,
> Lives thro' all life, extends thro' all extent,
> Spreads undivided, operates unspent,
> Breathes in our soul, informs our mortal part,
> As full, as perfect, in a hair as heart;
> As full, as perfect, in vile Man that mourns,
> As the rapt Seraph that adores and burns;

To him no high, no low, no great, no small;
He fills, he bounds, connects, and equals all.[37]

(1.267-80)

Pope himself admits that in these lines he exceeded the
bounds of natural knowledge. The whole paragraph, he
wrote to Caryll, proves the author "quite Christian in his
system, from *Man* up to *Seraphim*" (*Corr.*, III, 354). The
Twickenham notes, furthermore, show that the intellectual
background to the paragraph is theological: the New Testament, Augustine, Aquinas, Cardinal Bellarmine. Both
this passage and the earlier lines describing God's
plenitude (1.43-50) assume a theological perspective of the
world; both assert God's system to be "perfect," "the best."
But the later passage differs sharply in emotional effect.
The earlier lines form a rhetorical glissade through propositions grasped intellectually by contemporary cos-
mologists; the latter attempt to render in its fullness the
rapturous feeling of a participant in the "stupendous
whole" of nature. Although the lines lay implicit claim to
the mystic's special eminence and immediate contact with
God, they paradoxically return Pope to the level of his
readers, all of whom are filled and connected by God. The
lines are arguably Pope's most moving verse in the poem,
and the most effective vindication of God's ways. One of
the reasons may be that, in a poem built carefully on distinctions and discriminations, on scales of being and articu-
lated frames, these lines obliterate all distinctions (for all is
"one stupendous whole") and induce an oceanic feeling, a
sublime sense of being at one with, and in direct contact
with, the universe of God.

These lines present Pope's vindication in the sublime
mode. They would seem to provide the most conclusive
sense available—through reason and religion—that the

[37] In transcribing this passage, Joseph Warton, who doubted that Pope
had the true fire of a poet, felt almost tempted to retract his assertion
"that there is nothing transcendently sublime in Pope": *An Essay on the Genius and Writings of Pope*, 4th ed., 2 vols. (London, 1782), II, 77.

world is a single, ordered body, "and God the soul." But the passage does not come at the end of the *Essay*; it does not even form the conclusion of the first epistle. For in important ways this sublime vision of unity and coherence is not all that Pope wants to express. The first epistle in fact concludes with a balanced declaration that all nature is the art of God, but that the art is "unknown" to man; that all chance is God's direction, but cannot be "seen"; that all discord is God's harmony, but cannot be "understood" by man. The vision of the *Essay on Man* is double: the world is both pattern and puzzle, both accessible to our understanding and inaccessible. It is finally to further our sense of this double vision, I think, that Pope has focused our attention as much as he has on the figure of the poet-expositor, who shares with all men moments of intuited order and moments of observed chaos.

The most striking instance of such double vision comes at the end of the first epistle and the beginning of the second. Due attention to Pope's juxtaposition of these famous passages—the one concluding "Whatever is, is RIGHT," the other, "The glory, jest, and riddle of the world"—will tell us something important about the art of the *Essay*. The first epistle, as I have noted, moves from a vision of perfect coherence and unity to a reminder that the harmony of the universe must be accepted on faith and not on understanding. Nonetheless, the closing line is meant to convey our root sense that there is a single governing intelligence in the universe by whom all is ordered and to whom all is understood. And even erring man can see clearly that "whatever is" must be according to that plan. But the second epistle moves sharply away from such assurance. As the reader's eyes are directed from God to mankind, emphasis falls not on vision but on blindness, not on order but on chaos. Though in the first epistle man occupies his niche in the "scale of reas'ning life," Pope now focuses closely on that particular niche and finds not that man fulfills his tasks and himself within carefully defined limits, but that he is a chaotic, doubting creature, placed on a dark estate, not sure of his place but rising and falling, or hanging between. It is important to note, however, that the second of these famous passages does not cancel out the first. Nor does Pope make any attempt to *resolve* his sense of man as riddle and the universe as perfect order; rather, he is content to *juxtapose* the two. The second immediately succeeds the first, acting as a reminder that man sees the world both as order and as chaos, often at the same time, depending on his perspective and his focus.

This juxtaposition of pattern and puzzle recurs throughout the *Essay* and acts as its central organizing principle: "A mighty maze! but not without a plan"; "Tho' Man's a fool, yet GOD IS WISE." Epistles I and II most emphatically give us this juxtaposition. As Edwards has shown so convincingly of the second epistle, "Pope's dialectic moves away from synthesis when it seems to have been achieved—it unresolves what had seemed settled."[38] But such integration-disintegration shows, I think, not that Pope finds that the doctrine of harmony fails him, or that as poet he must resist his doctrinal impulses. Rather, it shows that Pope was aiming to convey the consolation that comes from our certainty of providential rule *and* the discontent, even the anxiety, that comes from our awareness that, within our proper sphere, we are pitifully deluded and suffering. Neither the comfort nor the distress cheapen or dilute each other, however. And despite the general movement in Epistles III and IV toward reintegration (the establishment of human governments, the real possibility for human happiness), the more mixed mood of Epistles I and II is not forgotten.

The idea that the *Essay on Man* sees double, sees both the splendor of the "cosmic setting" and the folly and the pain of "human littleness" (Brower's terms), is not new.[39] What needs emphasis, however, is the *care* Pope seems to have

[38] Edwards, "Visible Poetry," p. 312.
[39] Brower, *Alexander Pope*, p. 237.

taken to see double, to balance two different ways of looking at man without favoring either. And one of the means he employed is the figure of the poet-expositor: Pope himself. By manipulating his own relation to his reader and perspective on the scene of man, by standing apart from his readers as their far-seeing moral instructor or by huddling with the confused human herd on the dark isthmus, by allowing himself to see from a superhuman theological point of view or by restricting himself to a narrowly human vantage—Pope conveys both a sense of pattern and of puzzle, of maze and of plan.

Just as the poem begins with Pope setting out on a mental ramble with Bolingbroke, and thus focuses our attention on the poet and his powers as well as the "scene of man," so the poem closes with the same pair and again focuses on Pope's powers as poet. Once more he asks his muse to instruct him how to "steer / From grave to gay, from lively to severe," to be "Correct with spirit, eloquent with ease, / Intent to reason, or polite to please." Though it is often noticed that the final lines of the poem summarize the themes of all four epistles and thus present an overview of man, it is not enough noticed that they equally insist on the poet's role as expositor:

> urg'd by thee, I turn'd the tuneful art
> From sounds to things, from fancy to the heart;
> For Wit's false mirror held up Nature's light;
> Shew'd erring Pride, WHATEVER IS, IS RIGHT;
> That REASON, PASSION, answer one great aim;
> That true SELF-LOVE and SOCIAL are the same;
> That VIRTUE only makes our Bliss below;
> And all our Knowledge is, OURSELVES TO KNOW.
>
> (391-98)

The verbs—"turn'd," "held up," "shew'd"—remind us that though the world is God's order, to philosophize about it in poetry is a human activity.

··◦⊰|6|⊱◦··

Personal Drama in Pope's
Horatian Imitations

Poetic Autobiography

If we come to the *Horatian Imitations* of the 1730s from a study of Pope's earlier familiar epistles, we find that the poet's personal sensibility has now become not only the focus for the poems' climactic moments but also the very center of the poems themselves. In a series of poems, beginning in 1733 with the imitation of the first satire of Horace's second book (*To Fortescue*) and continuing through the *Epilogue to the Satires* (1738), Pope set about quite openly, like Montaigne, to present "my Self to my Self for Argument and Subject."[1] A number of the Horatian poems (I include under this heading both imitations and the original poems traditionally grouped with them) may properly be termed apologies, that is, defenses or justifications of the poet's practice as a satirist. It is on these poems—*To Fortescue* (*Sat.* II.1), the *Epistle to Dr. Arbuthnot, To Bolingbroke* (*Ep.* I.1), and the *Epilogue to the Satires*, Dialogues I and II—that I wish to concentrate. In them we can see more clearly than anywhere else in Pope's poetry that his own sensibility stands at the base of his poetic world and is, paradoxically, a means for Pope to encompass a wider world. Studying his own character and experience provides him a focus for exploring the kinds of moral and psychological demands and predicaments that confront all those who, like himself, must live in a world at once exhilarating, gratifying, and offensive.

The Horatian poems have aroused vigorous critical

---

[1] Montaigne, *Essays*, trans. Charles Cotton, 3 vols. (London, 1685-1686), II, 91.

interest in recent years. Among them, the *Epistle to Dr. Arbuthnot* has long been studied, particularly for its rhetorical structure, but lately the other Horatian satires have received overdue attention. We now know much of the poems' political, social, and theological dimensions, of the traditions of retirement that help shape Pope's sense of himself in the poems, and of his expert use of the Horatian adversarius and conversational raillery. Informed by these valuable discussions of Pope's poems, I wish to treat them now as poetic autobiography.

The primary objection to such a reading of the *Horatian Imitations* is that " 'tis all from Horace." Pope perhaps sufficiently answered that objection in his *Epilogue to the Satires*, Dialogue I, by placing the charge in the mouth of an "impertinent Censurer." Furthermore, both the *Epilogue* and the *Epistle to Dr. Arbuthnot* are not strictly imitations but poems of a "Horatian kind." Even where Pope is imitating a particular Horatian epistle or satire, as he does in *To Fortescue* and *To Bolingbroke*, he is not simply reproducing Horace. As John Butt notes, "presumably he selected for imitation those poems which most nearly 'hit his case,' and if he reproduced something of Horace's scepticism and epicureanism, it was because he recognized the sceptic and epicurean in himself."[2] It has been ably demonstrated too that Pope regularly diverges from his model to create poems more Christian in their religious coloration and more Juvenalian in their grave declamatory fury.[3] G. K.

---

[2] Butt, introduction to *Poems*, Vol. IV, *Imitations of Horace*, ed. John Butt, xxx.

[3] The Juvenalian quality of Pope's Horatian poems has been recognized since the mid-eighteenth century. Thus Warburton noted: "Nor was his temper less unlike that of Horace, than his talents. What Horace would only smile at, Mr. Pope would treat with the grave severity of Persius. And what Mr. Pope would strike with the caustic Lightening of Juvenal, Horace would content himself with turning into ridicule" (*Works of Pope*, ed. Warburton [London, 1751], IV, 51). See also Joseph Warton: "He clearly resembles in his style, as he did in his natural temper, the severe and serious Juvenal, more than the smiling and sportive Horace" (Warton, *An Essay on the Genius and Writings of Pope*, 4th ed., 2 vols. [London, 1782], II, 274). For an account of Pope's Christianizing alterations, see especially Thomas Maresca, *Pope's Horatian Poems* (Columbus, Ohio, 1966).

Hunter has also shown how Pope typically conceives himself as standing against the social order, and Horace standing with it.[4]

Other editors have noted how Pope elaborates on the Latin to fit his own case, as, for example, at the end of the seventh epistle of the first book, where Horace's *parvum parva decent* grows into a dozen lines on Pope's life of simplicity and independence. Similarly, *Singula de nobis*, from *Epistle* ii.ii, is transformed, by way of Montaigne, from matter-of-fact statement into moving elegy:

> Years foll'wing Years, steal something ev'ry day,
> At last they steal us from our selves away;
> In one our Frolicks, one Amusements end,
> In one a Mistress drops, in one a Friend:
> This subtle Thief of Life, this paltry Time,
> What will it leave me, if it snatch my Rhime?
> If ev'ry Wheel of that unweary'd Mill
> That turn'd ten thousand Verses, now stands still.[5]
>
> (72-79)

Elsewhere Pope will transfer words from one of Horace's friends to himself, as when young Ofellus's description of his life becomes Pope's own account of Twickenham: "in five acres now of rented land. / Content with little, I can piddle here / On Broccoli and mutton, round the year" (*Sat.* ii.ii.136-38). In the most significant of these examples, Pope takes the famous phrase, *uni aequus virtuti atque ejus amicis*, which Horace had applied to Lucilius, and assigns it to himself: "TO VIRTUE ONLY and HER FRIENDS, A FRIEND" (*Sat.*, ii.i.121).

The autobiographical approach to the *Horatian Imitations* is not entirely new. One hundred years ago W. J. Courthope found them "most deeply interesting" on their "autobiographical side, as reflecting Pope's ideas of his own

---

[4] Hunter, "The Romanticism of Pope's Horace," *Essays in Criticism*, 10 (1960), 601-3.
[5] On this point, see particularly Maynard Mack's review of Sherburn's edition of the *Correspondence*, in *Philological Quarterly*, 36 (1957), 398.

character, and his feelings towards his friends and his enemies" (*Works of Pope*, **v**, 256). But to read the poems as *poetic* autobiography is not simply to return to a nineteenth-century view of them. We now have a fuller sense of the art of the *Imitations*—and of Pope's richly diverse and conflicted self. The poems should be seen not simply as biographical documents but as personal dramas in which Pope attempts to work out and present in verse some of the conflicts within himself or between various of his selves—good man, professional poet, son and friend, defender of Virtue, lover of peace, irritable warfaring wit. The satires of the 1730s show, I think, that in the last decade of his life Pope had not resolved his discords into harmony, but had instead found them to be a rich poetic vein.

Adversarius as Foil

The dramatic form of these five satires is one of their most prominent characteristics. Two are explicitly labeled "Dialogues," two others, although called a "Satire" and an "Epistle," consist of conversations between Pope and an adversarius, Fortescue and Arbuthnot.[6] Even in the fifth, the epistle to Bolingbroke, Pope *responds* to a "voice" that "whispers in my ear," or to the imagined questions or reactions of his friend ("Ask not, to what Doctors I apply . . . You laugh, half Beau, half Sloven if I stand . . ."). In each poem Pope is playing off against each other two contrasting views of his own satiric practice. It has even been suggested recently that in the Dialogues of the *Epilogue to the Satires* both speakers represent contrasting views within Pope himself:

> Both "Fr." and "P." are versions of Pope himself, or of any man aware of the conflict between his social identity and his secret image of himself as autonomous

---

[6] In his edition of Pope's *Works* (1751), Warburton assigned to Arbuthnot six speeches (totaling sixteen lines) that in Pope's original edition had been imagined responses.

moral hero. The dialogue form articulates the inner debate between that skeptical self that "knows better" which like "Fr." stands by one's indiscretions murmuring "alas" with the sympathetic disapproval that identifies our elders and betters, and that other self which, passionately committed to its own free perception of truth, allows no concessions.[7]

Put more simply, Fr. is the self in Pope that is cautious, wary, alert to what is safe or politic in the world of Walpole's England, while P. is the morally fervent Pope, with his singing robes about him, declaiming against the vicious world in utter disregard of its power to strike back. When the matter is stated in these terms, we can see that the voice of caution in the *Epilogue* clearly has links with the roles played by Fortescue and Arbuthnot in the poems addressed to them. Insofar as a good orator-rhetorician must subsume the position of his opponent, must so thoroughly understand the opponent's argument that he can allow whatever merit it possesses and yet thoroughly defeat it on its merits, to this extent, I think, we can say that both speakers are aspects of Pope himself.

We can also see that the cautious adversarius may conceivably embody that side of Pope which clearly recognized his precarious situation as a Catholic member of the political opposition with a penchant for pouring himself out plain. However boldly Pope spoke out in his satires of the 1730s, he in fact took care to preserve his safety. He knew how much he could get away with, knew how to beard the lion in its den and yet skip nimbly away unharmed, how innuendo could serve to nettle his enemies, yet might easily be disavowed. The adversarius might also conceivably embody that worldly side of Pope, the skillful man of business, the prudent, calculating man who won for a disabled poet not only the recognition of the world but also a full meas-

[7] Thomas Edwards, *Imagination and Power: A Study of Poetry on Public Themes* (New York, 1971), p. 110. The passage is a minimal expansion of an earlier discussion of the poems in Edwards's *This Dark Estate*, p. 88.

ure of its rewards—wealth, material ease, rich and powerful friends, and the very liberty to speak out in opposition.

But there clearly are limits to the idea that the adversarius is a version of Pope himself. Fortescue and Arbuthnot, to begin with, are historically identifiable friends
of the poet.[8] The sentiments attributed to Fortescue are
quite appropriate to a lawyer and associate of Walpole.
Those attributed to Arbuthnot are, in at least one instance,
apparently the doctor's own.[9] In other instances Arbuthnot
is useful for putting a case that Pope wants presented, to
some extent accepted, and yet finally rejected: the danger
of naming names (lines 101-4), or the utter insignificance
of Sporus, a creature beneath the satirist's contempt and
insensible to his attack (lines 305-8). In the Fortescue and
Arbuthnot poems, then, we do not think of the adversarius
as a current version of Pope. Perhaps he may loosely embody views that Pope himself has considered or once held
about the appropriate way to respond to his literary enemies. The worldly, cautious advice of the adversarius—in
these poems, in the *Epilogue to the Satires*, and in the late
letters—is in any case roundly rejected; Pope determines to
speak out, to publish, to declaim despite the danger. He
prefers to present himself as a man of integrity who re-
nounces any suggested accommodation with the world
and, especially in these poems, as a fearless satirist who
does not hesitate to risk everything in declaring his mind.
In the poems to Fortescue and Arbuthnot, where the
worldly advice is either reasonably prudent or half-
facetious ("Then all your Muse's softer Art display, . . . Lull
with *Amelia*'s liquid Name the Nine . . . "), the relations between poet and adversarius are still cordial. But cordiality

[8] The Fortescue poem is subtitled, "In a Dialogue between Alexander
Pope of Twickenham in Com. Midd. Esq.; on the one Part, and his
Learned Council on the other."

[9] In the 1737 edition of his letters, Pope printed a letter from Arbuthnot dated 17 July 1734, some six months before the *Epistle to Dr. Arbuthnot* was published. In the letter, Arbuthnot cautions Pope, as he does
in the poem, to pay " a due regard to your own safety": *Corr.*, III, 417.

disappears in the *Epilogue to the Satires*, where the adversarius advocates a craven accommodation and the poet, Pope, is driven to his most impassioned pitch. One extreme, as it were, provokes its opposite. The reader, furthermore, unquestioningly identifies Pope himself with the P. of the poem.

The adversarius in the two Dialogues serves useful purposes but does not, I think, represent Pope's self, except in the way I have described. Fr. in the first Dialogue is given some substantial speeches and is allowed to develop a theory of toothless satire quite counter to what we know Pope had already adopted: "smile with Horatian delicacy, laugh at any but fools or foes, lash great men only when they've fallen." We have no reason to believe Pope had any commitment to this view of satire. Indeed, Fr. may be useful in underlining just how *un*-Horatian Pope's satire has become. It is not "from Horace," and it is not simply in Horace's "sly, polite, insinuating stile" (Pope preserves far more of Horace's style in the first Dialogue than in the second). Although P. professes ironically to share Fr.'s cynical worldly assumptions and tone, claiming as he does, for example, to defend "the Dignity of Vice," he does not accept his view of satire and, by the end, dissociates himself utterly from Fr.'s world: "Yet may this Verse (if such a Verse remain) / Show there was one who held it in disdain." In the second Dialogue Pope himself goes on the offensive, and Fr. is thrown off balance, reduced to a series of brief spluttering objections. Again Fr. pleads for general rather than particular satire and serves Pope chiefly as a rhetorical "straight man," who feebly puts the expected objections to Pope's own argument so that they may be rebutted.

Fr. is soundly routed by P.'s arguments and moral fervor. Yet, as often in Pope's satire, the enemy displays a kind of insensitivity and resilience that enables him to endure. That Fr. has the last word in the second Dialogue may be Pope's way of recognizing that his own voice is indeed unheard in the land, that the Fr.'s of the world will carry the day, while the P.'s cry in the wilderness, a different sort of licensed fools, who hurt nobody and who, like the "old Whigs," are permitted to "wear their strange old Virtue as they will" (1.44). Despite P.'s insistence on speaking out, his project is futile, as Fr. knows. Fools and foes will be neither reformed nor deterred: "These you but anger, and you mend not those" (1.54). Ironically, Fr.'s last words—"Alas! alas! pray end what you began, / And write next winter more *Essays on Man*"—are in effect taken up by Pope, who resolved, in a long footnote appended to the end of the poem, "to publish no more" (that is, no more poems of this sort) and who had thoughts of turning again to a continuation of the *Essay on Man*.[10]

Thus it is true that Fr. embodies the world's caution and the world's knowledge that lofty moral outrage is relatively harmless. As Johnson noted, "the man who threatens the world is always ridiculous; for the world can easily go on without him and in a short time will cease to miss him."[11] By including Fr. in the *Epilogue to the Satires* Pope may be assuring the reader that he knows perfectly well how the world will view him and that he can appreciate the force of the world's argument. He shares Fr.'s knowledge, but this is not to say that Fr. is really a "version" of Pope. We never question that P. is Pope. Fr. serves to further a process of self-definition, not as a principle within Pope, but as something to be excluded or refused. He defines himself in his intransigence and extravagance against the worldly knowledge and insensitivity of Fr. One might say, in fact, that P. (that is, Pope) is more clearly defined as himself *because* of the presence of the worldly Fr.

Adversary as Antiself

Fr. is not so much a version of Pope as a foil against which P. and his readers can see more clearly who Pope is. The same can be said of the adversarius in *To Fortescue* and

---

[10] See *Poems*, IV, 327n. [11] "Life of Pope," p. 153.

the *Epistle to Dr. Arbuthnot*. More important than the adversarius in Pope's process of self-definition, however, is a figure we might call the adversary. Seen especially in *Arbuthnot*, but occurring in other poems as well, this figure—Atticus, Sporus, Walpole, Cibber—is primarily designed as Pope's antithesis, an antiself, and thereby an aid to self-definition. For Pope's sense of himself seems to have been strengthened and clarified by the presence of a real or imagined other against which he himself might thrust. He seems most articulate, most himself, when he finds or places himself in opposition, whether in the personal literary quarrels that occupied most of his adult life, the political Opposition to Walpole in the 1730s, or the elaborate poetic fantasies in which an embattled Pope faces a world of vicious enemies.

But the effectiveness of the contrast between Pope and his antiselves may well depend on the striking resemblances each figure bears to Pope in a number of particulars. Consider first the portrait of Atticus in the *Epistle to Dr. Arbuthnot*:

> Peace to all such! but were there One whose fires
> True Genius kindles, and fair Fame inspires,
> Blest with each Talent and each Art to please,
> And born to write, converse, and live with ease:
> Shou'd such a man, too fond to rule alone,
> Bear, like the *Turk*, no brother near the throne,
> View him with scornful, yet with jealous eyes,
> And hate for Arts that caus'd himself to rise;
> Damn with faint praise, assent with civil leer,
> And without sneering, teach the rest to sneer;
> Willing to wound, and yet afraid to strike,
> Just hint a fault, and hesitate dislike;
> Alike reserv'd to blame, or to commend,
> A tim'rous foe, and a suspicious friend,
> Dreading ev'n fools, by Flatterers besieg'd,
> And so obliging that he ne'er oblig'd;
> Like *Cato*, give his little Senate laws,

And sit attentive to his own applause;
While Wits and Templers ev'ry sentence raise,
And wonder with a foolish face of praise.
Who but must laugh, if such a man there be?
Who would not weep, if *Atticus* were he!

(193-214)

Atticus is first of all a distinctly pointed version of Addison. And in the context of the entire poem, he is by and large what Pope claims *not* to be: a man of influence and power, but jealous, timorous, suspicious, so that he is ultimately concerned only with "his own applause." Atticus's deceptively restrained manner ("Damn with faint praise, assent with civil leer, / And without sneering teach the rest to sneer, . . . afraid to strike, . . . hint a fault, and hesitate dislike . . . reserv'd to blame, or to commend, . . . tim'rous foe") makes a clear contrast with Pope's manner as friend and as critic. When Pope-the-critic praises his friends Arbuthnot and Gay or his beloved parents, he does so openly and fully; when he blames, it is not by "faint praise" or by hinting and hesitating. He speaks out plainly and boldly; indeed, one might suspect that the outspoken manner Pope adopts in the poem derives in part from his wish to put as much distance as possible between himself and Atticus. He tells each fool "that he's an Ass" (80) and censures moral evil in the plainest possible terms (for example, "Eve's Tempter," [330]). Where Pope places deep value on friendship, declares himself a fearless Friend of Virtue, and does not hesitate to strike with his lash against his foes, Atticus is a "tim'rous foe, and a suspicious friend."

Cato and his "little Senate" also form an apt contrast to Pope amidst his literary circle. Atticus is a jealous ruler, tolerating no peers, conducting sessions of his "little Senate" not to pronounce clearly on the merits and faults of current writers or to encourage and promote excellence, but rather to receive the applause of the foolish "Wits and Templers" who flatter him. His "laws" and "sentences" are handed down only in order that the lawgiver's own wit may be applauded. For his part too, Pope receives the praise of a literary circle. He is not a dictator, however, but an apprentice who grows into an equal:

> *Granville* the polite,
> And knowing *Walsh*, would tell me I could write;
> Well-natur'd *Garth* inflam'd with early praise,
> And *Congreve* lov'd, and *Swift* endur'd my Lays;
> The Courtly *Talbot, Somers, Sheffield* read,
> Ev'n mitred *Rochester* would nod the head,
> And *St. John*'s self (great *Dryden*'s friends before)
> With open arms receiv'd one Poet more.
> Happy my studies, when by these approv'd!
> Happier their Author, when by these belov'd!
>
> (135-44)

The circle Pope joins is of course a distinguished one, while Atticus's is made up of fools and flatterers. More important, though, is that Pope is welcomed into a circle of presumed equals—"With open arms receiv'd *one Poet more*"—where no single figure strives for hegemony, where Pope has a vivid sense not only of the confraternity but also of the heritage of merit. As a poet he joins a tradition, while Atticus gains but a petty throne. The most important difference, however, lies in the interrelations of the literary circle. Pope's literary happiness comes through the approval and the love of his fellow poets: "by these approv'd . . . by these belov'd." Atticus wins only the "applause" of fools.

Even when Pope has later gained literary preeminence (and when many of his early literary friends are dead), he refuses to act the dictator. He *reluctantly* hears the appeals of flattering poetasters, dismisses them curtly when they become tiresome, seeks "no homage from the Race that write" (219). When a respectable, "sober" critic points to faults in his verse, Pope receives him with equanimity: "If wrong, I smil'd; if right, I kiss'd the rod" (158). In a position to help a writer in need, Pope does not hesitate to aid even his enemies:

This dreaded Sat'rist *Dennis* will confess
Foe to his Pride, but Friend to his Distress:
So humble, he has knock'd at *Tibbald*'s door,
Has drunk with *Cibber*, nay has rhym'd for *Moor*.[12]

(370-73)

The differences between Pope and Addison are especially significant because they exist within a ground of similarity. Both were in their times literary figures of great
power, in positions to influence the cultural, and perhaps
the moral, life of the nation. Possibly because he cannot
deny the apparent likeness, Pope is all the more anxious to
convince his readers (and himself too?) of the clear distinctions. Hence he takes some risks in describing Atticus in
terms that may recall his own case. That Pope was at least
covertly aware of the similarity is suggested by some parallels in phrasing and in ideas on lesser points. Atticus was
"born to write . . . and live with ease." Pope too was "dipp'd
in ink" at birth and "lisp'd in numbers, for the Numbers
came" (that is, with ease), and he claims that he has little
business else than to "Maintain a Poet's Dignity and Ease."
Indeed, the attempt to win some ease in a lifetime of
harassment and *dis*ease is a fair description of the poem's
action.[13] "Damn with faint praise, assent with civil leer, /
And without sneering, teach the rest to sneer" aims at Addison's deceptively polite critical manner, but might also
recall Pope's own ironic *Guardian* paper in feint (that is,
feigned)[14] praise of Ambrose Philips's pastorals.[15] "Willing

[12] Here, for once, Pope seems to have left *un*spoken some of his good
deeds. A reading of his correspondence shows him to have been constantly helping one friend or another, even relative strangers.

[13] Cf. "The Muse but serv'd to ease some Friend, not Wife, / To help me
thro' this long Disease, my Life" (131-32).

[14] An obsolete meaning of "faint" is in fact "feigned": *OED*, s.v. "faint,"
a.1.

[15] One significant variation between the versions of 1722 and 1727 and
that of 1735 is that Pope dropped from the latter the couplet, "Who, if
two Wits on rival Themes contest, / Approves of each, but likes the worst
the best," referring to Addison's equivocal praise of Pope's and of
Tickell's translations of the *Iliad*, Book I. Perhaps Pope thought that after

to wound, and yet afraid to strike" might come uncomfortably close to Pope's own treatment of Aaron Hill. When pressed, Pope removed Hill from *The Dunciad* (III.283), denying that he ever meant to satirize him. (Johnson later observed that Pope "first endeavours to wound, and then is afraid to own that he meant a blow.")[16] Likewise, Pope perhaps knew that, in the minds of his collaborators on the translation of the *Odyssey*, he could be something of a literary "Turk," unwilling to share his throne and anxious to conceal their part in the work.[17]

Even if Pope did not overtly recognize any secret affinity with Atticus, his enemies did. Soon after the first version of the Addison character was published piratically in 1722,[18] Tickell took up the defense of his patron, Addison, by charging Pope with the same literary vices—pride and equivocating malice:

> When soft Expressions covert-Malice hide,
> And pitying Satire cloaks o'er-weening Pride;
> When Ironies reverst right Virtue show,
> And point which Way true Merit we may know:
> When Self-conceit just hints indignant Rage,
> Shewing its wary Caution to engage;
> In mazy Wonder we astonish'd stand,
> Perceive the Stroke, but miss th' emittent Hand . . .

twenty years the allusion had become obscure. But is it possible that he saw—with the help of his enemies—that the lines might uncomfortably suggest Pope's commentary on his own and Phillips's pastorals?

[16] "Life of Pope," p. 151. That Johnson turned Pope's lines against him is suggested by C. J. Horne, "The Biter Bit: Johnson's Strictures on Pope," *Review of English Studies*, 27 (1976), 310-13. Hill complained in "The Progress of Wit" that Pope "sneakingly approves, / And wants the soul to spread the worth, he loves": Hill, *Works*, 4 vols. (London, 1753), III, 371.

[17] In a 1725 letter to Fenton, Broome characterized Pope as a "Caesar in poetry" who determined to keep for himself as much as possible of the credit and reward that the collaborative project might win: *Corr.*, II, 345. Pope would rightly insist, however, that, unlike Addison, he had no jealous fears that Fenton and Broome might supplant him. His motives were to preserve the prestige and increase the sale of the venture.

[18] For the text, in which there are some significant variants, see *Poems*, VI, 142-43.

So the skill'd Snarler pens his angry Lines,
Grins lowly fawning, biting as he whines;
Traducing with false Friendship's formal Face,
And Scandalizing with the Mouth of Praise:
Shews his Intention, but his Weakness too,
And what he would, yet what he dare not do;
Whilst launching forth into a Depth of Praise,
Whose kind Attempts the Mind attentive raise,
When suddenly the Pyrate Colours show,
Beneath the Friend's Disguise, the lurking Foe.[19]

Pope probably knew of this poem: he was an assiduous collector of attacks on himself, as the list appended to the *Dunciad* clearly shows.[20] We cannot argue that this pamphlet or any subsequent ones had any effect on the character of Addison/Atticus, for Pope's early sketch is undeniably without antecedents.[21] But when Pope revised and reprinted the portrait in 1727,[22] and finally found a place for it in the *Epistle to Dr. Arbuthnot* in 1735, he probably did so with the knowledge that his enemies and many of his readers would be aware of an alleged similarity between himself and Atticus. In the full-scale satirist's apologia the Atticus portrait serves to define and defend Pope by showing us his opposite; he admits to what similarities there are only to insist, in the end, on the differences.

Like Atticus, Sporus functions in the poem as a kind of antiself by which Pope may more clearly define himself.

---

[19] Tickell, "Answer to the foregoing Verses [the pirated first version of the character of Addison] Presented to the Countess of Warwick," in *Cythereia: or, New Poems upon Love and Intrigue* (London, 1723), pp. 92-94.

[20] See also *Corr.*, III, 11-12, and "Life of Pope," pp. 188, 209.

[21] Pope's enemies continued to beat him with weapons drawn from the Addison/Atticus portrait. One attack, *An Essay upon the Taste and Writings of the Present Time* (1728), simply adapts a couplet from the portrait: "When being grown too fond to rule alone . . ." (quoted in *Pamphlet Attacks*, p. 130; see also p. 313). Hervey's *Difference between Verbal and Practical Virtue* (1742) still remembers the Atticus lines in "Lying to blame, and sneering to commend" (p. 6).

[22] It was published in the Pope-Swift *Miscellany* and not printed in *Poems*, VI, 284-85; the variants introduced do not show the influence of printed attacks.

Again, the character is designed primarily to set off Pope's own manly virtue. One reason why the foil is so successful (and the portrait so venomous?) is that Sporus serves at the time as a covert self-parody:

> Let *Sporus* tremble—"What? that Thing of silk,
> "*Sporus*, that mere white Curd of Ass's milk?
> "Satire or Sense, alas! can *Sporus* feel?
> "Who breaks a Butterfly upon a Wheel?"
> Yet let me flap this Bug with gilded wings,
> This painted Child of Dirt that stinks and stings;
> Whose buzz the Witty and the Fair annoys,
> Yet Wit ne'er tastes, and Beauty ne'er enjoys,
> So well-bred Spaniels civilly delight
> In mumbling of the Game they dare not bite.
> Eternal Smiles his Emptiness betray,
> As shallow streams run dimpling all the way.
> Whether in florid Impotence he speaks,
> And, as the Prompter breathes, the Puppet squeaks;
> Or at the Ear of *Eve*, familiar Toad,
> Half Froth, half Venom, spits himself abroad,
> In Puns, or Politicks, or Tales, or Lyes,
> Or Spite, or Smut, or Rymes, or Blasphemies.
> His Wit all see-saw between *that* and *this*,
> Now high, now low, now Master up, now Miss,
> And he himself one vile Antithesis.
> Amphibious Thing! that acting either Part,
> The trifling Head, or the corrupted Heart!
> Fop at the Toilet, Flatt'rer at the Board,
> Now trips a Lady, and now struts a Lord.
> *Eve*'s Tempter thus the Rabbins have exprest,
> A Cherub's face, a Reptile all the rest;
> Beauty that shocks you, Parts that none will trust,
> Wit that can creep, and Pride that licks the dust.
>
> (305-33)

It seems clear that Pope intended Sporus as the very antithesis of the self he presented in the poem. Following hard upon the attack come lines in which Pope defines himself *against* the form of evil he has just described. Note first the emphatic negatives:

> Not Fortune's Worshipper, nor Fashion's Fool,
> Not Lucre's Madman, nor Ambition's Tool,
> Not proud, nor servile, be one Poet's praise
> That, if he pleas'd, he pleas'd by manly ways;
> That Flatt'ry, ev'n to Kings, he held a shame,
> And thought a Lye in Verse or Prose the same.
>
> (334-39)

"Manly" may be the crucial word here, for corrupt sexuality is one of Sporus's leading attributes, and Pope's attack—and the poem as a whole—enables him to display a kind of transformed sexual energy. Rhetorically, the portrait of Sporus is a foil, but at the same time it is clearly a portrait of John, Lord Hervey. As editors have pointed out, some of the details in Pope's attack derive from earlier printed attacks on Hervey, most prominently William Pulteney's *Proper Reply to a late Scurrilous Libel* (1731), where Hervey is described as a "Circulator of Tittle-Tattle, a Bearer of Tales, a Teller of Fibs, a station'd Spy" (p. 7). He is sexually ambiguous: "you know that He is a *Lady* Himself; or at least such a nice Composition of the two Sexes, that it is difficult to distinguish which is most praedominant, . . . a *delicate Hermaphrodite*, such a pretty, little, *Master-Miss*" (p. 5). His wit is laborious yet vapid: "the little, quaint Antitheses, the labour'd Gingle of the Periods, the great Variety of rhetorical flourishes, affected Metaphors, and puerile Witticisms" (p. 6). Similar details occur in other attacks printed in the next several years. A favorite target is Hervey's affected effeminate manner and his ladylike beautiful but painted face. In the anonymous *Tit for Tat*, a reply in 1734 to Hervey's *Epistle from a Nobleman*, he is

> The wonder of a Sunday croud,
> Affected, foppish, vain and loud,
> Poppet all o'er in dress and feature,
> A very linsey-wolsey creature;

Ne'er made for use, just fit for show,
Half-wit, half fool, half man, half beau . . .
So finely colour'd, such a grace,
One takes it for my Lady's face;
As highly touch'd with nicest care,
The self-same pert and silly air.

Another target is Hervey's suspected sexual impotence.
Pope was not the first to suggest that this ladylike creature
was less than "manly," nor the first to quibble on the word
"thing."[23] In *The Lord H-r--y's First Speech in the House of
Lords* (1734) also appears, in the same context, the rhyme
on "silk" and "ass's milk":

Tho' when I stand upright,
  You take me for a skein of silk;
And think me with a face so white,
  A perfect Curd of ass's milk.
. . . .
So I, the softest, prettiest thing,
  This honourable House affords,
Come here by order of the King,
  Created Lady of the Lords.[24]

In the face of such evidence, it is difficult to doubt that
Pope was aiming at a recognizable portrait of a public
figure, Lord Hervey, and was drawing on an available satiric vocabulary.

But at the same time, within the context of Pope's poem,
the Sporus portrait, as many critics have recognized, presents a type of Evil. It is no less a type for being a portrait
of a historical figure (and no less a portrait for being a type).

[23] *OED*, s.v. "thing," 19b, 11c: "in comtempt or reproach, implying un-
worthiness to be called a person"; "privy member, private parts." Pope
repeatedly puns on the latter sense in *Sober Advice from Horace*, 90, 103,
136, 154, and in the rondeau *You know where*.
[24] Quoted in Robert Halsband, *Lord Hervey, Eighteenth-Century Courtier*
(Oxford, 1973), p. 166. In a contemporary manuscript ballad, "The Court
Garland," Hervey is a "painted toy," a "doubtful he, she, je ne sais quoy."
One knows not "what kind of thing to name thee": quoted in ibid., p. 138.

To take over material originally designed for one purpose and to adapt it for a new context was, in Pope's mind, a proof of great judgment, and such practice more than once contributed to the success of his own work.[25] Likewise, the portrait of Sporus was a reworking of the portrait of an enemy into a portrait of the Enemy, Evil itself.

I think, however, that Pope perhaps saw more in Sporus than Hervey and Evil. He may well have seen a grotesque version of himself. Such an assertion must remain speculation, but there is reason to believe that Pope sensed a secret affinity between himself and the loathed John Hervey. As with Atticus, the antiself seems to stand outside and potentially inside Pope's self. Consider some of the details of the portrait. Sporus is an effeminate, androgynous figure; Hervey was notoriously "pretty"[26] and, as his latest biographer shows, publicly bisexual. His love for Stephen Fox was no secret.[27] We have no unequivocal evidence that Pope was, or imagined himself, sexually ambivalent. But there are grounds for speculation. A "little man," never physically manly, possessed of an unusually delicate sensibility (a "feminine" sensibility?), Pope humorously called himself "abhominably epicoene."[28] Once, after a visit to view a hermaphrodite, he remarked that "few proficients have a greater genius for Monsters than my self" (*Corr.*, I, 277); few, that is, have so acute an interest or sensitivity to this kind of monstrosity? In *The Rape of the Lock* Pope appears to declare some complicity with the "little men" of the poem, and he presents a bizarre mixing or reversal of the sexes, mighty Amazonian bosoms and weak foppish

[25] See Spence, I, 45, and the expansions and transformations of *Windsor Forest* and *The Rape of the Lock*.

[26] In *Tit for Tat* Hervey is a "sweet, pretty pratler of the C[ourt]" (p. 3).

[27] Halsband, *Lord Hervey*, passim.

[28] *Corr.*, II, 189. In this letter Pope parodies an Ovidian heroical epistle, playing banished wife to Peterborow's absent husband. Pope is of course joking, but jokes, we know, may reveal serious concerns. Perhaps only in such guise could Pope admit sexual ambivalence. It is noteworthy that in the famous tribute to Martha Blount at the end of the *Epistle to a Lady* sexual ambivalence is transformed from defect to virtue. Heaven's "last best work" is a combination of male and female sensibilities, a "softer man."

witlings. Like Hervey, Pope took ass's milk, a tonic, as Gay reports, for the "dwindling beau" (*Trivia*, II.16). Both were somewhat courtly figures, quite conscious of their physical appearance, and particularly of their faces. Though Pope did not paint his face, he was quite proud that his deformity had not affected his facial features, and he took care that all portraits showed his face prominently displayed, with his deformed body left outside the frame.

Many details, it is true, clearly allude to Hervey with no application to Pope. The mumbling spaniel who dares not bite, whose smiles betray "Emptiness," makes wonderfully witty fun of Hervey's false teeth. "Froth" may hint maliciously at Hervey's epilepsy. Puppet and prompter suggest Hervey as Walpole's mouthpiece in the House of Lords. The toad at the ear of Eve nicely aims at Hervey's easy access to Queen Caroline, perhaps even at his habit of riding behind her ear in a hunting chaise.[29]

Other significant details of the portrait, however, are more puzzling, and in fact seem more appropriate for Pope than for Hervey. The implied charge of sexual impotence, for example, is patently ridiculous. Hervey married the beautiful Molly Lepel, sired a large family (so much for "Beauty ne'er enjoys"), and carried on—apparently with some success—an affair or two. Pope, on the contrary, never married; there is no evidence that his "affairs" with Lady Mary and the Blount sisters, however passionately felt, ever went beyond words. His sexual experience was probably limited. How much of Cibber's famous story about the visit to the bawdy house is true we cannot say, but Pope's outrage at its publication may be due in part to the comically inadequate figure he made. Likewise, if Hervey notably wrote or spoke "Smut" or "Blasphemies," it did not become part of his reputation, but Pope was widely attacked for the alleged blasphemy of his version of Psalm 1, and the indecorous bawdry of *The Rape of the Lock* and the *Sober Advice from Horace* (1734). And though "vile Antithesis" and "Amphibious Thing" accord with Hervey's

[29] See *Poems*, IV, 119.

bisexuality, they perhaps may point with equal appropriateness to Pope's own antithetical or incongruous nature, which sometimes struck him as wretchedly unnatural: a vigorous mind trapped in a "crazy carcase," and a temper unable to attain "the soul's calm sunshine," the *aequus animus* he prized so highly in Patty Blount.

If Pope considered these points of similarity, he may have felt that a reader of ill will may have seen even more in the portrait as unflattering images of Pope himself. Hervey seems not to have been noted, as his friend Lady Mary was, for personal uncleanliness—he was not obviously a "Child of Dirt"—but the dwarfish Pope's weakness, as Johnson reported, "made it very difficult for him to be clean."[30] Might not the highly impressionable Pope in some respects seem to himself a "puppet"—as indeed he did to later critics—in the hands of the "prompter" Bolingbroke, versifying doctrine handed to him, and, in the *Essay on Man*, "blindly propagating opinions contrary to his own?"[31] Might not Pope's satires be dismissed as at once vicious and harmless, full of malice and yet hardly a threat to any person with power, in short, "Half Froth, half Venom," the splutterings of a poisonous toad?

If we find it difficult to believe that Pope would imagine such things of himself, his contemporaries easily did so for him. Indeed, a major "source" for the portrait of Sporus would appear to be the printed attacks on Pope. In the *Verses addressed to the Imitator of Horace* (1733) Pope is described as both wasp ("waspish strains") and reptile. In *Codrus* (1728) he is a splenetic toad, venomous and yet harmless, who spews satire:

> The stinking Venom flows around,
> And nauseous Slaver hides the ground.
> Yet not one Mortal, whom it hit
> 'Twas just as harmless as his Wit.

[30] "Life of Pope," p. 197. In his *Letter to a Noble Lord* (1733), Pope admitted some "natural faults." "I am short, not well-shaped, generally ill-dressed, if not sometimes dirty": *Works of Pope*, v, 428.

[31] "Life of Pope," p. 163.

For take away the filthy Part,
Of T--d, and Spew, and Mud, and Fart:
(Words which no Gentleman could use,
And e'en a Nightman would refuse.)
There nought remain'd, save to the Elf
A Disemboguement of himself.[32]

(138-47)

Elsewhere he is a spaniel:

And ever after, 'twas their Drift
(A Spaniel P-pe A Mastiff Sw--t)
To teize and bite whate'er came next 'em,
But of pure Spite, tho' nothing vext 'em,
To bark, to insult, to run stark wild,
And foam at Woman, Man, and Child;
To foul and dirt each Place they came in
And play some Pranks, unfit for naming.[33]

As early as Dennis's *True Character* (1716), Pope was portrayed as a Satan with an angel's face. "By his constant and malicious Lying, and by that Angel Face and Form of his, 'tis plain that he wants nothing but Horns and Tayl, to be the exact Resemblance, both in Shape and Mind, of his Infernal Father" (pp. 10-11). A common charge repeated throughout the pamphlet attacks is that Pope's misshapen body is an apt image of his mind (just as, in Pope's view, Hervey's amphibious sexuality is an emblem of his deceptiveness: he is a man "that none will trust"). This verse attack, in the form of instructions to a sculptor, is typical:

There carve a Pert, but yet a Rueful Face,
Half Man, half Monkey, own'd by neither Race . . .
This his Misshapen Form: but say, what Art
Can frame the monst'rous Image of his Heart.
Compos'd of Malice, Envy, Discontent.
Like his limbs crooked, like them Impotent.[34]

[32] Printed in *Pamphlet Attacks*, p. 155.
[33] Jonathan Smedley, *The Metamorphosis* (1728), printed in *Pamphlet Attacks*, p. 134.
[34] *Pope Alexander's Supremacy and Infallibility examin'd* (1729), p. vi.

Impotence, indeed, was another favorite charge. The impotent creature at the ear of Eve bears some resemblance to an earlier picture of Pope: "and those great Ladies who do nothing without him; admit him to their Closets, their Bed Sides, consult him in the choice of their Servants, their Garments, and make no scruple of putting them on or off before him: Every body knows they are Women of strict Virtue, and he a harmless Creature, who has neither the Will, nor Power of doing any farther Mischief than with his Pen, and that he seldom draws, but in defence of their Beauty."[35] Pope knew too that he had been mocked as a "little, abject Thing" in Dennis's *Remarks on Mr. Pope's Homer* (1717),[36] and that his own "things of little size" had been the subject of a lady's (or his own) joke.[37]

In some important respects, then, Sporus might seem as much a portrait of Pope (as the ill-willed might view him, and as Pope might fearfully view himself) as of Hervey. Primarily, of course, it is a portrait of Hervey, and at the same time, rhetorically speaking, a foil to the virtuous Pope presented in the poem. By drawing on the hostile image of himself propagated in the pamphlet attacks, Pope is no doubt in part throwing back in the faces of his enemies the mud that they attempted to sling on him, much in the same way that details from the Sporus portrait were later flung at Pope.[38] But it seems possible that Pope was doing more

[35] *Memoirs of the Court of Lilliput* (1727), printed in *Pamphlet Attacks*, p. 99.
[36] P. 8. Pope cites the attack in his parallel between Dryden and himself, appended to *The Dunciad* in 1729.
[37] See Pope's brief rondeau *You know where* (1726), discussed in Chap. 2 above. See also the letter, quoted in Chap. 3 above, p. 91, where Pope apparently notes his inadequate "Size and Abilities."
[38] See, for example, *Sawney and Colley* (1742): "I know thee, next, a Waspish Thing, / Whose Business is to buzz and sting; / Replete with Malice, Spleen and Spite. / But thus thy Satire's guiltless grown, / Who slanders all Men, slanders none, / As impotent in Spite as love / Contempt alone by each you move" (p. 7). See also Hervey's *Difference between Verbal and Practical Virtue* (1742): "For all the Taste he ever has of Joy, / Is like some yelping Mungril to annoy / And teaze the Passenger he can't destroy" (p. 6).

than this, that he deliberately inserted in his apologia the hostile view of himself held by his enemies, and perhaps even by himself, in order to confront, to include, and finally to repudiate that view. The process of self-defense and self-definition through the figure of Sporus is, as with the Atticus portrait, in part a matter of denying as well as affirming.[39]

Definition by denial may consist in refutation of an unjust charge. It may also take the form, as it does in the *Epilogue to the Satires*, of presenting oneself as the antithesis of a vilified other. This clearly operates, as I have suggested, in the Sporus portrait ("*Not* Fortune's Worshipper . . ."). The process may also help to account for a striking feature of the poem: Sporus's perverted sexuality and Pope's virtual sexlessness. Sporus's very name hints at impotence (castration, effeminacy) and homosexuality, and these features are repeatedly confirmed by further hints of weakness (inability to taste or bite, the fitful, puny spending and dispersal of energy implied in "Half Froth . . . spits himself abroad, / In Puns . . . ," etc.—perhaps an enfeebled ejaculation) and irregular intercourse (the toad "at the ear of Eve," the seesaw of "now Master up, now Miss"). Sporus having corrupted sexuality itself, Pope repudiates it, increasing the degree of opposition between them. As it happens, Pope's life, so far as we know, allowed him little opportunity to express a mature sexuality, so his sexlessness in the poem may simply reflect the biographical facts. But the odd emphasis on "Friend, not Wife" ("The Muse but serv'd to ease some Friend, not Wife" [131]) suggests that Pope needs to stress the point. Moreover, the women that he encounters (except for his mother) belong to the

---

[39] For a brief discussion of Sporus that is in some respects similar to mine, see John Trimble, "The Psychological Landscape of Pope's Life and Art" (Ph.D. diss., University of California, Berkeley, 1971), pp. 298-300. Trimble's emphasis falls on Pope's *unconscious* recognition of similarities between himself and Hervey, and on his attempt, by means of the portrait, "to annihilate . . . disapproved traits in himself." The idea that one attacks alleged qualities in others that one disapproves in oneself is, of course, a commonplace of modern psychology.

realm of art: a "Virgin Tragedy" (56); a pastoral "painted
Mistress" (150). He serves as moral protector rather than
sexual mate of the "soft-ey'd Virgin" (286), "Beauty in distress" (288), or "fair Virtue" (359). He is "belov'd" only by
male friends and judges of his poems (144), he has "kissed"
only the critic's rod (158), has been "close with" only Swift;
only from such a union will something "come out" (275),
and his only progeny will be poems.[40] And yet he claims to
be "manly" (337), clearly demonstrates a potency in standing firm against the foes of virtue,[41] and even attains a kind
of paternity in rocking "the cradle" (his mother's) "of re-
posing Age" (409). Indeed, one might say that, sexuality
having been disallowed by nature and corrupted by
Sporus, Pope redirects sexual energy into forms where he
can display mastery.

The self is more fully seen in the presence of the antiself,
its identity more clearly established. And for Pope to direct
his most bitter satiric thrusts against those antiselves is for
him to locate his self more firmly at the center of his poetic
and moral worlds. Curiously, while Pope so triumphantly
asserts his identity, Sporus virtually loses his in a prolifera-
tion of subidentities (thing, curd, butterfly, bug, child of
dirt, spaniel, manipulated puppet, toad). A shape-changer
with no single shape, his self is dispersed into unrelated objects or animals, literally spent as he "spits *himself* abroad"
into "puns, or politicks, or tales, or lyes," gathering not to a
conclusive whole (even an evil whole) but to a mere miscellany. Not unlike Dryden's Zimri, another "antithesis," his
arts are self-canceling, self-defeating: a lady and lord, a
cherub and reptile, a seesaw wit, a dust-licking pride.

[40] Pope took this idea quite seriously; see Chap. 1 above. He may also
have thought of his gardening projects as "vegetable children"; see *Corr.*,
IV, 94.

[41] His phallic force is seen more clearly in other satires, where he points
the pen (*To Fortescue*, 105), wields his sacred weapon, or draws the last pen
for freedom (*Epilogue*, II.212, 248). The pen, as Byron noted, thinking of
Pope and of himself, is "That mighty instrument of little men" ("English
Bards and Scotch Reviewers," 10).

Atticus and Sporus are the two most prominent examples of what I have called the antiself in Pope's satires. But one might argue that Pope often strikes out at parody versions of himself. Walpole is another of the great antipathists and secret brothers. As Maynard Mack has suggestively argued, Walpole can be seen as Pope's "Mighty Opposite," and yet his career bears some interesting resemblances to Pope's own: both sought power and fame, enjoyed eminence, displayed acute sensitivity to criticism, and excelled in manipulation of other men.[42] In their private lives both inspired great loyalty and made deep and diverse friendships. Pope had adequate ground to choose Walpole as his target; for the political Opposition, the prime minister himself symbolized all that had gone wrong in England. But might Pope have also focused on Walpole because he could see in him the dark underside of some of his own better qualities? The self-assurance Pope derived from his Horatian armor of conscious rectitude ("He's arm'd without that's innocent within") shades into the impudent Walpole's equally durable "Wall of Brass."[43] Then too, Walpole, as ruler of the political world, made an illuminating contrast to Pope, the ruler of a counterkingdom; and Walpole at Houghton made an instructive contrast to Pope at Twickenham.

There may be other antiselves as well. Timon makes a kind of anti-Pope, his villa a hideous corruption of the country life led at Pope's own villa. Bufo, in the *Epistle to Dr. Arbuthnot*, like Pope himself, is "puff'd by ev'ry quill," fed with dedications, plagued by poetasters "Who first his Judgment ask'd, and then a Place." Cibber, in his *Apology* (1742)—artlessly confessional, delighting in his "Nakedness of Temper" to expose himself, impudently vain even of his faults—makes an amusing parody of the Pope who

[42] *The Garden and the City*, pp. 201-6.

[43] *Imit. Hor. Ep.* 1.i.94-95. Pope must have remembered Horace's famous *Integer vitae* (Ode 1.22). He and other Opposition writers regularly associated "wall," "screen," and "brass" with the prime minister.

loved to pour out all himself and sought in his later poetry carefully to construct a different sort of apology. In *The Dunciad* Pope himself may figure as a kind of anti-Cibber, and the dunces in that poem may serve as images of the professional writer, like Pope, who never escapes the commercial treadmill of publishing, as Pope did escape.[44]

Public and Private Selves

From one perspective then, and it is not by any means the only one from which an interpreter might view these poems, Pope's apologies constitute a personal drama in which antiself and adversarius help to define Pope's self by opposition. To whatever extent the antiself is or was once part of Pope's own self, it is here, as it were, admitted to consciousness, confronted, and projected onto another figure. Thus, to speculate about the psychological dynamic, Pope may be able to acknowledge and at the same time deny certain aspects of his personality. From another perspective, however, and at another psychological level, an altogether different kind of drama is taking place in the Horatian apologies. Especially when read as a group, the poems show Pope dramatizing the same juxtapositions between man and poet, friend, son, Christian, and defender of Virtue that we find in the letters. Although the implied conflicts between various aspects of Pope's self take different forms, it is possible to group them roughly into a single recurrent conflict. On the one hand, there is the private man who is devoted to the pleasures of friendship and gardening, who delights in "pouring out all himself," who looks on poetry as a private pleasure, who is concerned equally, if not more, with the rest of his own life's "business," who is retiring and "soft by nature," who is a lover of quiet and peace. On the other hand, there is a man conscious of public responsibilities, who is devoted to the services of Truth, who delights in lashing out at villainy,

[44] See Chap. 7 below.

who looks on poetry as a career or sacred duty, who is concerned above all else with the defense of Virtue, a man aggressive, fierce, and quick to respond to provocation, a lover of the satiric battle. The former seems much more centered on himself and his own proper pleasures, what he owes to himself; the latter is centered rather on a moral absolute—Truth and Virtue—outside himself.

I hesitate to assign to either of these selves a label which would tend to make rigid and oversimple what appears to be a looser set of oppositions, now viewed from one aspect, now from another, able to accommodate not only his own personal experience but also, perhaps, the kinds of conflicting duties to which human beings have enduringly felt drawn. That is to say, the poems concern first of all the historical Alexander Pope—as he liked to think of himself and present himself to the world—and next the readers who might find that Pope's words hit their case too, as they ponder the proper response to the evil surrounding them. Such a view as I present here is close to, but may be distinguished from, I believe, what is still the most influential view of the different voices in Pope's satires: Maynard Mack's conception of the satirist as *vir bonus*, as *naif*, and as hero.[45] My notion of two selves bears some relation to Mack's three voices, the *vir bonus* and *naif* corresponding more or less to the private retiring man, and the hero to the public satirist. But I place more emphasis on the ways in which the two selves are at first in conflict, and finally in a kind of resolution. Second, I shall demonstrate as fully as possible that the two selves in the poems coincide with the selves in the letters.[46]

In the five apologies of the 1730s we can find the two aspects of Pope's self presented over and over again. Pope is not always concerned to play the two aspects off against one

---

[45] Mack, "The Muse of Satire," *Yale Review*, 51 (1951), 88-89.

[46] Instead of citing again the contrast in Pope's letters between a public and a private self, I refer the reader to my discussion in Chaps. 1 and 2 above.

another in a single poem, although he does just that in the poems to Fortescue and Arbuthnot. In the espistle to Bolingbroke (1738), however, the private Pope is chiefly on display, while in the two Dialogues from the *Epilogue to the Satires* (1738), we see little if any of that private Pope. There is no apparent progression within each poem or within the group of poems from the dominance of one self to the dominance of the other; there is no schematic resolution of opposites. Indeed, the images with which we are left at the end of the epistle to Bolingbroke—the demigod Pope ironically clouded by a most human "Fit of Vapours"—and at the end of the *Epilogue*—the declaiming satiric warrior drawing "the last Pen for Freedom"—could hardly be more opposed. Yet, curiously, the poems are alike in that Pope plays off lofty aspiration—the drive to make oneself into "That Man divine whom Wisdom calls her own," a warrior-priest in the "Temple of Eternity"— against ordinary human limitation, either a man's own daily inconstancy and fallibility, or the hardened insensitivity of a world that cannot or will not hear a poet's heroic words. Likewise, as I shall show, the private and public selves may only appear to be antithetical.

In the earlier poems, however, we are especially struck with the antithesis, partly because Pope builds the poems around a conflict. *To Fortescue* for the most part presents the private Pope, his needs and pleasures, but builds to his loftiest declamation—"TO VIRTUE ONLY and HER FRIENDS, A FRIEND"—before subsiding once more to the private man and his retired pleasures. The poem opens, for example, with Pope seeking advice from his "learned counsel." His poems have been criticized for their boldness and weakness. What is he to do? The lawyer's answer, "I'd write no more," provokes the remainder of the poem, a protestation, by turns ironic and impassioned, that he *must* write. Initially, the need to write is a psychological, almost a physiological, compulsion:

Not write? But then I *think*,
And for my Soul I cannot sleep a wink.
I nod in Company, I wake at Night,
Fools rush into my Head, and so I write.

(11-14)

In subsequent lines Pope refuses the poetry of panegyric
and lyric flattery. It is satire he must write. And why? Because it is his pleasure. After all,

Each Mortal has his Pleasure: None deny
Scarsdale his Bottle, *Darty* his Ham-Pye;
Ridotta sips and dances, till she see
The doubling Lustres dance as fast as she;
F-- loves the *Senate, Hockley-Hole* his Brother
Like in all else, as one Egg to another.

(45-50)

If any other man is permitted his pleasure, why not the
satirist? His pleasure is surely as innocent as any other's:

I love to pour out all myself, as plain
As downright *Shippen*, or as old *Montagne*.
In them, as certain to be lov'd as seen,
The Soul stood forth, nor kept a Thought within;
In me what Spots (for Spots I have) appear,
Will prove at least the Medium must be clear.[47]

(51-56)

---

[47] "Spots" confesses rather less than, say, "faults." Pope, however, may
have chosen it on other grounds: a self-enhancing memory of Lepidus's
praise of Antony—"His faults in him, seem as the spots of heaven, / More
fiery by night's blackness; hereditary, / Rather than purchas'd: what he
cannot change, / Than what he chooses" (*Antony and Cleopatra*, I.iv.12-15);
and the pun on an older meaning of "spots," "moral stains," and a new
one, "beauty marks" (*OED*, s.v. "spot," I.1, II.1b). (See *Epistle to a Lady*, 44,
where "happy Spots" set off a fine complexion.) The wit of the line, already apparent in Pope's mock-earnest insistence—"For spots I have"—
derives extra piquancy from the disparity between the two senses. And yet
the disparity helps to make Pope's point: the spot enhances. Characteristically, Pope turns defect to advantage.

At this point Pope's voice rises slightly, and his language becomes more formal and elevated:

> In this impartial Glass, my Muse intends
> Fair to expose myself, my Foes, my Friends;
> Publish the present Age, but where my Text
> Is Vice too high, reserve it for the next:
> My Foes shall wish my Life a longer date,
> And ev'ry Friend the less lament my Fate.
>
> (57-62)

In lines 51-56 Pope's sole interest is self-expression for the purpose of self-vindication. In lines 57-62 he combines that interest in self-expression ("expose myself") with concern for a wider sphere, "my Foes, my Friends . . . the present Age." We may observe, however, the personal nature of his undertaking, as signaled by the frequent use of "my"—my Muse, my Foes, my Friends, my Text. He still thinks in terms of a satiric sensibility that seeks to expose or reflect in the mirror of his own self ("this impartial Glass") the vice ("my Foes") and virtue ("my Friends") he finds around him. We can detect, in a phrase like "Publish the present Age" and in the implication that his "Text" will outlive vice, suggestions of that other self who serves Virtue and Eternity. But Pope quickly drops such suggestions and resumes his presentation of the satirist as a man who only seeks to please himself:

> My Head and Heart thus flowing thro' my Quill,
> Verse-man, or Prose-man, term me which you will,
> Papist or Protestant, or both between,
> Like good *Erasmus* in an honest Mean,[48]

---

[48] Pope here converts a Restoration satiric image of Erasmus into an honorific one. Because he refused to intervene either for or against Luther at Worms, though appealed to by both sides, Erasmus was said, in Dryden's words, to have been "hung 'twixt Hell and Heaven" (Prologue to *The Duke of Guise* [1682]). This between-stools position is ironically called "Erasmus' paradise" in Otway's *Souldier's Fortune* (1683), Act IV, and in Congreve's *Double Dealer* (1695), Act IV. In the introduction ("To the Reader") to his translation (1689) of Erasmus's *Select Colloquies*, Roger

In Moderation placing all my Glory,
While Tories call me Whig, and Whigs a Tory.
Satire's my Weapon, but I'm too discreet
To run a Muck, and tilt at all I meet;
I only wear it in a Land of Hectors. . . .

(63-71)

Peace is my dear Delight—not *Fleury*'s more:
But touch me, and no Minister so sore.
Who-e'er offends, at some unlucky Time
Slides into Verse, and hitches in a Rhyme.

(75-78)

Again, writing is a matter of self-expression: the head and heart flow out through the quill, sometimes in prose, sometimes in verse, sometimes a Papist tune, sometimes a Protestant. The uninhibited activity is what delights him. However, "Satire's my Weapon" introduces a new emphasis that Pope will develop later. Here the satirist is a knight-errant, a true lover of peace, but ready to strike out if his own sense of right is "offended." (Once again, the satirist measures vice by his own personal standard.)

The level of discourse—light, colloquial, colored by irony and occasional sarcasm—enforces a sense of an easygoing poet who does not look on his work with a grave eye. Yet, as he continues, hints again creep in to suggest that satire is more than Pope's idle diversion:

Then learned Sir! (to cut the Matter short)
What-e'er my Fate, or well or ill at Court,
Whether old Age, with faint, but chearful Ray,
Attends to gild the Evening of my Day,

L'Estrange likened himself to Erasmus: "Some will have him [the translator] to be a Papist in Masquerade, for going so far: Others again will have him to be too much a Protestant, because he will go no farther: So that he is crush'd betwixt the Two Extremes, as they hung up Erasmus himself, betwixt Heaven and Hell." Note that Pope once more converts liability into strength, a painful, suspect, and dangerous hanging-between into a proud, pleased, and "honest mean."

Or Death's black Wing already be display'd
To wrap me in the Universal Shade. . . .

(91-96)

Once more Pope extends his eye beyond the present moment and contemplates his "Fate," old age or death. "Evening of my Day," "black Wing," and "Universal Shade"
surprise by their sudden somberness and figurative
heightening. But this loftier mood is immediately dissi-
pated:

Whether the darken'd Room to muse invite,
Or whiten'd Wall provoke the Skew'r to write,
In Durance, Exile, Bedlam, or the Mint,
Like *Lee* or *Budgell*, I will Rhyme and Print.

(97-100)

The poet is now, ironically, the inmate of a madhouse or a
debtor's sanctuary (note how the low "Bedlam, or the
Mint" makes comic contrast with the high, almost epic "In
Durance, Exile"). Again, however, Pope suddenly shifts
gears. From low irony and a cumulative view of satire as a
means of pouring forth the self to satisfy some personal
needs, Pope leaps suddenly to the poem's loftiest point and
a view of satire as the armed service of Virtue:

What! arm'd for *Virtue* when I point the Pen,
Brand the bold Front of shameless, guilty Men,
Dash the proud Gamester in his gilded Car,
Bare the mean Heart that lurks beneath a Star;
Can there be wanting to defend Her Cause,
Lights of the Church, or Guardians of the Laws?
Could pension'd *Boileau* lash in honest Strain
Flatt'rers and Bigots ev'n in *Louis'* Reign?
Could Laureate *Dryden* Pimp and Fry'r engage,
Yet neither *Charles* nor *James* be in a Rage?
And I not strip the Gilding off a Knave,
Unplac'd, un-pension'd, no Man's Heir, or Slave?
I will, or perish in the gen'rous Cause.

Hear this, and tremble! you, who 'scape the Laws.
Yes, while I live, no rich or noble knave
Shall walk the World, in credit, to his grave.
TO VIRTUE ONLY and HER FRIENDS, A FRIEND.

(105-121)

Here the satirist devotes himself to the cause of Virtue, not
to the gratification of his own sensibility. Now too he is
fiercely engaged in a public and political world of Church,
Court, and laws, doing battle with gamesters and knaves
and "shameless, guilty Men." No longer the lover of peace
and retirement, he revels in the fight, frankly admitting the
aggressiveness in his nature and the plain fact that satire
hurts—"point the Pen," "Brand," "dash," "bare," "strip."

And yet this mood too gives way with the same sudden-
ness with which it arrived. At the lofty moment of "TO VIR-
TUE ONLY and HER FRIENDS, A FRIEND," Pope pivots, as it
were, on the word "friend," turns his back on the world in
which he had, for the moment, declared himself so fully
engaged, and retires to his grotto, his friends, and the
pleasures of private life:

TO VIRTUE ONLY and HER FRIENDS, A FRIEND,
The World beside may murmur, or commend.
Know, all the distant Din that World can keep
Rolls o'er my *Grotto*, and but sooths my Sleep.
There, my Retreat the best Companions grace,
Chiefs, out of War, and Statesmen, out of Place.
There *St. John* mingles with my friendly Bowl,
The Feast of Reason and the Flow of Soul:
And He, whose Lightning pierc'd th' *Iberian* Lines,
Now, forms my Quincunx, and now ranks my Vines,
Or tames the Genius of the stubborn Plain,
Almost as quickly, as the conquer'd *Spain*.

(121-32)

The public world is now but a "distant Din," while Pope enjoys the delights of another world, the counterkingdom of
"Chiefs, out of War, and Statesmen, out of Place," where

the lone warrior pointing his pen yields to the festal companion handing round the "friendly Bowl." Where that
world once provoked the sleepless Pope to distraction and
compelled his satiric response (lines 11-14), it now "sooths"
him to sleep. The destructive violence of the satirist is now
redirected, along with the warchief's piercing lightning,
into the gardener's gentler campaign to "form" the quincunx and "rank" the vines—building and ordering rather
than tearing away. Likewise, he seeks out not "guilty Men"
to brand, but friends and men of merit to encourage:
"Fond to spread Friendships, but to cover Heats, / To help
who want, to forward who excel" (136-37). His reward is
not his own approbation but the recognition and love of
friends. "This, all who know me, know; who love me tell"
(138).

From this point the poem moves quickly to its conclusion, where Pope sounds for a moment like the public cen-
sor, insisting that his poems are "grave *Epistles*, bringing
Vice to light, / Such as a *King* might read, a *Bishop* write, /
Such as Sir *Robert* would approve" (151-53). Yet the sly
irony in "approve" ("approve of," but also "prove to be
true") keeps the tone light and does not pretend to resolve
the disparity between Pope's public and private selves. Indeed, Pope seems quite content to let the two selves sit side
by side, even pointing up the difference between them by
the abruptness with which he moves from one to the other
(see lines 106 and 121).

The *Epistle to Dr. Arbuthnot* dramatizes even more clearly
the conflict between Pope as defender of Virtue, sallying
forth into a world of knaves to lash the vicious and rescue
Truth in distress, and Pope as contemplative recluse,
shrinking from contact with the loud, impudent, importu-
nate world, seeking the consolations of quiet, books,
friendship, and family. It has long been recognized that
the poem is a masterpiece of modulation, a "rising and falling of emotion, from equanimity to violence and back

again,"[49] presenting a Pope harassed and plagued by fools
and knaves, patient and enduringly tolerant until he can
no longer hold back explosive anger. Having lashed out, he
again recovers a measure of calm.[50] What has not been
sufficiently recognized is that the ebb and flow of the poem
articulates an unresolved debate, corresponding to a debate carried on in his letters and in the epistle to Fortescue.
What are his obligations as a man, as a poet?[51] How can he
reconcile his public and private roles?

The dilemma of the reluctant public man of letters, comically dramatized for some 250 lines, comes to a crisis when
Pope exclaims:

> Heav'ns! was I born for nothing but to write?
> Has Life no Joys for me? or (to be grave)
> Have I no Friend to serve, no Soul to save?[52]
>
> (272-74)

Here, as throughout the poem, the incipient pathos is
checked by irony, but the issue raised is still a serious one.
Although Pope emphatically wants to answer "yes, there
are other joys and duties," doubt remains that the private
self can assert its claims with success. "To write well, lastingly well, Immortally well," Pope had once reflected,
"must one not leave Father and Mother and cleave unto
the Muse? Must one not be prepared to endure the re-
proaches of Men, want and much Fasting, nay Martyrdom
in its Cause. 'Tis such a Task as scarce leaves a Man time to

[49] Edwards, *This Dark Estate*, pp. 105-6.
[50] See Elias Mengel, "Patterns of Imagery in Pope's *Arbuthnot*," *PMLA*,
69 (1954), 189.
[51] Pope writes in the "Advertisement" that the poem contains an "Apology for the Author and his Writings" in response to attacks on his "Morals, Person, and Family" as well as on his writings. In Gilliver's announce-
ment of the forthcoming second volume of the 1735 *Works*, the *Epistle to
Dr. Arbuthnot* is entitled, "Of Himself and his Writings to Dr. Arbuthnot":
Pope Bibliography, I, pt. 2, 282.
[52] Cf. "D'ye think me good for nothing but to rhime?": *Imit. Hor. Ep.*
II.ii.32.

be a good Neighbour, an useful Friend, nay to plant a
Tree, much less to save his Soul" (*Corr.*, II, 227).

In *Arbuthnot* the conflicting claims of the private life and
of a larger world are finally unreconciled. Immediately
after this plaintive appeal for the private self, Pope turns
quite abruptly to present himself as a virtuous writer and
lashing satirist:

> Curst be the Verse, how well soe'er it flow,
> That tends to make one worthy Man my foe. . . .
>
> (283-84)
>
> A lash like mine no honest man shall dread,
> But all such babling blockheads in his stead.
>
> (303-4)

These lines are followed by the Sporus portrait, a passage
to rival anything Pope wrote in its violence and aggressiveness, in the focused intensity of its fury. And the attack
leads in turn to a renewed declaration of Pope's public mission:

> Welcome for thee, fair Virtue! all the past,
> For thee, fair Virtue! Welcome ev'n the *last*.
>
> (358-59)

He has built up to a moment of lofty enthusiasm. As at a
similar point in the poem to Fortescue, Pope declares his
deepest allegiance to Virtue. But within ten lines (the parallel with *Fortescue* continues) we are back once more with the
private self. As if to emphasize the contradiction, Pope
turns abruptly:

> Yet soft by Nature, more a Dupe than Wit,
> *Sapho* can tell you how this Man was bit.
>
> (368-69)

He has put away his weapons, is by nature "soft," forbear-
ing, forgiving. He never sought a battle, never enjoyed it.
For the remainder of the poem Pope presents only the private self—the friend of distressed enemies, the son of good

and honest parents, the comforter of his dying mother and the seriously ailing Arbuthnot. He has retreated once more into a smaller, private world.

Again, significantly, that world is associated with Pope's past.[53] It is a world and a possible self, so the poem suggests, that may be passing. Pope's request that he too may live the quiet, "healthy," innoxious life of his father ("O Grant me thus to live, and thus to die!") will plainly go ungranted. He has made clear already that his own life has been both a "long Disease" and a battle against evil. Yet Pope clearly *recognizes* the claims of piety, friendship, and family and genuinely wants to believe that, except for the force of circumstances, he might have been that simple "good Man" that he was fitted by nature and heritage to be. The juxtaposition of pious son and heroic defender of public virtue may recall an earlier hero famed for *pietas*. Aeneas had found it nearly impossible to be both a public and a private man, to reconcile all the senses of *pietas*— honor of one's family and household gods on the one hand, honor of one's country and the laws on the other. In the *Epistle to Dr. Arbuthnot* Pope retains a lively sense of all those obligations,[54] and has not yet so identified himself with his public mission that he risks losing his private self. Indeed, although he sets in opposition his public and private selves, Pope does not in this poem insist that he must choose one or the other. He holds on to both, yet spares nothing to present the distance between them.

When Pope turned next to extended self-description, in

---

[53] It is only by rearranging facts that Pope can conclude the poem in the present. As his own note indicates, Mrs. Pope had actually died in 1733.

[54] Dryden's gloss of *pietas*—it "comprehendeth the Whole Duty of Man towards the Gods, towards his Country, and towards his Relations"—and his elaboration of the term in describing the "manners" of Aeneas—"Piety to the Gods, and a dutiful Affection to his Father; Love to his Relations; Care of his People; Courage and Conduct in the Wars; Gratitude to those who had oblig'd him; and Justice in general to Mankind"—might well describe Pope's character in the poem: Dryden, dedication to the *Aeneid*, in Dryden, *Poems*, ed. James Kinsley, III (Oxford, 1958), 1010, 1020.

the imitation of Horace's *Epistle* i.i (1737),[55] it was largely the private self that he presented. But even there the more public Pope emerges (though not to be commented on) in the broad satire on human worldliness. The *Epistle to Bolingbroke* begins with Pope's lament that he has been "Publick too long." Like the harassed poet at the opening of *Arbuthnot*, he is "sick . . . of envy and of Praise." But this time Pope (following Horace, of course) puts emphasis not on the pious son and lover of quiet, but on the man whose chief "business" is private virtue—to make himself into the ever-constant "Man divine whom Wisdom calls her own." A variety of obstacles to this goal are considered: St. John's advice that he continue to write, his own lingering fondness for "Verse and Love, and ev'ry Toy," the world's counsel that he seek instead "Wealth and Place"—these obstacles are easily thrown aside—and his temperamental inconstancy and "incoherent" mind.

In this poem Pope finally claims to adopt the advice of Fortescue that he "write no more." His grounds, however, are different: not satire's dangers, but the rival claims of "Life's instant business," the care of his soul or "self" demand it. Now in the cool evening of his life,

So slow th'unprofitable Moments roll,
That lock up all the Functions of my soul;
That keep me from Myself; and still delay
Life's instant business to a future day:
That task, which as we follow, or despise,
The eldest is a fool, the youngest wise;
Which done, the poorest can no wants endure,
And which not done, the richest must be poor.

(39-46)

[55] The imitation of Horace's *Epistle* ii.ii (1737) contains some interesting autobiographical passages (quoted above, p. 30). The poem deals with, among other matters, the conflicting claims of poetry—"my Rhime" (72-79)—and the private self—the need to "smoothe and harmonize my Mind," to "keep the equal Measure of the Soul," (198-211).

The claims of the private self could hardly be put more strongly. With allusions to Scripture providing discreet reminders,[56] Pope presents the traditional classico-Christian argument for the self-centered, even self-absorbed, life. Every man is responsible above all for his own soul. No man dare leave undone "that task," whatever his service to public morality:

> What right, what true, what fit, we justly call,
> Let this be all my care—for this is All:
> To lay this harvest up, and hoard with haste
> What ev'ry day will want, and most, the last.
>
> (19-22)

The "last" is, of course, the Day of Judgment, when each individual account is rendered. It is as if Pope has returned to and answered a question asked in *Arbuthnot*: "Have I no . . . soul to save?"

In this theological context, to write satire is not, as it was in *To Fortescue*, to serve the needs and honest pleasures of the private self. Rather, it is a trifle to be outgrown. But one senses that Pope's dismissal is a fond one: "Farewell then Verse, and Love, and ev'ry Toy, / The rhymes and rattles of the Man or Boy" (17-18). And, of course, as the poem continues it gives the lie to this pretended farewell. The world, whose voice urges Pope to "get Mony," to "be but Great, / With Praise or Infamy, leave that to fate, / Get Place and Wealth, if possible, with Grace; / If not, by any means get Wealth and Place" (101-4), provides him a ready target for satire. Whatever his protestations to the contrary (see lines 134-35), fully half of the poem consists of Pope's rigorous satire against worldly accommodation and against every man's inability "to act consistent with himself an hour" (137). Human inconsistency leads Pope back to his own case and his own efforts to get wisdom. Earlier in the

---

[56] Prov. 13:7, Luke 12:19-21, Phil. 4:8. See Maresca, *Pope's Horatian Poems*, p. 175.

poem he had presented an engaging portrait of his own inconstancy, there viewed as eclecticism and flexibility:

> But ask not, to what Doctors I apply?
> Sworn to no Master, of no Sect am I:
> As drives the storm, at any door I knock,
> And house with Montagne now, or now with Lock.
> Sometimes a Patriot, active in debate,
> Mix with the World, and battle for the State,
> Free as young Lyttelton, her cause pursue,
> Still true to Virtue, and as warm as true:
> Sometimes, with Aristippus, or St. Paul,
> Indulge my Candor, and grow all to all;
> Back to my native Moderation slide,
> And win my way by yielding to the tyde.
>
> (23-34)

But later in the poem, after viewing the pageant of human inconsistency, Pope sees his own variability more ironically, more skeptically. Eclecticism is now not richly various, but self-canceling:

> no Prelate's Lawn with Hair-shirt lin'd,
> Is half so incoherent as my Mind,
> When (each Opinion with the next at strife,
> One ebb and flow of follies all my Life)
> I plant, root up, I build, and then confound,
> Turn round to square, and square again to round.
>
> (165-70)

Even his person is at odds with itself: "half Beau half Sloven . . . Coat and Breeches strangely vary, / White Gloves, and Linnen worthy Lady Mary!" (161, 163-64). This is no well-accorded strife that expresses an underlying harmony, but the incongruity and inconstancy that Pope, in the letters, found to be an essential feature of his very self. As if in confirmation, the poem concludes with Pope's wry chagrin at the disparity between his aspirations to divine wisdom and his human foibles. Bolingbroke, he says,

> ought to make me (what he can, or none,)
> That Man divine whom Wisdom calls her own;
> Great without Title, without Fortune bless'd,
> Rich ev'n when plunder'd, honour'd while oppress'd,
> Lov'd without youth, and follow'd without power,
> At home tho' exil'd, free, tho' in the Tower.
> In short, that reas'ning, high, immortal Thing,
> Just less than Jove, and much above a King,
> Nay half in Heav'n—except (what's mighty odd)
> A Fit of Vapours clouds this Demi-god.[57]
>
> (179-88)

The "Fit of Vapours," whatever its mocking allusion to the clouds that veil the pagan or Old Testament gods, is plainly an equivalent of Horace's *pituita* and an apt emblem of Pope's wretched carcase, his constantly aching head, his variable temper—all the clogs of an earthly body.[58]

If the emphasis in the epistle to Bolingbroke falls on Pope's private self, the two Dialogues of the *Epilogue to the Satires*, published in the following year (1738), present the public Pope once more, not the wry, self-mocking man of inconstancy, but the heroic defender of Virtue. The question at issue is not whether, but how to write satire— general or personal?—in an age of such egregious corruption. The answer is a firm defense of personal satire and a vigorous display of Pope's willingness to offend sensibilities, to disturb the peace, to engage in battle with weapons that do injury. With a pointed pen, Pope will

[57] The closing lines are sometimes thought to allude to Bolingbroke; grammatically, however, they clearly refer to Pope, the "me" of line 179. Even those lines that seem to allude to Bolingbroke ("Great without Title . . . plunder'd . . . follow'd without power . . . At home tho' exil'd") can refer equally to Pope, plundered, powerless, and exiled as a Catholic in Protestant England. Perhaps the lines apply to both men: Bolingbroke is best able to "make" Pope into a man of wisdom precisely because he is one himself.

[58] Plainly, I dispute the conclusions of Maresca that Pope in the Horatian poems presents himself as a properly Christian "concordant character" and that in the epistle to Bolingbroke he has in fact become the demigod man of Wisdom (*Pope's Horatian Poems*, pp. 53, 182-86).

"maul" a minister's tools (1.147), "rowze . . . provoke . . . and goad" the sluggish "Watchmen of the Publick Weal" (217-19). The poet himself stands a lonely vigil against the imagined triumph of Vice, joins in the glorious triumph of Truth over the "tinsel Insects" of a court. Only at one moment in the *Epilogue* do we get a glimpse of that other Pope, the soft, quiet man of peace. In defending himself against the charge of "spleen," Pope claims he distributes praise where he can. He pauses to recall good men:

> Oft in the clear, still Mirrour of Retreat,
> I study'd SHREWSBURY, the wise and great:
> CARLETON's calm Sense, and STANHOPE's noble Flame,
> Compar'd, and knew their gen'rous End the same:
> How pleasing ATTERBURY's softer hour!
> How shin'd the Soul, unconquer'd in the Tow'r!
>
> (II.78-83)

Their friendship is among his most cherished possessions:

> Names, which I long have lov'd, nor lov'd in vain,
> Rank'd with their Friends, not number'd with their
>   Train;
> And if yet higher the proud List should end,
> Still let me say! No Follower, but a Friend.
>
> (90-93)

Yet friendship does not hold the place of honor, as it does, for example, in *To Fortescue* and the *Epistle to Dr. Arbuthnot*. It is merely one of several motives, and far less important than Virtue itself, which serves as Pope's chief guide and prompter. Where the earlier poems end as Pope communes with a dear friend, the two Dialogues of the *Epilogue to the Satires* end with Pope in grand isolation and alienation, without even an ally.

"The Testimony of His Own Conscience"

As in the earlier apologies, Pope makes no explicit attempt in the *Epilogue* to reconcile his two selves. He acknowledges both, and decides for neither. The private self is concerned above all with things close at hand—friends, family, Pope's own soul, the pleasures of retirement. The public self looks toward the state of public morality, the health of the nation, toward Virtue and Truth themselves. Both selves, as we saw earlier, correspond to versions of Pope in the letters; both represent distinct sides of his character. But just as in the letters one can discover some reconciliation between competing impulses, so in the Horatian poems some resolution is suggested between the public and private selves. For even when Pope in his most "public" voice cries out in defense of Virtue, he makes it clear that the villainy he decries is a personal provocation, an offense to his personal sensibility. In this light, to write satire for private pleasure, as an outpouring of the self, is not, after all, so different from writing as Virtue's public defender. In each case the self's needs are consulted and its desires gratified.

In the epistle *To Fortescue*, for example, the public moralist defines the world around him by reference to himself, that is, as "my Foes" or "my Friends" (58). All is to be reflected in the "impartial Glass" (57) of the self. Even his proudest cry, "TO VIRTUE ONLY and HER FRIENDS, A FRIEND" (121), as I have argued earlier, transforms public morality into a matter of friendship. Public self and its concerns here merge with private. In the *Epistle to Dr. Arbuthnot* the public defender can again be seen to be acting from essentially private, self-regarding motives. Traditionally, the satirist claims to write out of public-spirited good will, seeking to reform, or at least to deter, the foolish or vicious.[59] Pope himself occasionally offered this defense of his satire.[60] But in *Arbuthnot* Pope several times makes it clear that he knows satire to be ineffectual, that his motive is not to reform:

'Tis sung, when *Midas'* Ears began to spring,
. . . .

[59] See, for example, the recent discussion in P. K. Elkin, *The Augustan Defence of Satire* (Oxford, 1973).

[60] For example: "And heals with Morals what it hurts with Wit" (*Epistle to Augustus*, 262). See the *Correspondence* generally.

His very Minister who spy'd them first,
(Some say his Queen) was forc'd to speak, or burst.
And is not mine, my Friend, a sorer case,
When ev'ry Coxcomb perks them in my face?
. . . .
Out with it, *Dunciad*! let the secret pass,
That Secret to each Fool, that he's an Ass.
(69, 71-74, 79-80)

The motive here is self-satisfaction, as Pope makes plain by
claiming that his satire is in fact not cruel, for "no creature
smarts so little as a Fool." (Codrus is unconcerned as peals
of laughter break over his head.) No scribbler is shamed by
Pope's words, no poet or peer hurt. Sporus himself can feel
neither "Satire or Sense" (307) and is perhaps not worth
flapping. But Pope flaps anyway. Amendment, the traditional goal of satire, is clearly not his interest. He will write
satire, whether or not evil men are touched:

A Knave's a Knave, to me, in ev'ry State,[61]
Alike my scorn, if he succeed or fail,
Sporus at Court, or *Japhet* in a Jayl,
A hireling Scribler, or a hireling Peer,
Knight of the Post corrupt, or of the Shire,
If on a Pillory, or near a Throne,
He gain his Prince's Ear, or lose his own.
(361-67)

What matters then is Pope's own integrity. He must as a
matter of principle declare where he stands, without reference to the outcome of his protest. The same point is made
more forcibly in the first Dialogue of the *Epilogue*. Despite
the fact that Vice triumphs over a willing world, that nothing is sacred but villainy,

Yet may this Verse (if such a Verse remain)
Show there was one who held it in disdain.
(171-72)

[61] Cf. *"Virtue* may chuse the high or low Degree, / 'Tis just alike to Virtue, and to me" (*Epilogue to the Satires*, 1.137-38).

Pope's action here is, from a worldly point of view, nobly irrelevant, perhaps even foolishly pompous ("held it in *disdain*"), a measure of his alienation and failure.[62] Yet we do not, nor does Pope himself, view his action from the world's point of view. From his own perspective, his action is the proper one, whether or not it makes any difference. He seeks only to bear witness, regardless of the consequences, to his own principles.

In the second Dialogue Pope develops this position more fully and explicitly:

> Ask you what Provocation I have had?
> The strong Antipathy of Good to Bad.
> When Truth or Virtue an Affront endures,
> Th' Affront is mine, my Friend, and should be yours.
> Mine, as a Foe profess'd to false Pretence,
> Who think a Coxcomb's Honour like his Sense;
> Mine, as a Friend to ev'ry worthy mind;
> And mine as Man, who feel for all mankind.
>
> (197-204)

Viewed one way, he identifies himself with Good, Virtue, and Truth, and responds as a member of a class (the good). But viewed another way, Good, Virtue, and Truth are embodied in him as their champion. He writes satire out of personal "antipathy,"[63] and takes every instance of evil as a personal "affront" to him. He does not shrink from the charge of pride. Indeed, he declares it:

> *Fr*. You're strangely proud. *P*. So proud, I am no Slave:
> So impudent, I own myself no Knave:
> So odd, my Country's Ruin makes me grave.
> Yes, I am proud; I must be proud to see
> Men not afraid of God, afraid of me:
> Safe from the Bar, the Pulpit, and the Throne,
> Yet touch'd and sham'd by *Ridicule* alone.
>
> (205-11)

[62] On this point see Edwards, *This Dark Estate*, p. 93.

[63] Pope may here be reshaping for his own use an insult once hurled at himself. In the *Verses address'd to the Imitator of Horace* (1733) God declares an "antipathy" between serpentlike Pope and the entire "human race" (56).

Again Pope emphasizes the personal nature of his battle. His enthusiasm leads him to claim for his effort some success. Bad men will be "afraid" of him, will be "touch'd and sham'd" by his ridicule. But by the end of the poem, even this degree of success is doubted,[64] and his stance is once again measured with reference only to his own conscience and to poetic immortality. Bad men may momentarily triumph as insects of the day, but it is Pope's idealistic hope that the good, with his help, will ultimately gain fame in the "Temple of Eternity."[65] The poem concludes, however, not with the imagined heavenly triumph of Virtue, but with the earthly vigil of her defender:

> Yes, the last Pen for Freedom let me draw,
> When Truth stands trembling on the edge of Law:
> Here, Last of *Britons*! let your Names be read;
> Are none, none living? let me praise the Dead.
>
> (248-51)

His role is to praise virtue wherever it is found. If no virtuous men live, he himself will be one of the "Last of Britons" praising the dead. Like the succession of virtuous Old Testament figures in the last books of *Paradise Lost*, Pope presents himself as the "one just man" in a world of evil, who speaks out, heard or unheard. Like his own Codrus, Pope will stand "unshook amidst a bursting World." For the most part, he permitted himself few illusions about the difference that "one just man" might make. But occasionally he rose to the belief that he himself might be the "Sole Dread of Folly, Vice, and Insolence!" that "one man's honesty" might "redeem the land."[66]

[64] Pope does not overstate, even in enthusiasm. He does not necessarily claim, even here, that bad men will be deterred from vice.

[65] The conclusion to the second Dialogue is thus the complement, and not the reverse, of the conclusion to the first, where vice triumphs in the world.

[66] One wonders indeed whether while writing the unfinished *1740* in praise of Frederick, Prince of Wales, as the only political hope of the nation, Pope perhaps thought also of himself: "Whatever his religion or his blood, / His public virtue makes his title good. / Europe's just balance and our own may stand, / And one man's honesty redeem the land" (95-98).

More often, Pope looked at the fallen world as finally shameless and unshakable. In this mood he wrote not to terrify, far less to redeem, but simply to protest. Indeed, he referred to the *Epilogue to the Satires* as "my Protest" (*Corr.*, IV, 178). At the conclusion to its second Dialogue he added a valedictory note:

> This was the last poem of the kind printed by our author, with a resolution to publish no more; but to enter thus, in the most plain and solemn manner he could, a sort of PROTEST against that insuperable corruption and depravity of manners, which he had been so unhappy as to live to see. Could he have hoped to have amended any, he had continued those attacks; but bad men were grown so shameless and so powerful, that Ridicule was become as unsafe as it was ineffectual. The Poem raised him, as he knew it would, some enemies; but he had reason to be satisfied with the approbation of good men, and the testimony of his own conscience.

He hopes now not to amend the bad but to be commended by good men and by the ultimate arbiter, his own conscience.[67] For many of Pope's readers, myself included, such displays of integrity are among his best moral and poetic moments. Not surprisingly, since a parading righteousness is almost inherently offensive, others prefer the witty attack to the high-minded defense. They claim furthermore that the *poetry* is better—denser, wittier, more animated, more concrete—in Pope's satiric passages than in his outbursts of moral idealism, which, it is thought, flatly declare or float free of the particularities and contingencies of moral experience.[68] Without undertaking a full scale defense of the high-minded Pope, I would briefly

[67] Cf. "The greatest Comfort of life, next to a good Conscience, is the Good Opinion of Good Men" (*Corr.*, II, 279).

[68] I put here a case that I have not seen argued at length in print, but that I take nonetheless to be currently entertained. Modern distaste for Pope's high-mindedness is common. For a recent example, see F. M. Keener, *An Essay on Pope* (New York, 1974).

respond by recalling that at its best moments Pope's lofty idealism does not float free from his satiric world and that the verse likewise remains in touch with felt particularity.

The presence of the enemy almost always excites Pope; he flourishes in opposition, sings best when his hands and feet are manacled. Only when he turns to imagine an immortal "Temple of Eternity" beyond the contingencies of human struggle does his verse lose density and life:

> Not so, when diadem'd with Rays divine,
> Touch'd with the Flame that breaks from Virtue's
>   Shrine,
> Her Priestless Muse forbids the Good to dye,
> And ope's the Temple of Eternity;
> There other *Trophies* deck the truly Brave,
> Than such as *Anstis* casts into the Grave;
> Far other *Stars* than * and ** wear,
> And may descend to *Mordington* from *Stair*:
> Such as on HOUGH's unsully'd Mitre shine,
> Or beam, good DIGBY! from a Heart like thine.
> Let Envy howl while Heav'n's whole Chorus sings,
> And bark at Honour not confer'd by Kings;
> Let Flatt'ry sickening see the Incense rise,
> Sweet to the World, and grateful to the Skies:
> Truth guards the Poet, sanctifies the line,
> And makes Immortal, Verse as mean as mine.
>
> (232-47)

Here the scene fails to visualize, and the lines are eked out with formulaic phrases ("Rays divine," "Heav'n's whole Chorus," "Sweet to the World, and grateful to the Skies"). The particulars here—Anstis, Mordington, etc.—merely clog the verse without providing illuminating contrast. Only the puns on "line" and "makes Immortal" (perpetuates a lineage, "sanctifies" a "mean" verse and makes it live eternally) save the final couplet.

In his best verse Pope insists that the corrupt world and the man of integrity impinge on each other in several respects. First, the defender of Virtue firmly thrusts against a vividly realized countervailing force, the triumph of Vice or the threat of Sporus: "Not Fortune's Worshipper, nor Fashion's Fool, / Not Lucre's Madman, nor Ambition's Tool, / Not proud, nor servile, be one poet's praise / That if he pleas'd, he pleas'd by manly ways." Second, Pope firmly plants the moral idealist in a body that, by its frailties, impedes an aspiring will (*Epistle to Bolingbroke*), and in a world that decides whether or not he may speak (*To Fortescue*), refuses to listen (*Epilogue to the Satires*, II), and rewards nothing but villainy (*Epilogue to the Satires*, I). Third, Pope does not forget that the moral idealist fights his battles with the tools of the satirist.

> What? arm'd for *Virtue* when I point the Pen,
> Brand the bold Front of shameless, guilty Men,
> Dash the proud Gamester in his gilded Car,
> Bare the mean Heart that lurks beneath a Star. . . .
>
> Yes, while I live, no rich or noble knave
> Shall walk the World, in credit, to his grave.
> (To Fortescue, 105-8, 119-20)

Pope, the self-appointed scourge of Virtue, does not shrink from a highwayman's violence. Here too is vividly, concretely imagined moral warfare:

> O sacred Weapon! left for Truth's defence,
> Sole Dread of Folly, Vice, and Insolence!
> To all but Heav'n-directed hands deny'd,
> The Muse may give thee! but the Gods must guide.
> Rev'rent I touch thee! but with honest zeal;
> To rowze the Watchmen of the Publick Weal,
> To Virtue's Work provoke the tardy Hall,
> And goad the Prelate slumb'ring in his Stall.
> (Epilogue to the Satires, I.212-19)

As he addresses his "Weapon"—the pen—Pope is first a zealous priest, reverently handling the "sacred" relics somehow left to men by Heaven for holy war. This figure blends with the Homeric warrior taking up his spear and praying to the gods before battle. "Touch" is the focus of the passage.[69] "Rev'rent . . . touch" suggests the pious soldier's deliberateness, purity of purpose, perhaps even humility.[70] Bad men, Pope had earlier said, are "touch'd" by ridicule, censured, or affected in mind or feeling.[71] That figurative wounding becomes sharply literal when Pope's weapon "touches" his enemies. The scene becomes an allegorical fantasy of inverted order: public watchmen (presumably Parliament) who fail to watch; judges (Westminster "Hall") who abet the law's delay; prelates sunk in sloth and oxlike oblivion. Although they retain figurative senses, "rowze," "provoke," and "goad" are also made to seem powerfully literal: in a preview of the *Dunciad*, we envision parliamentary committees yielding to yawns, judges who need to be petitioned (one "provokes" a court to take up a case),[72] bishops asleep in port.

Here, as not uncommonly in Pope's high-minded mood, the verse has a rich and powerful density, and often a lurid fantasy effect (for example, the allegorical pageant of the triumph of villainy). As in the *Dunciad*, abstractions become vividly concrete, old metaphors are re-enlivened:

> Ye tinsel Insects! whom a Court maintains,
> That count your Beauties only by your Stains,
> Spin all your Cobwebs o'er the Eye of Day!
> The Muse's Wing shall brush you all away.
>
> (*Epilogue*, II.220-23)

The poet's effortless triumph is vividly realized in the metaphorical meeting of grubby insect and soaring bird. Moral idealism does not spoil Pope's gifts as a poet.

---

[69] Is Pope half-thinking of the lyrist (i.e., poet) "touching" the strings of his lyre?

[70] As if in response, Pope is later "Touch'd with the Flame that breaks from Virtue's Shrine" (233).

[71] Cf. "Ev'n those you touch not, hate you" (*To Fortescue*, 41), and "In *Sappho* touch the *Failing of the Sex*" (*Epilogue to the Satires*, I.15). The word "touch" (as verb and noun) is used unusually often in Pope's poems.

[72] *OED*, s.v. "provoke," I.2.

Egocentric Satire

Pope's late satires set forth what might be called a self-centered or egocentric theory of satire, which perhaps constitutes his distinctive contribution to the form. The claim that one writes for oneself in response to something within one's own nature is not Pope's invention, but no other English satirist has made that claim with such clarity and power. Horace says he writes for his own pleasure, but he typically passes off his satires as mere diversions. When he does make a lofty claim for the dignity and immortality of art (for example, "Exegi monumentum," Ode III.20), he is celebrating something outside the self. Pope is closer to Juvenal, who says it is difficult *not* to write satire (*Sat.* 1.30). Corruption forces his offended sensibility to respond: "Facit indignatio versum" (*Sat.* 1.79). The apologiae of Juvenal and Persius may have provided Pope with hints for his own apologies,[73] just as they contributed to his lofty declamatory tone. Whatever he found in his Roman predecessors, Pope made openly self-centered satire his special stance as a satirist.

Swift and Pope are sometimes contrasted in their attitude toward the function of satire, with Swift considered to be profoundly skeptical and subversive of the traditional satirist's moral high ground that Pope continues to occupy and defend. But in fact, their analyses of satire's function and effectiveness are not dissimilar. Pope sees as plainly as Swift that satire is ineffective in amending or deterring vicious men, that the satirist can be vindictive, cruel, proud, concerned above all, like Swift's critic, with "forcing into the Light, with much Pains and Dexterity, [my] own Excellencies and other Men's Defaults, with great Justice to [my]self and Candor to them" (*A Tale of a Tub*, v). But while Swift conveys a sense of anxious uncertainty about his role as satirist,[74] Pope is not uncomfortable with that role. In an

[73] Compare Persius, *Sat.* 1.120-21, with the *Epistle to Dr. Arbuthnot*, 69-82.
[74] See Gardner Stout, "Speaker and Satiric Vision in Swift's *Tale of A Tub*," *Eighteenth-Century Studies*, 3 (1969), 175-99.

Intelligencer paper (no. 3, 1728) Swift spoke of two ends in writing satire, "one of them less noble than the other, as regarding nothing further than the private Satisfaction, and Pleasure of the Writer; but without any View towards personal Malice: The other is a public Spirit, prompting Men of Genius and Virtue, to mend the World as far as they are able."[75] One suspects that Swift rarely felt he was accomplishing both ends at once and that he was uneasy if he thought he was satisfying only himself.[76] But Pope seems to have believed that "private Satisfaction" and "publick Spirit" might well house together—"the way to have a Public Spirit, is first to have a Private one"—and he was content, where there was no chance of mending the world, to please himself. Satire serves Virtue and the satirist may justifiably derive pride and pleasure from his service: "There is a pleasure in bearing Testimony to Truth; and a Vanity perhaps, which at least, is as excusable as any Vanity can be" (*Corr.*, ii, 90). In the Horatian poems he practices, with an apparently free conscience, a form of writing that is assertively—and in his view quite properly—self-concerned, self-centered, and ultimately self-defining.

[75] Swift, *Prose Works*, ed. H. Davis, 14 vols. (Oxford, 1939-1968), xii, 34.
[76] This is in spite of his claim in the *Intelligencer* to be quite pleased with the "innocent" pleasure of "laughing with few Friends in a Corner." See Stout, "Speaker and Satiric Vision."

·❧|7|❧·
Pope in *The Dunciad*

To turn from the *Horatian Imitations* to *The Dunciad* is to turn from poems in which Pope himself is often the explicit subject to a poem whose subject is the world of dulness and dunces, and in which Pope himself appears to figure very little. Yet the *Dunciad* is also richly self-expressive. As W. J. Courthope wrote, "Pope himself, his power, his weakness, and his passion, is felt in every line."[1] It is "personal satire," not only in the sense that Johnson and Courthope meant, that is, a satire against persons and personal enemies,[2] but also in that it is as powerfully self-assertive as the *Epilogue to the Satires* and perhaps more complexly self-revelatory than any of the Horatian poems.

Insofar as the *Dunciad* presents a partisan history of Pope as embattled satirist, it is an autobiographical document. In other ways too the poem centers on Pope; it is not so much an exploration of self as a display of powers. Some features of self persist: the sense that Pope alone stands vigil against a world of chaos; the need to register a moral protest against a dulness that, finally, "sees all in self." These features are especially prominent in the fourth book, where, not surprisingly, most interpreters have felt most comfortable, in part because they can apply to it categories developed from comment on the moral satires of the 1730s. But the *Dunciad* is a different kind of poem, and not only generically. More than his other works, it is a poem of several levels or layers, one half-buried beneath

[1] In *Works of Pope*, IV, 19.
[2] Johnson described it as "Personal satire ludicrously pompous": "Life of Pope," p. 241. Courthope said that "It must be regarded simply as the culminating incident in a war of authors. Like all Pope's satires its distinguishing feature is its personality": *Works of Pope*, IV, 19-20.

another. Its subject matter stimulates something in Pope's imagination besides moral idealism and releases other kinds of energies. While the triumph of Vice in the *Epilogue to the Satires* calls forth an impassioned Friend of Virtue, the impending triumph of Dulness calls forth a champion of Wit whose concerns are only partly moral. To be sure, we have something of the virtuous Pope in the *Dunciad*—the honest, benevolent, outraged moralist. But alongside this figure emerges a less purely moral self, who revels in his own creative powers, exults in his witty supremacy over the duncery he imagines, and may even be attracted to the sensual oblivion that Dulness promises her devotees. Here more than anywhere else in his poetry, Pope indulges a freely playing, almost anarchic, imagination, ordinarily so carefully harnessed to the demands of his moral intelligence.

Such a view of the *Dunciad* is at odds with orthodox interpretations of the poem. Most modern critics, with some recent exceptions,[3] see the poem as a mighty and solemn protest against the decay of civilization and play down its role in the war against the duncery. Aubrey Williams, recognizing that the poem is "involved with the local, personal, and contemporary" at its origin, removes the *Dunciad* from its "matrix of history" so that we can see "the literary perversion of duncery, whether biographical or imaginary, as the correlative of greater disorders in a wider realm of values." The author of a more recent book on the poem simply assumes that the impersonality of the poem

[3] See especially Howard Erskine-Hill, "The 'New World' of Pope's *Dunciad*," *Renaissance and Modern Studies*, 6 (1962), 47-67, reprinted in *Essential Articles: Alexander Pope*, ed. Maynard Mack, rev. ed. (Hamden, Conn., 1968), pp. 803-24, and Emrys Jones, "Pope and Dulness," *Proceedings of the British Academy, 1968* (London, 1969), pp. 231-63, reprinted in *Pope: A Collection of Critical Essays*, ed. J. V. Guerinot (Englewood Cliffs, N.J., 1972), pp. 142-45. Both articles are discussed below, pp. 229-30. See also Donald T. Siebert, "Cibber and Satan: *The Dunciad* and Civilization," *Eighteenth-Century Studies*, 10 (1976-1977), 203-21, which appeared after this book was in press.

has been solidly established and need not be further discussed.[4] Without denying that "larger issues" are under Pope's consideration in the poem, especially in Book IV, I wish to examine the ways in which Pope himself is richly present.

"Present in the poem" is, however, a problematic notion, for it is not easy to decide what or where "the poem" is, whether we mean the 1728 three-book version, the 1729 *Variorum*, or the 1743 four-book poem, and whether we include the elaborate notes and cumbrous apparatus that swell a poem of some 1,750 lines into a large bound volume. The nature of the poem and its attacks on dozens of Pope's contemporaries and predecessors, many of them obscure even in Pope's time and all but forgotten now, requires an explanatory key and draws into the poem's sphere a series of *vitae obscurorum virorum* and the whole subculture of Grub Street. Furthermore, the nature of much of the apparatus—testimonies of authors, a list of attacks on the Pope, a parallel between the characters of Pope and Dryden—makes the poem open out into Pope's own life. It is very difficult in fact to draw the poem's boundaries, to decide what is "in" it, what is not in it, where poem leaves off and biography begins. This has direct consequences on our reading. How much information about Pope is an informed reader expected to have and bring to bear on his reading of the poem? Some recent interpreters and most class-text editors have assumed that virtually no information is needed, that the "poem itself," shorn of apparatus and most of the notes, stands as an autonomous poetic object. Nineteenth-century critics, on the other hand, tended to read the poem and the poet's biography as continuous. If, however, we carefully read the material that Pope supplies us in the *Variorum*, consider the notes and apparatus as an integral part of the poem, and include

---

[4] Williams, *Pope's Dunciad: A Study of Its Meaning* (Baton Rouge, 1955), p. 15; John E. Sitter, *The Poetry of Pope's Dunciad* (Minneapolis, 1971), p. 66.

the correspondence dealing with the *Dunciad* (which became by his own choice part of Pope's public record in 1737), and the public quarrels in which he engaged, we will have a full context providing a clear image of Pope and valuable clues for interpreting his role in the poem.

Friends and Enemies

The *Dunciad* clearly has roots in Pope's career as a literary man of the 1720s. It is very much a book of "friends and enemies." As later editors have noted, the poem may have originated in the projects of the Scriblerians in 1714, and it was perhaps in progress when Swift visited Pope in the summers of 1726 and 1727. Arbuthnot may have had a hand in the apparatus. After the publication of the *Variorum*, Pope wrote to Swift, to whom the poem was dedicated, emphasizing how the *Dunciad*, like the later letters, was to stand as a monument to their friendship: "It was my principal aim in the entire work to perpetuate the friendship between us, and to shew that the friends or the enemies of the one were the friends or enemies of the other."[5] A note in Book III commemorates Pope's friendship with another Scriblerian, John Gay. As Settle foretells Gay's death—"Gay dies unpension'd with a hundred friends" (III.330)[6]—Pope adds the note: "This gentleman was early in the friendship of our author, which has continued many years." Another note commends his friend Garth: "It must have been particularly agreeable to him to celebrate Dr. *Garth*; both as his constant friend thro' life,

[5] *Corr.*, III, 57. Swift's delighted response confirms that the poem was so received: "I am one abstracted from every body, in the happiness of being recorded your friend, while wit, and humour, and politeness shall have any memorial among us" (ibid., 64).

[6] All quotations from the *Dunciad* are from *Poems*, Vol. v, the *Dunciad*, ed. James Sutherland. I cite the 1743 version unless otherwise specified. In quoting Pope's footnotes, I also cite the 1743 edition for the sake of uniformity, even though most of the notes to Books I-III are printed in the Twickenham edition only in the 1729 *Variorum* version and simply cross-referenced in the 1743 version.

and as he was his predecessor in this kind of Satire" (ii.140n.).

Enemies are of course much more apparent in the poem. Pope admitted their role in prompting the *Dunciad*. "This Poem will rid me of those insects," he wrote to Swift,[7] and the list of "Books, Papers, and Verses in which our Author was abused" clearly implies that the *Dunciad* was Pope's rejoinder. William Cleland's letter assumes that the dunces named in the poem are Pope's "enemies,"[8] and contemporary reception of the *Dunciad* makes it plain that it was taken by the dunces as Pope's personal attack on them. So much is now perhaps common knowledge, but it needs to be recalled as we begin to consider a poem whose art has been said to be loftily "impersonal." To judge by Pope's own declarations, he quite unashamedly saw the poem, at least in part, as a means of complimenting his friends and punishing his enemies.[9]

The Apparatus

Another circumstance concerning the first publication of the *Dunciad* needs to be emphasized. Although in 1728 it carried only a handful of notes, Pope intended, perhaps from the beginning, to publish the poem with full commentary.[10] The *Variorum* apparatus has received compara-

[7] *Corr.*, ii, 481. Cf. the motto Pope originally planned to use for the poem, a stanza from *The Faerie Queene* (1.23) in which a shepherd brushes away a "cloud of cumbrous gnattes" that try to "molest" him with their "feeble stings": *Poems*, v, 9n.

[8] "A Letter to the Publisher," *Poems*, v, 16.

[9] When publication was delayed, Swift complained: "Why does not Mr Pope publish his dullness, the rogues he mawles will dy of themselves in peace, and So will his friends, and So there will be neither punishment nor reward" (*Corr.*, ii, 475).

[10] See *Poems*, v, xx, and *Corr.*, ii, 467. It is clear that within a month of the poem's publication Pope was at work on the *Variorum*; see his letter to Swift, 28 June 1728, *Corr.*, ii, 503. The poem first appeared anonymously, and Pope did not publicly admit his authorship until the 1735 *Works*. But he made it clear, by means of Cleland's "Letter" and the "Testimonies of Authors," that the poem was his.

tively little critical attention. Commentators have remarked how the notes in particular parody the labors of textual critics like Theobald and Bentley,[11] point up the Virgilian parallel by means of citations from the *Aeneid*, and provide the detailed evidence to support Pope's satire on individual dunces, particularly information about their printed attacks on Pope. However, another important function needs to be stressed. James Sutherland has remarked how the apparatus serves to "justify" and to "aggrandize" the poet:

> the notes were intended to justify the personal satire of the poem, and to convince the public that the author was a good writer (of which the poem itself was a hilarious demonstration) and a good man, and that of the two he valued the second more highly than the first. The commentary, in fact, has considerable biographical value; it supplements the picture of the self-righteous poet that one meets so often in the Letters, and it makes clearer than ever the care that he took to preserve and to extend his literary reputation. To those two ends the various prefaces, notes, and appendices were all to contribute: Pope's enemies were to be humbled, but—equally important—Pope himself was to be aggrandized.[12]

Although he took a scornful view of the apparatus, Cibber had long ago made the same point. He sneered at "those *vain-glorious* encumbrances of Notes and Remarks," which were prompted by Pope's ruling passion, a *"low avarice of Praise."*[13]

But the function of the apparatus is more fundamental

[11] See James Sutherland, " 'The Dull Duty of an Editor,' " *Review of English Studies*, 21 (1945), 202-15.

[12] Sutherland, in *Poems*, v, xl. These "two ends" help to account, for example, for an epigram complimenting Pope and satirizing his enemies that was included in a note at the end of Book i (p. 94). The poem is apparently by an admirer of Pope. See also the epigram at II.143n.

[13] Cibber, *Letter to Mr. Pope*, cited (so as to disclaim the charge) in the *Dunciad* Appendix, "The PUBLISHER to the READER," p. 203n.

than apology for the poem and its poet. The basic point needs to be stressed that the apparatus is not a mere appendage but an integral part of the *Dunciad* (prefaces and appendices alone fill nearly half of the *Variorum*'s pages). And its effect is also more basic than apology: it permits Pope to establish his presence clearly and openly in the poem. The reader of the *Variorum* and of all subsequent editions of the *Dunciad* finds his way into the poem blocked, it might be said, by an imposing thicket of prefatory matter: the publisher's "Advertisement," the "Letter to the Publisher" signed by a William Cleland, a substantial collection of "Testimonies of Authors concerning our Poet and his Works," and an essay on the poem by Martinus Scriblerus. It might be better to say that the reader is escorted into the poem by these aids, his attention focused above all on the figure of the poet. Likewise, the reader at the conclusion is escorted *out* of the poem by more than forty pages of appended apparatus: indices, a "List of Books, Papers, and Verses of Mr. Dryden and Mr. Pope," and more. The reader's attention is shifted from poem back to poet.

Throughout the *Dunciad* then, in preface, notes, and appendix, Pope himself serves as a kind of counterweight to the lurid Grubaean chaos. On the one hand, the fantasy world of the Cave of Poverty and Poetry is counterpointed by the plain facts and mundane quarrels that entangled Pope and the literary hacks, booksellers, and party writers. On the other, the madness and squalor of the dunces is countered by Pope's sanity and decency.

The commentary never lets the reader forget that Pope has been the victim of an almost unceasing stream of attacks from the beginning of his literary career. Cleland's letter is motivated, so he claims, by the unwarranted attacks on Pope's "moral character." The notes quote repeatedly from Dennis's several attacks, especially from the malicious and hysterical *Character of Mr. Pope* (1716)[14] and from Cib-

---

[14] See especially Pope's note to II.142.

ber's *Letter to Mr. Pope* (1742). The cumulative effect of such attacks is noted at one point: "The reader, who hath seen in the course of these notes, what a constant attendance Mr. Dennis paid to our author . . ." (II, 271n.). What material Pope could not, or chose not to, fit into the notes, he included in the "Testimonies of Authors," where virulent attacks from Dennis, Welsted, and Theobald are answered by the praises of Addison, Prior, and others, including many of the dunces themselves. "The Parallel of the Characters of Mr. Dryden and Mr. Pope" likewise presents in topical form the common charges made against Pope and against his poetic predecessor (for example, "His Politicks, Religion, Morals," "Mr. Pope trick'd his Subscribers," "Names bestow'd on Mr. Pope"). The Index too contains many entries under the heading "Personal abuses on our Author."

To publicize the fact that he was the object of constant attack, of course, serves Pope's purposes in several ways. First, it tends to justify any harsh response he might now make. Second, it discredits the attackers themselves, especially when they can be shown to have praised Pope's anonymous work and then attacked him when his authorship was made known, or when the denunciations of minor hacks can be juxtaposed with the praises of established arbiters of taste like Addison. Third, it permits Pope to claim as poetic ally, father, or even version of himself, a revered figure like Dryden. Finally, it clears the way for praise of "our author." Thus Cleland feels bound to answer groundless attacks on Pope's moral character. In this duty he claims both a "public" and a "private" concern. Pope's attackers are the same who have "made free with the greatest Names in Church and State," and thus it is an "act of justice to detect" them. But more important, Cleland declares himself a personal friend: "I am one of that number who have long lov'd and esteem'd Mr. POPE, and had often declared it was not his Capacity or Writings (which we ever thought the least valuable part of his character) but the honest, open, and beneficent Man, that we most esteem'd and lov'd in him" (p. 13). Cleland's letter, almost certainly written by Pope himself,[15] provides good evidence of the way in which Pope wanted to present himself to the world in the *Dunciad*. As we have seen, during the years in which the poem was being written and revised, Pope in his letters was expressing identical sentiments.[16]

The *Dunciad* offered Pope few opportunities of displaying his honesty, openness, and beneficence, but he made several occasions, going out of his way to do so. As Dulness boasts that her realm has its own Garths and Addisons, Pope's note remarks his own "love of praising good writers," even in a poem on dulness (II.140n.). More significant perhaps are the several instances of Pope's beneficence toward his enemies, the bad writers. After describing the Cave of Poverty and Poetry, Pope notes his own endearing "*Candour* and *Humanity* . . . to those unhappy Objects of the Ridicule of all mankind, the bad Poets" (1.43). He imputes their wretched productions "not so much to Malice or Servility as to Dulness; and not so much to Dulness, as to Necessity," and thus "at the very commencement of his Satyr, makes an Apology for all that are to be satyrized." This is, of course, in part humorously mock-pious, the aggressor's deadpan assurance of good will. The strategy is not unlike his use elsewhere of innuendo; in each case the satirist can lay claim to innocence even as he inserts the knife. Then too, his note does not tell the whole story. In Cleland's letter Pope adopts a bluffer pose: "Men are not bunglers because they are poor, but they are poor because they are bunglers" (p. 15). Their poverty itself, he suggests, may become "a just subject of satyre, when it is the consequence of vice, prodigality, or neglect of one's lawful call-

[15] See Sutherland, in *Poems*, V, xxv.

[16] "I am very sensible, that my *Poetical* Talent is all that may make me *remember'd*: But it is my *Morality* only that must make me *Beloved*, or *Happy*. . . . I much more resent any Attempt against my moral Character (which I know to be unjust) than any to lessen my poetical one (which, for all I know, may be very just)": *Corr.*, III, 172. See above, Chap. 2, p. 57.

ing." But Pope's claim in the note to humanity and candor should not be dismissed altogether. He might easily have been much harsher on the dunces, specifying malice and venality as their motives, much as his enemies, the dunces, had said of him.

"Good nature of our Author; Instances of it, in this work" appears as a heading in the poem's Index.[17] One of the entries cited is Pope's note on a line quoted from Ogilby: "Our author shows here and elsewhere, a prodigious Tenderness for a *bad writer*. We see he selects the only good passage perhaps in all that ever *Ogilby* writ; which shows how candid and patient a reader he must have been" (1.328n.). This too is an ironically exaggerated protestation of good will ("prodigious Tenderness") that manages to insult Ogilby by claiming to show him favor. But Pope goes on, citing at length a passage from his own 1717 Preface, "where he labours to call up our humanity and forgiveness toward these unlucky men by the most moderate representation of their case that has ever been given by any Author." Wittily deploying once again a defense that had first been made on behalf of his own work, Pope can here claim to look with sympathy on the labors of his Grub Street enemies: "Much may be said to extenuate the fault of bad Poets: What we call a *Genius* is hard to be distinguished, by a man himself, from a prevalent inclination." It would be naive to believe that such toleration represents Pope's dominant attitude toward his dunces. The poem itself presents them much more mockingly. Many of the notes, furthermore, are bluntly contemptuous. But we will oversimplify the *Dunciad* if we dismiss such moments of tolerant sympathy as *mere* irony. Pope's attitude toward

[17] In two instances Pope draws attention to his readiness to retract any charges that can be shown to be false or to remove from the *Dunciad* any person "who could give him the . . . assurance, of having never writ scurrilously against him." See III.146n. (1729 edition), and especially II.295n. (1743 edition), where Pope points out his own "Tenderness" in removing any evidence of Aaron Hill's name, noting too that the lines on Hill form "a Panegyric instead of a Satire."

duncery, as I will try to make clearer, is above all ambivalent.

Antagonistic Kinship

If there are ironic suggestions in the notes to the poem that Pope is tender-minded and tolerant, a beneficent observer of his dunces, there are suggestions, equally strong though not so explicit, that he acts as a great counterweight to them, as their antithesis. Put another way, they act as anti-Popes, ludicrous parodies of the brilliant man of letters. For such hacks and wouldwits Pope shows the scorn of the first-rate for the third-rate, the same jealous superiority that a true genius like Dryden, invoking the names of Jonson and Etherege, displays toward false pretenders like Shadwell. Just as Dryden stands in "MacFlecknoe" as the true standard of wit, so Pope in the *Dunciad* provides the measure of excellence.

Though we look back on Pope and his contemporaries to find his literary eminence amply confirmed, he himself may have taken another view. No doubt he looked down on the dunces in confident contempt. But with another part of his mind he may have been less sure. Perhaps the dunces receive such scorn because of their threatening similarity to Pope.[18] Like him, they were men who wrote for their bread, propagandized for politicians, dealt with printers, contracted to translate for booksellers, intrigued with the disreputable Curll, had their names bandied about without ceremony in the gutter press, and risked the penalties of libel and treason laws. Pope of course had succeeded

---

[18] Maynard Mack has recently suggested another similarity between Pope and his dunces. Noting Pope's fastidious attention to "exact learning" in his marginal annotations to the volumes in his library and in his early correspondence, Mack suspects that "particularly in his younger days Pope shows signs of the interest in word-catching that he scorned in others." In the *Dunciad*, Mack goes on, Pope "exorcises all his impulses of this sort by holding them up to laughter." See "Pope's Books: A Biographical Survey with a Finding List," in Maximillian Novak, ed., *English Literature in the Age of Disguise* (Berkeley, 1977), pp. 224-25.

while they had for the most part failed.[19] They had not made their fortune from Homer and were thus compelled, like Theobald, to keep up the steady stream of pantomimes, plays, potted biographies, occasional poems, and compilations.[20] But at times, and especially in the 1720s, as he struggled with the tasks of translating, editing, and commentary, Pope, even though a successful writer, seems to have wondered whether he was anything more than a dull drudge himself. He speaks in the Preface to his *Shakespeare* (1725) of "the dull duty of an editor." At work on Homer, he complains in a letter that he "must undergo the Drudgery of an author in correcting Sheets."[21] He feels himself become "by due Gradation of dulness, from a poet a translator, and from a translator, a mere editor" (*Corr.*, II, 140). Does the *Dunciad*, which Pope first called his "Poem of dulness,"[22] spring in part from his own need to distance himself from a decade in which he published no new major original poem—his fate "ten years to comment and translate" (*Dunciad* III.331)?[23] In flinging back at the dunces the

[19] Just after the publication of the first *Dunciad* Pope wrote to praise Swift: "every stick you plant, and every stone you lay, is to some purpose; but the business of such lives as theirs [the scribblers] is but to die daily, to labour, and raise nothing" (*Corr.*, II, 522).

[20] Johnson took note of this: "His effusions were always voluntary, and his subjects chosen by himself. His independence secured him from drudging at a task, and labouring upon a barren topick" ("Life of Pope," p. 219). For Theobald's varied production, see R. F. Jones, *Lewis Theobald* (New York, 1919), Appendix D.

[21] *Corr.*, I, 281. See also an early letter to Parnell: "You are a Generous Author, I a Hackney Scribler. You are a Grecian & bred at a University, I a poor Englishman of my own Educating" (ibid., 226).

[22] "After I am dead and gone, [the poem] will be printed with a large Commentary, and letterd on the back, *Pope's Dulness*" (*Corr.*, II, 468). In another letter to Swift from the same year (1728) Pope notes that he is decayed in constitution and spirits, no fit companion, except for Swift: "Your Deafness wou'd agree with my Dulness" (ibid., 480).

[23] Did some of the unusual circumstances of the poem's publication likewise arise from Pope's wish to keep himself untainted by the commercial publishing world? Pope assigned the copyright of the *Variorum* to Oxford, Burlington, and Bathurst, who in turn assigned it to Gilliver, but not before initiating the distribution process themselves, sending some copies to their friends, selling others privately and collecting money, and getting

charges they had made against him from the beginning of his career—that he was vain, dull, mercenary, obscene, monstrous—does Pope attempt to confirm his belief in his own superiority to them? Does he see in the visionary madness of crack-brained Cibber or a "moon-struck Prophet" (IV.12) a distorted image of his own poetic "raptures," his share of "that *Excellent* and *Divine Madness*, so often mentioned by *Plato*, that poetical rage and enthusiasm" (I.106n.)?[24] Contempt, together with a sense of secret affinity, may produce in Pope an ambivalence—an antagonistic kinship with a world of dulness.

Some critics have recently come to see that Pope does not view dulness with unequivocal disgust. Howard Erskine-Hill has noted Pope's delight in exploring the "world" of dulness, "strange, fascinating, and complex, surrealistically awe-inspiring or beautiful as well as ridiculous and offensive."[25] And Emrys Jones has acutely remarked Pope's fascination with the low, the gross, the obscene. His claim that

---

their friends to do the same. By remaining anonymous, and by making his noble friends act as his publishers, Pope no doubt sought to protect himself against libel and to gain valuable publicity, as Sutherland suggests (*Poems*, v, xxviii, 460-63). But did Pope also perhaps see such practices, like the subscriptions to Homer and the letters, as a way of somehow maintaining or establishing his status as a gentleman amateur, in some way free from or above the dirty business of commercial publishing? See further, Ian Watt, "Publishers and Sinners: The Augustan View," *Studies in Bibliography*, 12 (1959), 3-20. For a full account of Pope's relations with his publishers, we may look forward to the eventual publication of David Foxon's 1976 Lyell lectures at Oxford on "Pope and the Early Eighteenth-Century Book Trade."

[24] Though Pope was suspicious of poetic enthusiasm, he was no drily rationalistic versifier and did not deny—even in his own creative processes—the role of "rapture." On this point see Maynard Mack's introduction to Pope's translation of the *Ilaid*, in *Poems*, VII, ccxxi-xxiv. Note too how the "Poet's vision of Eternal Fame," which Pope long shared, is one of the dreams that overflows Cibber's sleeping brain (*Dunciad* III.12). In a letter written while he was preparing the four-book *Dunciad*, Pope perhaps only half-facetiously remarked that "whatever I publish, (past, vamp'd, future, old or revived) it shall surely be sent you": *Corr.*, IV, 441. See also *Dunciad* I.284.

[25] Erskine-Hill, "The 'New World' of Pope's *Dunciad*," pp. 803-24 (quotation from p. 812).

Pope is ambivalent about and excited by dulness seems so right that I will simply quote from him:

> Pope is keenly stimulated by images of solidity and inertness—he has a remarkably sensitive insight into insensitivity. . . . The poet of consciousness and wit can be said to be contemplating a form of the mindless. . . . Pope seems to be communicating, however obscurely and momentarily, a sense of non-conscious life—a form of vitality which is alien to the conscious mind and felt to be a threat to it. . . . What Pope as a deliberate satirist rejects as dully lifeless his imagination communicates as obscurely energetic—states of being densely, but often unconsciously, animated.[26]

What I want to develop here is Jones's remark that the *Dunciad* enables Pope to "indulge feelings of an infantile nature." He has in mind particularly Book II, where Pope makes his dunces, in their pissing, tickling, and shouting contests, seem like "unabashed small children." Pope too delighted (unnaturally, growled Johnson) in "ideas physically impure,"[27] in excrement, in monsters and freaks, and occasionally the decorous poet found ways of incorporating such material in poetry, chiefly by associating it with his satirical targets.[28] The use of low materials—in their "negated" form—thus enables Pope to express more fully his creative potential and his imaginative delight. Consider, for example, the passage Joseph Warton described as "The Adventures of Smedley, and what he saw in the Shades below":

> lo! a burst of thunder shook the flood.
> Slow rose a form, in majesty of Mud;
> Shaking the horrors of his sable brows,

---

[26] Jones, "Pope and Dulness," pp. 142-45.

[27] "Life of Pope," p. 242.

[28] Freud might have described the process as "negation," in which "the subject matter of a repressed image or thought can make its way into consciousness on condition that it is denied": Freud, *Collected Papers*, ed. James Strachey (New York, 1959), V, 181-85.

And each ferocious feature grim with ooze.
Greater he looks, and more than mortal stares:
Then thus the wonders of the deep declares.
First he relates, how sinking to the chin,
Smit with his mien, the Mud-Nymphs suck'd him in:
How young Lutetia, softer than the down,
Nigrina black, the Merdamante brown,
Vy'd for his love in jetty bow'rs below,
As Hylas fair was ravish'd long ago.
Then sung, how shown him by the Nut-brown maids
A branch of Styx here rises from the Shades,
That tinctur'd as it runs with Lethe's streams,
And wafting Vapours from the Land of dreams,
(As under seas Alphaeus' secret sluice
Bears Pisa's off'rings to his Arethuse)
Pours into Thames: and hence the mingled wave
Intoxicates the pert, and lulls the grave:
Here brisker vapours o'er the Temple creep,
There, all from Paul's to Aldgate drink and sleep.

(III.325-46)

"Finely imagined, and one of the most poetical passages in any part of his work," says Warton rightly. The unspeakable Fleet Ditch has virtually disappeared, transformed by the imagination of Pope (not Smedley) into a Spenserian "bower." Fascinated with the poetic possibilities of excrement, Pope had prepared for this passage with the "brown dishonours" of Curll's face (II.108),[29] the impetuous spreading stream that "smoking flourish'd o'er his head" (the urinating contest [II.179-84]), and the imperial couplet on the ditch itself—"The king of dykes! than whom no sluice of mud / With deeper sable blots the silver flood" (II.273-74). Now Pope is led by his fascination, beyond Smedley (who is almost forgotten) and beyond the mere

---

[29] "Brown" tends to suggest excrement elsewhere, even when that is not the primary meaning. Cf. "Dishonest sight! his breeches rent below; / Imbrown'd with native bronze, lo! Henley stands" (III.198-99). Pope enjoyed smearing the faces of his enemies in excrement.

scatalogical joking about names, to the fine imagining of a dark and attractive/repulsive eroticized underworld. Such warm caverns—one thinks also of the Cave of Spleen and the Cave of Poverty and Poetry—are a favorite territory for psychic exploration in Pope. In all three caves Eros is dirty, perverse, monstrous. Maids call aloud longingly for corks (*Rape of the Lock*, IV.53); the Cave of Poetry (I.34-64) is clearly womblike ("chaste press," "genial," "spawn," "dark" and "deep," "embryo," "new-born nonsense");[30] and Smedley, "suck'd in" by mud-nymphs, is "ravish'd," Hylas-like, in dark bowers below. One can add the excremental fantasy of Cloacina's "black grottos" (II.93-108), where Curll's search through jakes for publishable scandal or wit is crudely sexualized: he "fishes" Cloacina's "nether realms."[31] In response, she "favours" him (the word still carried suggestions in Pope's time of sexual favours).[32] Just as Curll, Antaeus-like, "imbibes new life" from "th' effluvia strong," so Pope enjoys his rich linguistic play with ordure and its magical "sympathetic force." By contrast (or denial), Pope's own grotto at Twickenham was devoid of sexual connotations, was purged indeed of all natural cavernlike qualities: darkness (the grotto was carefully lit),[33] earthiness (it was paved with shells and reflecting stones), closeness (Pope contrived artful views from within of the river and the garden). Its female tutelary spirits are judiciously selected: the grotto was associated in his mind and verse with the wise counselor Egeria and a chaste sleeping "nymph of the grot."[34] Its "sacred floor" became a place for *poetic* creation or inspiration, and for meetings of idealistic patriots whose ardor is political: their "British Sighs" and

[30] I should add that in Pope's multidimensional vision the womblike cave is also a throne room (lines 46-54) and a dunce's brain (see below, p. 263).

[31] Cloacina figures elsewhere in Augustan mock-mythology. In Gay's *Trivia* bootblacks are said to spring from the intercourse of the sewer goddess with a dustman (II.106-68).

[32] Cf. *Rape of the Lock*, II.11.

[33] Pope later provides the "chaos dark and deep" with "glitt'ring" icy hills (I.75) and "gilded" monsters (I.83-84).

[34] Cf. Mack, *The Garden and the City*, pp. 69-79.

"bright Flame" mark them as men who "love their country."[35]

In elaborating on Jones's perception, I want also to suggest why Pope might have had such interest and insight into mindlessness. It seems plausible that Pope—hypersensitive and irritable, tremblingly,[36] feverishly, painfully conscious, indeed a man who makes a "fundamental association of consciousness with physical and moral pain,"[37] a craftsman whose "incessant and unwearied diligence" Johnson remarked[38]—might write so well of dulness because he could comprehend its "sure Attraction" (IV.75), perhaps even long to exchange his eternal vigil for the surrender of consciousness. Perhaps he could vividly imagine laying down his self-imposed burden of being Virtue's friend and relaxing into the delights of mere sensation and sleep.[39] As his friend William Kent said, Pope was "the greatest glutton I know."[40] Warton called him "a great sleeper."[41] Indeed, it is noteworthy that elsewhere in

[35] Cf. *Verses on a Twickenham Grotto*, discussed in Chap. 1 above.

[36] "Tremble" and its derivatives appear 48 times in Pope's verse (excluding translations), only 15 times in the stabler Dryden (excluding translations). But Pope may have picked it up from Dryden's *Virgil*, in which the word appears 91 times!

[37] Thomas Edwards, *Imagination and Power: A Study of Poetry on Public Themes* (New York, 1971), p. 106.

[38] "Life of Pope," p. 217.

[39] Thomas Edwards, *This Dark Estate*, pp. 126-27, makes the point that in the *Dunciad* sleep is "a kind of peace that Pope does not simply despise. . . . Sleep and intelligence are in a sense antitheses, and yet the latter may often long for the former."

[40] Quoted in "Life of Pope," p. 199n. See also Bathurst's remark that Pope "makes himself sick every meal at your most moderate and plain table in England (ibid., p. 200n.), and Johnson's belief that Pope was "too indulgent to his appetite" and "loved too well to eat" (ibid., pp. 199, 200).

[41] Warton, *An Essay on the Genius and Writings of Pope*, 4th ed., 2 vols. (London, 1782), II, 229n. Warburton also commented on Pope's "constant custom of sleeping after dinner": *Works of Pope*, ed. Warburton (London, 1757), IX, 6n. Marchmont adds that "if the conversation did not take something of a lively or epigrammatic turn he fell asleep, or perhaps pretended to do so": quoted in "Life of Pope," p. 198. Mrs. Piozzi stated that "he only sate dozing all day . . . and made his verses chiefly in the night" (ibid., p. 199), and Johnson said that when Pope "wanted to sleep, he 'nodded in company,' and once slumbered at his own table while the Prince of Wales was talking of poetry" (ibid., p. 198).

Pope's work, sleep has very positive associations of peace and contentment:

> Know, all the distant Din that World can keep
> Rolls o'er my *Grotto*, and but sooths my Sleep.
>
> *(To Fortescue*, 123-24)

> I wrap myself in the conscience of my integrity, and sleep after it as quietly as I can.
>
> *(Corr.*, I, 162)

> health of body, peace of mind,
>   Quiet by day,
> Sound sleep by night. . . .
>
> *(Ode on Solitude)*

Sleep is particularly imagined as release or escape from pain or passion:

> Peaceful sleep out the Sabbath of the Tomb.
>
> *(To Mrs. M. B. on her Birthday*, 19)

> Receive, and wrap me in eternal rest! . . .
> But all is calm in this eternal sleep.
>
> *(Eloisa to Abelard*, 302, 313)

> Not balmy sleep to lab'rers faint with pain.
>
> *(Autumn*, 44)

Poets, perhaps because like the dunces they keep "painful vigils" *(Dunciad* II.93), are attracted to the relief of sleep.[42] For Keats, sleep and poetry are near allied, but for Pope they are antagonistic:

> I pay my Debts, believe, and say my Pray'rs,
> Can sleep without a Poem in my head.

> The truth once told, (and wherefore shou'd we lie?)
> The Queen of *Midas* slept, and so may I.
>
> *(Epistle to Dr. Arbuthnot*, 268-69, 81-82)

[42] Pope comically associated poetry and sleeplessness in his own life. See, among other examples: a letter to Caryll while the Homer translation was under way—"I charitably take pains for others' ease, and wake to make you sleep" *(Corr.*, I, 462); the *Epistle to Fortescue*—"I cannot sleep a wink, / I nod in Company, I wake at night" (12-13); and a later letter—"I sleep in company, & wake at night: which is vexatious. If you did so, you, at your Age, wou'd make Verses" *(Corr.*, IV, 484).

Sure I should want the Care of ten *Monroes*,
If I would scribble, rather than repose.[43]
(*Imit. Hor. Ep.* II.ii.70-71)

It seems not implausible then that in the *Dunciad*, a great poem of sleep (the word and its derivatives appear there fourteen times; "rest" appears five times), Pope might have imagined both the moral emptiness and the amoral pleasures of somnolent oblivion.[44]

Surrender to the power of Dulness seems to be imagined, furthermore, as a kind of sexual surrender. More precisely, the secret relation with Dulness seems partly sexual, partly filial: "Suspend a while your Force inertly strong, / Then take at once the Poet and the Song" (IV. 7-8). Pope's note speaks, perhaps not merely mockingly, of his "Impatience to be re-united to her" (IV.1n.). Cibber's relation to Dulness, his mother, likewise may be partly sexual. His slumbering refuge on her lap is lovingly (even longingly?) described by Pope:

But in her Temple's last recess inclos'd,
On Dulness' lap th' Anointed head repos'd.
Him close she curtains round with Vapours blue,
And soft besprinkles with Cimmerian dew.

(III.1-4)

Pope genuinely imagines the bliss of this quasi-sensual

---

[43] In the beginning of his career, however, Pope sometimes associated poetry with states of reverie. See Mack, *The Garden and the City*, pp. 42-44, on Pope's early description of a trancelike imaginative reverie: "I seem to sleep in the midst of the Hurry, even as you would swear a top stands still, when 'tis in the Whirle of its Giddy motion. . . . my Days & Nights are so much alike, so equally insensible of any Moving Power but Fancy" (*Corr.*, I, 163). See also Pope's remark on the "amusing power of Poetry": "It takes me up so intirely that I scarce see what passes under my nose. . . . My Rêverie has been so deep" (ibid., 243).

[44] Cf. Thomas Mann's Aschenbach: "His love of the ocean had profound sources: the hard-worked artist's longing for rest, his yearning to seek refuge from the thronging shapes of his fancy in the bosom of the simple and vast; and another yearning, opposed to his art and perhaps for that very reason a lure, for the unorganized, the immeasurable, the eternal—in short for nothingness" (Mann, *Death in Venice and Seven Other Stories*, trans. H. T. Lowe-Porter [New York, 1954], p. 31).

swooning in a protected bower. The "last recess" is primarily the inner sanctum of Dulness's temple, in which sits the person of the god (its statue) curtained from the eyes of the laity. But Pope envisions this scene of religious ecstasy in sexual terms. Head-on-lap is said to be "a position of marvelous virtue" ("Argument to Book the Third"). Emphasis falls on a lap's maternal comforts (earlier Dulness is a "Nursing-mother" [1.312]) and suggests ultimately the passive safety of a dark, moist womb (the last "inclosure" or "recess").[45] Pope himself is never so intimate with Dulness, but the falling "curtain" at the end of the poem perhaps brings him to the condition that Cibber had reached at the beginning of Book III. So aware of an imperfect body, so conscious of his defects as a sexual being, and so attached well into maturity to his mother—Pope may have longed, or at least imagined longing, to be enveloped by a figure both maternal and sexual, to be swallowed at last, "covered" or "buried" by universal dulness/darkness.[46]

Such ambivalent involvement with the world of Dulness—if it is there at all—of course lies beneath the level of fully conscious and deliberate satire. If the poem expresses, as I think it does, Pope's secret sense of affinity, it also expresses more fully his denial and contempt of such delights. The predominant purpose of the poem is to declare Pope to be the antithesis of the dunces and the great adversary of Dulness. In establishing distance between himself and the dunces, Pope puts great emphasis on the Grub Street scene. Animated from his early work with a

[45] Her devotees who feel the "sure Attraction" of Dulness and "hang to the Goddess," "conglob'd" close around her (IV.75-80), make another image of ambiguous (sexual?) union. Compare also the all-encompassing embrace of Dulness, who "gathers" England "to her wings again" (III.126). Pope compares Dulness with Berecynthia, the Magna Mater, who in the *Aeneid* (VI.784-87) is seen embracing a hundred of her offspring (*Dunciad* III.131-34).

[46] In 1728 the line read, "And universal Dulness cover all." In 1729, "And universal Darkness covers all." In that period, "to cover" still could mean "to copulate with," but it refers to males. On curtains, see below, pp. 251-53.

sense of the poet in his setting,[47] he paints vividly the urban squalor and deprivation of the Cave of Poverty and Poetry. He implicitly contrasts this scene with his own setting at Twickenham, a prominent subject of his *Imitations of Horace* and already in the 1720s a proud concern in his letters—rural beauty, independence from all constraints, a bountiful supply of simple "broccoli and mutton," a "feast of reason," and, more importantly, "a flow of soul," and a poetic grotto that was later to be called the Cave of Pope.[48] Pope's Twickenham setting does not, of course, form part of the *Dunciad* itself, but he could surely expect his readers, especially in the later 1730s and 1740s, to bring it to mind as they read the poem.

Likewise, the moral portrait of the dunces is implicitly contrasted with Pope's own continuing portrait of himself in the Horatian poems. Pope as the man of virtue—and thus the dunces' antithesis—makes some oblique appearance in the notes to the *Dunciad*, as we have seen, and also in the text. Consider the presentation of the "Four guardian Virtues" of Dulness's throne:

> Fierce champion Fortitude, that knows no fears
> Of hisses, blows, or want, or loss of ears:
> Calm Temperance, whose blessings those partake
> Who hunger, and who thirst for scribling sake:
> Prudence, whose glass presents th' approaching jayl:
> Poetic Justice, with her lifted scale,
> Where, in nice balance, truth with gold she weighs,
> And solid pudding against empty praise.
>
> (1.47-54)

The four cardinal virtues, here parodied, may have been chosen, as Sutherland notes, because they were a recurring feature of the pageantry on a Lord Mayor's Day.[49] But

---

[47] *Windsor Forest, A Hymn Written in Windsor Forest.* See also Mack's chapter on "A Poet in his Landscape" in *The Garden and the City.*

[48] See Robert Dodsley, *The Cave of Pope. A Prophecy* (London, 1743).

[49] Sutherland, in *Poems*, v, 65n.

Pope may have thought them appropriate in other ways. Although the duncus pervert fortitude into impudence, temperance into enforced abstinence, prudence into worldly wiliness and criminal cunning, and blind justice into open-eyed weighing of gold against truth, Pope claimed these virtues, in their unadulterated form, for himself.[50] Fortitude is perhaps the most prominent characteristic of his heroic defiance of villainy ("For thee, fair Virtue! welcome ev'n the last!"); temperance a key to the portrait of himself at Twickenham ("content with little") and the portrait of the father he would emulate ("Healthy by Temp'rance"); dedication to impartial justice a leading attribute of the satirist who claims to denounce vice *wherever* he finds it ("on a Pillory, or near a Throne"). Prudence is a virtue Pope affected to scorn; it is Arbuthnot, Fortescue, and the interlocutor of the *Epilogue to the Satires* who urge Pope to be discreet, to "learn Prudence of a Friend." But, as Johnson noted, Pope excelled in "poetical prudence"; he *was* cautious, preferring the carefully phrased innuendo to the impulsive, reckless affront and managing, by prudent consideration, to overcome his political, religious, and physical liabilities and win for himself a full measure of comfort, esteem, influence, and material reward.[51]

[50] Pope may have been familiar with the tradition that each virtue has its counterfeit. For a contemporary expression of this commonplace, see Benjamin Hoadly's letter to the *London Journal*, 20 April 1723: "There is hardly any one Vertue, or Excellence, in the Best Part of Mankind, but what is attempted to be imitated, or mimicked, by Something in the Worst; designed to make the same Appearance, but in reality as distant in Nature from it, as Evil is to Good, or as a monstrous Defect is to Perfection itself" (Hoadly, *Works*, ed. John Hoadly [London, 1773], III, 105). A parallel tradition held, in Fielding's words, that "there are . . . so narrow bounds between some virtues and some vices, that it is very difficult to distinguish between them. Covetousness and thrift, profuseness and liberality, cowardice and caution, rashness and bravery, praise and adulation have been all very often mistaken for one another": *The Champion*, 4 March 1739/40, in Fielding, *Complete Works*, ed. W. E. Henley, 16 vols. (London, 1902), xv, 229.

[51] Johnson's remark on Pope's "poetical prudence" might be given *in extenso*: "he wrote in such a manner as might expose him to few hazards.

Thus Pope presents himself in several respects as a counterbalancing force in the poem, a true version of the virtues parodied by the rabble of dunces. At the same time, he may appear in the 1743 *Dunciad* as a virtual counterhero to the enthroned Cibber. Again the evidence must be sought in large part outside the strict confines of the poem. Cibber had newly provided an egregious instance of duncely fortitude or impudence with his artless *Apology* (1742), a parody, as I have already suggested, of Pope's own "apologies." If the parallel with Cibber had not yet occurred to Pope,[52] then it was brought to his attention in Hervey's *Letter to Mr. Cibber* (1742), a response to Cibber's own letter to Pope of the same year. In his letter Hervey drew at some length an elaborate parallel between the two antagonists, contrasting their characters always to Cibber's advantage. In the "parallel" both Cibber and Pope are seen as performers in their professional and private lives. "Neither of you," Hervey writes to Cibber, "pique yourselves much upon your Extraction, and both of you came into the World to make that Fortune you were not born to. You chose to be an Actor on the Stage, he a Performer in the Press." Up to a point, their merits are equal. "When you spoke the Sense and Thoughts of other People, you always succeeded as a Player. When he wrote the Sense and Thoughts of other People, he always succeeded as a Translator." But thereafter Pope's failings are illuminated by Cibber's successes. Pope's presentation of himself as man of virtue, for example, is dismissed as bad acting:

He used almost always the same fabrick of verse. . . . Of his uniformity the certain consequence was readiness and dexterity" ("Life of Pope," p. 219). Pope also excelled as a prudent poet-businessman, calculating well when and on what terms to publish, how best to advertise, etc. See R. H. Griffith's remark that Pope is "the greatest advertiser and publisher among English poets": *Pope Bibliography*, 1, pt. 2, xlvi-xlvii.

[52] Pope may have been measuring himself against Cibber for some time. Cf. "Better be Cibber, I'll maintain it still, / Then ridicule all Taste, blaspheme Quadrille" (*To Fortescue*, 37-38), and "Publick too long, ah let me hide my Age; / See Modest Cibber now has left the Stage" (*To Bolingbroke*, 5-6).

whereas you in whatever Character you have put on
have always been lik'd and applauded: his Fate has
been just the Reverse; for whenever he has endeavour'd to personate that of Benevolence, Disinter-
estedness, Humanity or Virtue, he has play'd them so
ill, they have sat so awkwardly upon him, and the
Mimickry has been so coarse, that all his Attempts
have been constantly exploded, the Cheat seen
through, and the wretched Actor despised.[53]

As men of wit, Cibber's "Conversation is always flowing
and easy; his [Pope's] affected and constrain'd." Pope
forces his nature; Cibber always talks "in the Character for
which Nature designed you; he in That, which in Spite of
Nature, he designed himself for, and is constantly labouring to obtain, and keep up by Art." By such means Cibber
seeks only to "amuse and entertain" and to promote
"chearful social Connection," while Pope endeavours to
"tax the admiration, and excite the Flattery" of whomever
he is with. Cibber, a natural, almost artless actor, "gaily and
laughingly" contributes to "mirth and pleasure." Pope, by
contrast, is "cooly and deliberately meditating how in his
next Performance he may damp both by ridiculing, vexing,
and aspersing ev'ry one who has the Misfortune of being
known to him." As a consequence, "No Wonder then whilst
you [Cibber] are sought and introduced into Society, he is
shunn'd and excluded from it: that whilst you are heard
and lik'd, he is only read and fear'd."

Such blows could hardly be better aimed. They strike at
several of Pope's favorite conceptions of himself—
benevolent and virtuous lover of the artless "language of
the heart," the warm friend who values and enjoys the
social pleasures.[54] Did Hervey's Letter and its parallel

---

[53] Hervey, Letter to Mr. Cibber (London, 1742), pp. 16-22.
[54] The parallel between Cibber and Pope was a natural one to draw.
W. L. Bowles compares their vanity: "The vanity of the one, silent, disdainful, and always appearing, though artfully endeavoured to be concealed. The vanity of the other, though I do not mean that their char-

perhaps contribute—together with Cibber's *Letter* and *Apology*—to Pope's decision to replace Theobald with Cibber as the King of Dunces in the revised 1743 *Dunciad?*[55] Although Pope, as I have argued, found a proper self-regard to be a valuable virtue, he perhaps saw in the foolish Cibber, recently presented to the literary world as Pope's great opposite, an apt image of the folly of self-love—as Dulness herself is an image of its evil—and at the same time the very antithesis of Pope himself, the heroic challenger of Dulness's empire.

Cibber, no man to refuse an opening, of course responded to his own coronation as Laureate of Dulness by warning Pope that he himself might have a more rightful claim to the honor. Pointing out Pope's own stupidity, impudence, vanity—charges Pope had advanced against Cibber as king—and his ridiculous performance as a lover, the laureate gaily noted that "the Qualities of thy Hero are close at thy Heels, and if thou dost not make some better shift to conceal thyself, will soon be within [thy] haunches."[56] Pope's implicit answer was already present in the *Dunciad Variorum* of 1729. He would wrap himself in

acters can be compared, open, pleasant, good-humoured, and never offensive, even where it appears strongest." And their laughter: "The laugh of Pope is that of a man, who *affected* raillery and contempt, whilst he boiled with anger; the laugh of Cibber is hearty, careless, and natural." In *Works of Pope*, ed. W. L. Bowles, 10 vols. (London, 1806), v, 67-68n., 71n.

[55] The author of the "Advertisement to the Reader" in the 1743 *Dunciad* (probably Pope himself) suggests that Cibber's *Letter*, *"which furnish'd him with a lucky Opportunity of improving* this Poem, *by giving it, the only thing it wanted*, a more considerable Hero," led to the change; see *Poems*, v, 251. Sutherland suggests that Pope may have long had it in mind to make Cibber his hero (ibid., xxxiii-xxxvi).

[56] *Another Occasional Letter from Mr. Cibber to Mr. Pope, wherein the New Hero's Preferment to his Throne, in the Dunciad, seems not to be Accepted. And the Author of that Poem Has More rightful Claim to it, is Asserted* (London, 1744), p. 49. Dennis had already written a pamphlet to show that Pope is the true King of Dunces, "by Right of Merit, . . . highly Qualify'd for that Supream Office" by his impudence and ignorance: Dennis, "Advertisement," in *Remarks Upon Several Passages in the Preliminaries to the Dunciad* (London, 1729), reprinted in *Critical Works of John Dennis*, ed. E. N. Hooker (Baltimore, 1939), II, 353.

the robes of Virgil and Milton; by parodying or echoing their works, he might claim them as legitimate ancestors. In similar fashion he declared his affinity not with Grub Street hacks but with "Great Dryden," in the lengthy and elaborate "Parallel of the Characters of Mr. Dryden and Mr. Pope,"[57] and with Boileau, in the "remarkable parity" between the two poets, which Cleland observes, "in Qualities, Fame, and Fortune."[58]

An addition to the 1743 *Dunciad* apparatus may be designed to further the parallel and contrast between Cibber and Pope. In the dissertation of Ricardus Aristarchus, "Of the Hero of the Poem," Pope figures almost as a shadow-hero to Cibber, or Cibber as a parody of Pope's own epic virtues. In all Bentleyan gravity, Aristarchus opines that as "little epic" (comic or mock-epic) differs from the "greater epic," so should their heroes differ: "Thus it being agreed that the constituent qualities of the greater Epic Hero, are *Wisdom, Bravery*, and *Love*, from whence springeth *heroic Virtue*; it followeth that those of the lesser Epic Hero, should be *Vanity, Impudence*, and *Debauchery*, from which happy assemblage resulteth *heroic Dulness*, the never-dying subject of this our Poem."[59]

The virtues of heroic dulness are subsequently illustrated with citations from Cibber's *Apology*. Those of the "greater epic" hero are described in such a way as to call to mind the portrait of himself that Pope had painted in the *Horatian Imitations*. Thus Wisdom: "It is the character of true *Wisdom*, to seek its chief support and confidence within itself; and to place that support in the resources which proceed from a conscious rectitude of Will. And are

[57] The "Parallel" was first published in the *Dunciad Variorum* (1729).

[58] Cleland also compares the similar "distinctions shewn to them by their Superiors," the "general esteem of their Equals," and "their extended reputation amongst Foreigners." "But the resemblance holds in nothing more, than in their being equally abus'd by the ignorant pretenders to Poetry of their times." Quoted in *Poems*, v, 17. Dennis pounced on this self-aggrandizing parallel and attempted to refute it point by point in his *Remarks upon the Dunciad* (*Critical Works*, ed. Hooker, II, 375-76).

[59] *Poems*, v, 256.

the advantages of *Vanity*, when arising to the heroic standard, at all short of this self-complacence?" (pp. 256-57).
One could scarcely do better than "the resources which
proceed from a conscious rectitude of Will" in describing
the animating strength of Pope's satires. Likewise, "the
second attribute of the true Hero, is Courage manifesting
itself in every limb; while, in its correspondent virtue in the
mock Hero, that Courage is all collected into the *Face*"
(p. 257). Pope's courage, both moral and physical, in the
presence of danger from enraged dunces or offended
politicians, is one of the remarkable and admirable features of his life.[60] The third heroic virtue, Love, significantly receives little emphasis: "*Gentle Love*, the next
ingredient in the true Hero's composition, is a mere bird of
passage, . . . and evaporates in the heat of *Youth*" (p. 258).
Love, except in its generalized form of friendship and benevolence, played little role in Pope's adult life, while Cibber (in Pope's view) was an aging and debauched
whoremaster. Pope, of course, is never named in Aristarchus's dissertation, but the alert reader, familiar with
Pope's literary career, may have sensed the oblique presence of Pope in the discussion of Cibber's heroic qualifications, standing, here and throughout the poem as a constant reminder of the dignity of letters and a measure of
Cibber's prostitution of that dignity.

Narrator as Hero

The decorum of the *Dunciad*, as Pope himself admits, does
not allow him many chances to intrude openly into his
poem and establish a presence in it. In part because of his
subject (dunces), in part because of the mock-heroic narrative, in which there is no room for him to figure as a char-

---

[60] Pope scorned the threats of physical reprisal. His sister remarked
that "my brother does not seem to know what fear is," and even though
threatened, "loved to walk out alone" with Bounce and a brace of pistols.
He told Spence that "he thought it better to die than to live in fear of such
rascals": Spence, 1, 116.

acter, in part because the poem is fantasy rather than realistic description, Pope *in propria persona* would be out of place. In this light, it is remarkable how much he does intrude into the body of the poem itself. As epic narrator, of course, he establishes something of a presence simply by virtue of the fact that he is the bard telling the story. But an epic poet may nonetheless, like Homer and Virgil, be quite reticent about himself and his art.[61] Mock-heroic poets, too, can be quite unobtrusive. Dryden in "MacFlecknoe" and Pope himself in *The Rape of the Lock* (both poems, it is true, much shorter than the *Dunciad*) intrude either not at all or very little.[62] Pope in the *Dunciad* follows instead the example of *Paradise Lost*, where Milton inserts himself, his hopes and aims as man and artist, in the proems to Books I, III, VII, and IX. Especially at the beginning or end of a book, Pope as narrator draws attention to himself, his project, and his poetic powers, not so much the power of conscious rectitude as the power of wit.

This project puts Pope from the beginning in a paradoxical relationship with Dulness, his subject. Whatever his half-revealed affinity, on the surface he is her mock-celebrant, and at the same time her great antagonist. To write a mock-heroic poem about Dulness is thus to write both for and against her. But in either case the poet's powers of writing, of narrating, are exercised. "The Mighty Mother, and her Son who brings, / The Smithfield Muses to the ear of Kings, / I sing." Consider the persons brought together in these two lines: Dulness and her son, the kings of England, the poet. Pope stands here in exalted company, as Virgil does in "Arma virumque cano" (cf. "Books and the Man I Sing"). The implication is that in some respect the epic poem deals both with its ostensible subject and with its

---

[61] Virgil follows the classical convention that epic poetry is impersonal. No reputable scholar, notes William Anderson in *The Art of the Aeneid* (Englewood Cliffs, N.J., 1969), p. 2, now believes that Virgil began his epic, as Servius had claimed, with the lines, "Ille ego, qui quondam gracili modulatus avena / carmen."

[62] See Chap. 3 above.

singer—his powers, his involvement with his story, his mighty task of telling and comprehending it.[63] Just as Milton as narrator might himself be said to be one of the heroes of *Paradise Lost*, and the poem to record his spiritual progress along with Adam's,[64] so too, though on a more modest scale, Pope might be said to be, if not the hero, then the shadow-hero in the *Dunciad*.

The opening of the poem thus announces the subject and introduces the "principal Agent," Dulness, and her son. But it also introduces an opposing presence, that of the poet. Pope chooses the self-assertive "I sing" over the equally traditional "Sing, O muse," and adopts a tauntingly curt and possibly disdainful imperative—"Say you"[65]—in addressing Dulness's chief supporters, "the Great." These are minor touches, to be sure, but they help to suggest a poet confident of his satiric powers, though in the midst of Dulness's impending triumph. The dedication to Swift, following soon after, aids in establishing this counter-presence:

> O Thou! whatever title please thine ear,
> Dean, Drapier, Bickerstaff, or Gulliver!
> Whether thou chuse Cervantes' serious air,
> Or laugh and shake in Rab'lais' easy chair,
> Or praise the Court, or magnify Mankind,
> Or thy griev'd Country's copper chains unbind;

---

[63] Cf. the invocation to Pope's projected epic *Brutus*: "The Patient Chief, who lab'ring long, arriv'd / On Britain's Shore and brought with fav'ring Gods / Arts Arms and Honour to her Ancient Sons: / Daughter of Memory! from elder Time / Recall; and me, with Britain's Glory fir'd, / Me, far from meaner Care or meaner Song, / Snatch to thy Holy Hill of Spotless Bay, / My Countrys poet, to record her Fame" (*Poems*, VI, 404). This extraordinarily interesting fragment is all that Pope wrote of the poem he fully planned to write in 1743; see Spence, I, 117. Its pronounced emphasis on "me," "My Countrys poet," and the implied relation between the country's founder and its recording poet, suggest that Pope conceived of the epic poet as a kind of hero himself.

[64] See, for example, William Riggs, *The Christian Poet in Paradise Lost* (Berkeley, 1973).

[65] Sharpened from the "Say from what cause" of the 1728/29 version.

From thy Boeotia tho' her Pow'r retires,
Mourn not, my SWIFT, at ought our Realm acquires,
Here pleas'd behold her mighty wings out-spread
To hatch a new Saturnian age of Lead.

(I.19-28)

Pope here celebrates and invokes the power of a great fellow satirist, whose supple shape-changing and easy alteration of poetic manner makes a sharp contrast to Dulness, "Laborious, heavy, busy, bold, and blind." As with Pope, Swift's strength lies in opposition to the ironically praised Court, even to ironically magnified "Mankind." That such opposition is not merely futile rhetoric Pope indicates by recalling Swift's success, through the *Drapier's Letters*, in ridding Ireland of Wood's copper halfpence. So too, Pope implies, Swift has to some extent driven Dulness from Ireland (Boeotia). It is now Pope's turn to display his satiric powers.[66] Swift may look on, pleas'd, not alarmed, may with Pope behold the scene which is now ironically to be presented.

It is important to note here that within the poem itself Pope steps, as it were, out of the frame of the fiction (the triumph of Dulness) and as poet addresses the dedicatee of his poem. Granted, the intrusion is conventional; any poetic dedication interrupts narrative illusion. But the address to Swift is nonetheless the result of an artistic choice, and the intrusion seems all the more significant because it comes not in the opening lines but after Pope has already begun his epic *narratio*. (Compare *The Rape of the Lock*, where the brief dedication occurs in the opening lines: "This Verse to Caryll, Muse! is due.") Just as the apparatus blurs the line between what is in the poem and what is in Pope's own life as man and poet, so here too the line is blurred between poet inside the fiction, subject to Dulness's "Force inertly strong," and triumphant poet who has com-

[66] In a letter to Swift (September 1725), just after the last of the *Drapier's Letters* and just prior to the publication of *Gulliver's Travels*, Pope promised an "investigation of my own Territories, . . . something domestic, fit for my own country, and for my own time": *Corr.*, II, 321-22.

posed the fiction and now beholds it and sees that it is good.

Pope announces the next narrative intrusion in the "Argument" at the beginning of Book IV: *"The Poet being, in this book to declare the* Completion *of the* Prophecies *mention'd at the end of the former, makes a new* Invocation; *as the greater Poets are wont, when some high and worthy matter is to be sung. He shews the Goddess coming in her Majesty. . . ."*[67] The argument goes on to present the triumph of Dulness, but Pope does not let slip the opportunity to present his own strength as actively shaping artist—"poet," "book," "declare," "makes . . . invocation," "greater Poets," "matter to be sung," "he shews." In like manner, the invocation itself balances Pope's power against that of Dulness:

> Yet, yet a moment, one dim Ray of Light
> Indulge, dread Chaos, and eternal Night!
> Of darkness visible so much be lent,
> As half to shew, half veil the deep Intent.
> Ye Pow'rs! whose Mysteries restor'd I sing,
> To whom Time bears me on his rapid wing,
> Suspend a while your Force inertly strong,
> Then take at once the Poet and the Song.
>
> (1-8)

This intrusion is perhaps the most striking in the poem; Pope imagines himself, as poet, literally borne toward "Chaos, and eternal Night" and subject to a "Force" assuredly greater than his own. We think, inevitably, not only of the poem's fictional apocalypse, but also of Pope's imminent death. But in fact there is little evidence that in 1742, when these lines were first published, Pope was (like the old view of Shakespeare in Prospero) taking leave of his art.[68] And to recall the personal context suggests how the lines, after all, serve to declare the poet's strength. A com-

[67] The narrator intrudes very briefly at the end of Book II: "Why should I sing what bards the nightly Muse / Did slumb'ring visit, and convey to stews" (421-22).

[68] He had plans for new poems (see note 62) and extensive revisions to his published work.

parison with Milton's sonnet, to which Pope probably alludes,[69] is instructive:

> How soon hath Time, the subtle thief of youth,
> Stol'n on his wings my three and twentieth year. . . .

> Yet be it less or more, or soon or slow,
> It shall be still in strictest measure ev'n,
> To that same lot, however mean, or high,
> Toward which Time leads me, and the will of Heav'n.
>
> > (Sonnet VII, 1-2, 9-12)

Setting aside the fact that Milton's poem recognizes the
overarching power of "The will of Heav'n," and Pope's
lines the ultimate power of Chaos and Night, both poets
declare themselves subject to time. Milton, still a young
man who had written little, complains first of time's thefts
and his own "late spring," with no "bud or blossom"
(poems) to show for it, but he finally yields willingly to the
"lot" that awaits him. "Yet" signals the turn from complaint
to compliance; the poet's assertion ("It shall be . . .") serves
only to affirm God's power (*Thy* will be done). Pope, a
middle-aged man who had written much and could look
back on a life of success and fame, determines to write yet
one more "song." That determination, caught in the
prayerful imperatives, carries an ironic note of pretended
submission—"one dim Ray of Light / Indulge," "so much
be lent"—and of defiant, countervailing power—"Suspend
a while your Force." The onrush of Chaos itself, which
comes to all, is held off ("Yet, yet") as Pope wins his "moment," suspends or arrests its "Force" (we will return to
this), and directs that only "Then" shall the "Pow'rs" take
him.

Again, allusions to the poet's power balance themselves
against the power of Dulness. The "Powers" may have their
"Mysteries," but the poet too has his "deep Intent." The
Powers may be restored, but the poet will "sing" their res-

[69] Wakefield notes that at IV.6, "The poet had in his memory Milton's
Sonnet, vii": Wakefield, *Observations on Pope* (London, 1796).

toration. Before being swallowed up, "The Poet and the Song" will declare themselves.[70] The presence of that shaping poet is emphasized too in the flurry of allusions to the poet's art in the Scriblerian notes to the first twenty lines of the poem. At line 4, a knowing wink: "The Author in this work had indeed a *deep Intent*; there were in it *Mysteries* . . . which he durst not fully reveal." At lines 11-12, a mocking note on poetic decorum: "The Poet introduceth this . . . with a peculiar propriety." Again, at line 20, a commendation of the poet's skill: "With great judgment it is imagined by the Poet, that. . . ." And the following line, a reminder of Pope's *ordonnance*: "We are next presented with the pictures of those. . . ." If a reader can bear in mind all that is happening on the page, he must see both the unfolding triumph of Dulness *and* the figure of the poet who is singing the song, imagining and presenting the scene.

The closing lines to Book IV strike most readers as the most overwhelming declaration of the power of "uncreating" Dulness. But even there we have a countervailing sense of Pope's *creating* word. Even as the poet declares that he is prevented from singing the final triumph of Dulness in full detail—"In vain, in vain,—the all-composing Hour / Resistless falls: The Muse obeys the Pow'r" (627-28)—his own note is busy hinting that he might have completed the poem after all:

> It is impossible to lament sufficiently the loss of the rest of this Poem, just at the opening of so fair a scene as the Invocation seems to promise. It is to be hop'd however that the Poet compleated it, and that it will not be lost to posterity, if we may trust to a Hint given in one of his Satires. *"Publish the present Age, but where the Text / Is Vice too high, reserve it for the next."* (626n.)

What Pope does present is a report of cultural apocalypse,

[70] The Scriblerian note which completes the effect of the line in fact denies that Pope is borne toward oblivion on rapid wing: "Fair and softly, good Poet! . . . For sure in spite of his unusual modesty, he shall not travel so fast toward Oblivion, as divers others of more Confidence have done."

not in leisurely detail ("who first, who last resign'd to rest") but in magnificently compressed fashion, where abstractions vividly concretized are made to bear the poetic burden ("Fancy's gilded clouds decay . . . Art after art goes out"). Of the conclusion, Emrys Jones has commented that "the poet at once succumbs to and defies the power of Dulness." He writes also of Pope's "imaginative desire for completeness" and his "poetic delight in images of cataclysmic destruction."[71] One might agree that Pope defies Dulness, but I suggest that the defiance lies in the way Pope summons and controls the end of his poem and the end of culture, in the masterful orchestration in which all of human order and of uncreating dulness are channeled into some fifteen closed couplets. The passage displays well what C. J. Rawson calls Pope's delight in "decisive summary." Pope's couplet rhetoric "suggests not denial but containment of powerful and subtle forces."[72] The hour is indeed "all-composing," not only because all is brought to the composure of sleep, but also because the poet here artistically disposes his material, setting "all" in order.[73] Although the subject is universal dissolution, Pope presents it as a stately procession ("she comes! she comes! . . . Thus at her felt approach . . . lo thy empire is restor'd") or a carefully staged and spaced series of events (stars fade "one by one," "art after art goes out") in which each allegorical figure does its turn and disappears (Truth flees, Philosophy shrinks, Physic begs defense, etc.). The result, as verbal shaping and framing of chaos, is profoundly exciting and satisfying to read (as it must have been to write), for it displays and exercises the mind's power over formlessness, indeed, over the ultimate threat to form.

The *Dunciad* is inescapably a *poem* about dulness and thus

---

[71] Jones, "Pope and Dulness," p. 154.

[72] Rawson, *Gulliver and the Gentle Reader* (London, 1973), p. 54.

[73] Compare the pun on "compose" at 11.389-90: "Soft creeping, words on words, the sense compose, / At ev'ry line they stretch, they yawn, they doze." Pope may have half-remembered Crashaw's "the sweet peace of all-composing night" ("Steps to the Temple," stanza 62).

inherently a containment of it. By that measure, of course, any and every artifact that forecasts or announces the destruction of civilization denies, or at least qualifies, the doom. Artistry becomes important critically when it is self-conscious or obtrusive. To draw attention to the act of singing, as Pope does at "all-composing" and earlier, is to increase our sense of the poet's controlling presence. And to write pompous scholarly notes as the curtain falls, a play-by-play commentary as it were, is to make a virtual mockery of the imagined destruction and a denial of Dulness's triumph. And since the *Dunciad* does *not* in fact conclude with the ringing phrase, "universal Darkness buries all," but itself carries on for more than forty pages of appendices—many of them directing our attention to Pope or to earlier editions of the poem—we are impressed again with the fact that the celebration of Dulness is a poem, a thing made by Pope. Especially at the close of the 1743 *Dunciad*, since it once formed the end of Book III in the poem Pope had written in 1728, we are struck with Pope's control, his powers of making, of remaking, of rearranging his materials—even when they include the end of all culture.[74]

Master of the Show

What in fact happens at the end of the *Dunciad*? The usual answer is that the "restoration of the empire of chaos" means the end of the world, or at least the extinction of culture. Literally, the hand of the "Anarch" (Chaos) lets fall a "curtain," and darkness buries (first edition, covers) all. Few critics have commented on that odd word "curtain." Warton alleged its inappropriateness in his note to IV.654: "After this noble and energetic line, the expression in the next, of 'lets the curtain fall,' is an unhappy descent in style

[74] The observations in this paragraph derive from common sense, but they need to be spelled out again to recall Pope's comic control of his poem and to dispel some of the excessive cosmic gloom that, due to the efforts of twentieth-century commentators, has gathered around the end of the *Dunciad*.

and imagery." Is this mere metaphor, and if so, why speak of curtains bringing darkness here when Pope has spoken so effectively of sunsets, fading stars, fires veiled, and sparks extinguished, even light dying? The fallen curtain brings a strange, gentle dissolution, as if the cosmos simply goes to sleep. Indeed, the imagery of the conclusion suggests that this may be what happens. Dulness herself yawns and "All Nature nods" (605), and a yawn spreads "o'er all the realm" (613). The Muse is urged to relate "who first, who last resign'd to rest" (621), and, like a mother singing a lullaby, to "hush the Nations with thy song" (626). In the final paragraph night arrives slowly, the last lights go out, the curtain falls, and all is dark. Is this perhaps a bed-curtain allowed to drop and obscure the sleeping world? Is the line the culmination of a process that began in Book I, where Dulness looks forward to the day when the king himself shall be her servant, when she as "Nursing-mother" may

'Twixt Prince and People close the Curtain draw,
Shade him from Light, and cover him from Law. . . .

'Till Senates nod to Lullabies divine,
And all be sleep, as at an Ode of thine.

(1.313-14, 317-18)

At the end of Book II the looked-for moment is closer. Dulness's subjects—critics and poets—sleep one by one, until "all was hush'd" (418).[75] Cibber himself, as we have seen, sleeps on Dulness's lap at the beginning of Book III. At the opening of Book IV, he still reclines "soft on her lap" (20), and at the end of Book IV he is merely joined behind the curtain by more sleepers. One question remains: if, as Pope hints, Dulness blesses some heads "completely" and others only "partly" (IV.621), are there some "heads" still awake? Does the end of the poem dramatize the death of human culture, or the death-sleep of culture *in the minds of*

[75] Two verbal echoes make the end of Book II a kind of preview of the end of Book IV: compare the references to Argus's eyes (II.374 and IV.637) and the infectious yawn or nod *spreading round* (II.409 and IV.613).

individual dunces?[76] The poem gives no unequivocal answer, and the intriguing ambiguity is only intensified if we follow out other suggestions of the word "curtain."[77] The word perhaps evokes the image of the *theatrum mundi*, of human life as a play upon the world's great stage, on which the final curtain now falls.[78] But at the same time, the word "curtain" is perhaps also intended to call up a consciously staged scene in a London theater, and if so, on which side of the curtain has darkness fallen, and who if anybody is watching the play? Can we perhaps say that the final couplet is designed as one last reminder that Pope has always been present in and behind the poem, that he has presented to us, the readers, a bizarre, monstrous spectacle, a staged triumph of Dulness and de-creation of the world? What may we do, as spectators in the well-lit Augustan playhouse but applaud Pope's magnificent artifice?[79] The hint here that Pope serves not only as narrator of past events but also as master of the show, presenter of a stage spectacle which we observe in the present (that is, we watch as "Darkness buries all"), receives some slight confirmation in other parts of the poem.

[76] See the end of Book II, a kind of parallel or foreshadowing of the end of Book IV: "What Dulness dropt among her sons imprest / Like motion from one circle to the rest; / So from the mid-most the nutation spreads / Round and more round, o'er all the sea of heads" (II.407-10).

[77] The image also carries strong political connotations. As Fielding noted in *Tom Jones* (VII, 1), "When Transactions behind the Curtain are mentioned, St. James's is more likely to occur to our Thoughts than Drury Lane." In a recent book, *Walpole and the Wits* (Lincoln, Nebr., 1976), Bertrand Goldgar discusses the well-established parallel between "the states political and theatrical" (p. 158). The image may also be an apt part of Pope's de-creation scene. In Samuel Boyse's account of the Last Judgment in *The Deity* (1740), God "shall bid the curtain of Omniscience rise" and show his creatures that "all his ways are right" (*Chalmers's Work of the English Poets* [London, 1810], XIV, 547). Boyse's poem postdates the first appearance (1728) of Pope's image, but do Boyse and Pope perhaps use a traditional Judgment-scene image? If so, Pope here parodies it: at the end of the world, Chaos bids a curtain not rise but fall.

[78] This is Aubrey Williams's view in his influential *Pope's Dunciad*, pp. 87-103.

[79] For illumination of playhouses, see *The London Stage, 1660-1800*, ed. E. L. Avery, Pt. 2, *1700-1729* (London, 1960), p. xlviii.

The "dramatic qualities" of Book IV have been commonly remarked,[80] and editors have noted the references to contemporary stage pantomime, even the way in which we behold a series of "episodic situations which might have been taken from the very Smithfield farces the poem celebrates,"[81] always to note, following Warburton's lead,[82] that Pope deplores such corruption of taste.[83] But no one, surprisingly, has drawn the conclusion that Pope may indeed be presenting a staged scene and may wish us to sense that he is doing so. The bardic "Lo!" or "Behold" may be a device of the epic poet, but it might also suggest the imagined stage producer present, along with the reader, at the unfolding scene.[84] "Scene" is a recurrent term, and Pope stresses its theatrical connotations. In Book I, Dulness, observing the Cave of Poverty and Poetry, "Beholds thro' fogs, that magnify the scene" and responds with "self-applause" (80-82). The Argument to Book III describes the prophecy from the Mount of Vision as a stage spectacle: *"On a sudden the Scene shifts, and a vast number of miracles and prodigies appear."* In Book III itself, Dulness draws a curtain to discover a scene: "Now look thro' Fate! Behold the scene she draws!" (III.127).[85] More important than these slight

---

[80] See Williams, *Pope's Dunciad*, pp. 87-103, and n. 84 below.

[81] Ibid., p. 91. It should be noted that "Smithfield farces" and legitimate stage pantomime are two quite different forms of popular theatre; see *The London Stage*, Pt. 2, pp. cxviii-xx. Pantomimes appeared first in the London theatres of Covent Garden and Lincoln's Inn Fields, and only later at Bartholomew Fair and other popular fairs; see Sybil Rosenfeld, *The Theatre of the London Fairs in the Eighteenth Century* (Cambridge, 1960), p. 146.

[82] See Warburton's note on "Smithfield Muses," at I.2, in *Poems*, v.

[83] Malcolm Goldstein, *Pope and the Augustan Stage* (Stanford, Calif., 1958), pp. 87, 99, 113.

[84] See, for example: I.27, "Here pleas'd behold her mighty wings outspread"; IV.629, "She comes! she comes! the sable Throne behold"; IV.653, "Lo! thy dread Empire, CHAOS! is restor'd." Significantly, each of these instances occurs in a context where Pope is emphasizing his own presence as artist and the present tense of the action. See also lines IV.45, 139.

[85] Williams notes these and other "suggestions of the theatrical," but his emphasis differs sharply from mine. Where he finds the function of the

suggestions, however, is a passage in the dissertation of Ricardus Aristarchus which confirms our sense that Pope is presenting a stage spectacle. Aristarchus, in discussing the kind of poem the *Dunciad* is, speaks of the Greek dramatists,

> who in the composition of their *Tetralogy*, or set of four pieces, were wont to make the last a *Satyric Tragedy*. Happily one of these ancient *Dunciads* (as we may well term it) is come down to us amongst the Tragedies of Euripides. . . . May we not then be excused, if for the future we consider the Epics of Homer, Virgil, and Milton, together with this our poem, as a complete *Tetralogy*, in which the last worthily holdeth the place or station of the *satyric* piece?[86]

By its relation as afterpiece to tragedy (pantomimes in Pope's day often served as afterpieces to tragedy) and as satiric afterpiece to epic (in an era when mock-epic poems excelled all serious efforts at the heroic), the *Dunciad* is in some respects like a stage piece, both a "Satyric Tragedy" and a "farce."

Contemporary theatrical fare would have provided Pope and his audience with similar shows. Fielding's farces during the 1730s may well have served Pope as a model. Sherburn suggested thirty years ago that Fielding's *Author's Farce* (1730, 1734) and *Pasquin* (1736) may have given Pope the device of using a mock queen enthroned as the focal point for a farcical episode.[87] But Fielding may have given Pope more. Just as *Pasquin* contains within it "The Life and Death of Common Sense," so the *Dunciad*, complete with apparatus, contains its own play-within-the-play, "The

---

theatrical elements in the poem to convey delight in the world's diverse spectacle and to recall the proper moral role of man on the world's stage—to play his part well—I would emphasize Pope's role as artificer, as stage presenter. See Williams, *Pope's Dunciad*, pp. 90-103.

[86] *Poems*, v, 255-56. Aristarchus also calls this ancient *Dunciad* a "Farce."

[87] Sherburn, "The Dunciad, Bk. iv," *Texas Studies in Language and Literature*, 24 (1944), 174-90.

Triumph of Dulness."[88] Fustian's play concludes with the triumph of Queen Ignorance over the Queen of Common Sense, whose death speech, like the close of the *Dunciad*, prophesies the end of order and reason:

> Farewel vain World! to Ignorance I give thee.
> Her leaden Sceptre shall henceforward rule. . . .
> Henceforth all things shall topsy turvy turn.[89]

Just as Pope's report of Dulness's arrival is cut short, so Common Sense dies in mid-prophecy:

> Statesmen — but Oh! cold Death will let me say
> No more — and you must guess et cetera. *Dies*.

But the triumph of Ignorance is neatly contained. Within the frame of Fustian's play, the ghost of Common Sense rises to expel Ignorance and to "get the better at last." Fustian then presents his epilogue, which serves as epilogue to the larger *Pasquin* as well. Common Sense, who speaks it, begs "a serious word or two to say" and urges Englishmen to banish "Childish Entertainments" and "the Tumbling Scum of every Nation," and to support instead "sense," "Poor Poetry," and the best of native English drama, "Shakespear, or immortal Ben." Fielding's very popular play may have helped prepare Pope's audience for the *Dunciad*, another triumph of Nonsense in which Sense "gets the better at last."

Fielding's farces at the Haymarket are one form of contemporary stage entertainment that may provide a metaphor for understanding the *Dunciad* and Pope's role

---

[88] Fielding's *The Author's Farce* also contains a play-within-the-play that might have interested—and originally have been inspired by—Pope. Published as by "Scriblerus Secundus" (announcing the Popean link), *The Author's Farce* presents a rabble of booksellers and scribblers, among them, Luckless, "Master" and "presenter" of a puppet show, "The Pleasures of the Town," whose "chief business," in the revised 1734 version, "is the election of an archpoet, or as others call him a poet laureate, to the Goddess of Nonsense." Fielding, *The Author's Farce*, ed. C. B. Woods (Lincoln, Nebr., 1966), p. 94.

[89] Fielding, *Pasquin*, ed. O. M. Brack et al. (Iowa City, Iowa, 1973), p. 49.

in it as presenter of the show. For another form, one might point not (with Warburton) to the "shews, machines, and dramatical entertainments" in the booths at Bartholomew Fair,[90] but to the highly popular pantomimes being staged by John Rich at Lincoln's Inn Fields and by Cibber at Covent Garden.[91] In the form Rich made popular, pantomime contained two parts: a "serious" part, usually based on a mythological love story; and a comic or "grotesque" part, based on the *commedia dell'arte* figures, Harlequin and Colombine. Elaborate sets, machinery, dancing and clowning all helped to direct the viewer's attention from language or action to spectacle. Pantomime was loftily disapproved by every critic with any interest in serious drama. Even Cibber called them "monstrous Medlies."[92] But he, along with several of Pope's leading dunces—Theobald and Settle—was ready to give the public what it seemed to want and made major contributions to the success of the form.[93]

In the *Dunciad* the pantomimes figure most prominently

[90] Warburton's note to 1.2, in *Poems*, v.

[91] For information on pantomime in the 1720s, see *The London Stage*, Pt. 2, pp. cxviii-cxx, cxl-cxlii, and M. P. Wells, "Some Notes on the Early 18th Century Pantomime," *Studies in Philology*, 32 (1935), 604-7.

[92] *An Apology for the Life of Mr. Colley Cibber*, ed. R. W. Lowe (London, 1889), II, 180.

[93] Cibber produced pantomimes regularly throughout the 1720s to rival those of Rich, and he acted in them himself. Theobald contributed the "serious" part to nearly a third of Rich's pantomimes and supplied verse for two of Settle's productions. Even though much is known of Theobald's popular hack work (see R. F. Jones, *Lewis Theobald*), critics of the *Dunciad* usually see him too simply as the heavy word-catching textual critic. His *Shakespeare Restored* (1726) was in fact dedicated to Rich. Settle had long been writing popular spectacles, for Bartholomew Fair shows, for Lord Mayor's pageants (as City Poet), and for the London theatres. His most elaborate work, *The Siege of Troy*, though not strictly a pantomime, makes use of a vast set, a seventeen-foot-high Trojan horse, trick statues for transformation scenes, and "illuminations and transparent Painting" (transparencies) to present the burning of the city. The spectacle, first presented at Drury Lane in 1701 as *The Virgin Prophetess, or the Fate of Troy*, was performed regularly at Bartholomew Fair from 1707 to 1720. See Rosenfeld, *The Theatre of the London Fairs*, pp. 161-65, and Pat Rogers, "Pope, Settle, and the Fall of Troy," *Studies in English Literature*, 15 (1975), 447-58.

in Settle's prophecy. To judge by frequency of reference, Pope's idea of the form derived from the *Harlequin Dr. Faustus* plays (1723), from Theobald's *Rape of Proserpine* (1727), and in general from John Rich's repertoire.[94] It is usually assumed that Pope's attitude toward pantomime was uniformly hostile. Yet it is evident from the quality of his description that his imagination responded excitedly to them:

> [He] look'd, and saw a sable Sorc'rer rise,
> Swift to whose hand a winged volume flies:
> All sudden, Gorgons hiss, and Dragons glare,
> And ten-horn'd fiends and Giants rush to war.
> Hell rises, Heav'n descends, and dance on Earth:
> Gods, imps, and monsters, music, rage, and mirth,
> A fire, a jigg, a battle, and a ball,
> 'Till one wide conflagration swallows all.
>   Thence a new world, to Nature's laws unknown,
> Breaks out refulgent, with a heav'n its own:
> Another Cynthia her new journey runs,
> And other planets circle other suns.
> The forests dance, the rivers upward rise,
> Whales sport in woods, and dolphins in the skies;
> At last, to give the whole creation grace,
> Lo! one vast Egg produces human race.
>
> (III.233-48)

Pope's note reads: "All the extravagancies in the sixteen lines . . . were introduced on the Stage, and frequented by persons of the first quality in England to the twentieth and thirtieth time" (233n.). Recent critics too have seen in the lines a foreshadowing of the onset of chaos. And yet surely this is not the whole story. For Pope has presumably not only seen these shows, he has vividly reimagined them and

[94] In the 1728 text Pope alludes to Faustus at III.229n., 306, 310n., to Theobald's pantomimes (Pope never in fact uses the word "pantomime"; the plays are always "farces") at I.68n., 106n., 208n., III.229-44, 233n., 244n., 307n., 308, 310n., to Settle's farces at I.106n., III.229-44, 281n., and to Rich at III.251-60.

shaped the "extravagancies" into a virtuoso vision of apocalypse and recreation of a "new world."

Pope's attitude toward John Rich is likewise not simply ridicule. The "matchless Youth" (in fact, Rich was somewhat older than Pope), presenter of the show, is a godlike figure, all-powerful, detached, and somehow not touched by the silliness he produces:

> In yonder cloud behold
> Whose sarsenet skirts are edg'd with flamy gold,
> A matchless Youth! His nod these worlds controuls,
> Wings the red lightning, and the thunder rolls.
> Angel of Dulness, sent to scatter round
> Her magic charms o'er all unclassic ground:
> Yon stars, yon suns, he rears at pleasure higher,
> Illumes their light, and sets their flames on fire.
> Immortal Rich! how calm he sits at ease
> 'Mid snows of paper, and fierce hail of pease;
> And proud his Mistress' orders to perform,
> Rides in the whirlwind, and directs the storm.
>
> (III.253-64)

Pope parodies here a famous simile in Addison's *The Campaign*, in which Marlborough, directing the war, is compared with an angel of Providence who, "pleas'd th' Almighty's Orders to perform, / Rides in the Whirl-wind, and directs the Storm" (291-92). Pope's lines mock-aggrandize Rich, the "Angel of Dulness," by comparing him with Marlborough, "unmov'd in peaceful Thought," and the "calm and serene" angel, but at the same time, Pope endows him with genuine power and grandeur. The suggestion here that Rich was a witty man making conscious use of vulgar materials is borne out by a half-ironic tribute from a contemporary and friend of Pope. James Miller dedicated *Harlequin-Horace* to Rich, that Horatian rule-giver of modern poetry, a man who knows his audience:

> You prudently look on Mankind to be one half
> Knaves, and t'other Fools, and conclude justly, that to

entertain both Sorts, there must be a joint-mixture of
Trick and Buffoonry, every one delighting in the Representation of what is most natural to him, or in which
he labors to excel. . . . You have Wit enough to make
your Advantage of the Follies of others, and Chymis-
try enough to extract Gold out of every thing but
common Sense. . . . You can by the single wave of a
Harlequin's Wand conjure the whole Town every
Night into your Circle; where, like a true Cunning
Man, you amuse 'em with a few Puppy's tricks while
you juggle 'em of their Pelf, and then cry out with a
Note of Triumph, Si Mundus vult Decipi, Deci-
piatur.[95]

Rich himself seems to have preferred to produce serious
drama but knew it was not economically profitable. No
leader in matter of taste, his choice of play was governed by
the town's applause: "Whenever the public taste shall be
disposed to return to the works of the drama, no one shall
rejoice more sincerely than myself."[96] Whatever Pope's attitude toward this theatrical pragmatism, he seems to have
remained on good terms with Rich. In 1727 he probably
recommended to Rich a play by David Lewis, subsequently
performed at Rich's Lincoln's Inn Fields theater.[97] In 1728
Rich was of course the producer of Gay's *Beggar's Opera*,
and in 1733 Pope promised to recommend to him Robert
Dodsley's *The Toy-Shop*.[98]

Of course, this is not to say that Pope admired Rich's
pantomimes; but he seems to have understood and ap-

[95] Miller, dedication to *Harlequin-Horace* (London, 1730). Pope knew
this poem and approved it; see *Corr.*, III, 173.
[96] Rich, dedication of *The Rape of Proserpine* (1726), quoted in R. F.
Jones, *Lewis Theobald*, p. 24. Cf. Miller, *Harlequin-Horace*: "Long labour'd
Rich, by Tragick Verse to gain / The Town's Applause—but labour'd long
in vain; / At length he wisely to his Aid call'd in, / The active Mime and
checker'd Harlequin" (pp. 30-31).
[97] See Goldstein, *Pope and the Augustan Stage*, p. 44. Lewis dedicated the
play, *Philip of Macedon*, to Pope and thanked him for the recommenda-
tion.
[98] *Corr.*, III, 346. The play was produced by Rich in 1735.

preciated Rich's role as producer or presenter.[99] As a presenter of folly, Rich may have seemed to Pope a figure for
the poet-celebrant of Dulness, a kind of "Angel of Dulness"
who performs his mistress's orders and yet retains a teasing
supremacy over an "unclassic" world, a calm, easy director
of the busy whirling storm, controlling worlds of dunces
with a nod. The *Dunciad* is indeed like some vast pantomime where "Tragedy and Comedy embrace" (1.69), a
monstrous medley of serious (the genuine threat of Dulness) and comic parts (the puny antics of dunces), a Virgilian mythology and Grub Street harlequinade. It has its
splendid settings—The Cave of Poverty and Poetry, the
Dome of Dulness, the Underworld—and sudden shifts of
scene—its goddess and her attendants, a coronation scene
and a great masquelike tableau of Dulness enthroned.
Dulness, who sits to "hatch a new Saturnian age of Lead"
(IV.28), outdoes all stage creation-pieces, from *The World's
Creation*, a popular Bartholomew Fair puppet show,[100] to
Rich's own famous egg trick.[101] And the poem's de-creative
spectacle outdoes any previous stage destruction. Indeed,
the "universal darkness" which covers all seems to echo (as
if to outdo) the "wide conflagration" which "swallows all"
(III.240),[102] the latter perhaps Pope's reimagining of the
spectacular stage fires, volcanoes, and earthquakes in Settle's *Siege of Troy* and Theobald's *Rape of Proserpine*, and the
Harlequin Dr. Faustus hellfire.[103]

[99] Rich was also an actor in his own shows, indeed, was one of the most
renowned Harlequins of his day. But Pope's interest in Rich seems to
focus on his producing activities (*Dunciad* III.249-60).

[100] First produced about 1682, this play held the fair stage for many
years.

[101] See Pope's note to *Dunciad* III.244 (1728 edition).

[102] See *Peri Bathous*, Chap. 15, the "Receipt to make an epic poem": "For
a burning Town, . . . old Troy is ready burnt to your Hands . . . [or] a
Chapter or two of the theory of the Conflagration [Burnet's *Sacred Theory
of the Earth* and its prophecy of the world destroyed by fire] done into
verse."

[103] The sense of artifice or performance is perhaps stronger when it is
recognized that the end of the *Dunciad* parodies the current fashion for
"Last Day" poems. Isaac Watts (1709), Edward Young (1713), and Aaron
Hill (1721), among many others, found an ideal sublime subject in the dis-

Creator and Destroyer

Like Rich, then, Pope seems to revel in his role as presenter and master of the show. He also delights in his own powers to create new worlds and to imagine fantastic landscapes. The transformation in Book II of Grub Street and Fleet Ditch into the scenes of heroic games, and the visionary power of Books III and IV, are Pope's own. We see through the eyes of Settle and other dunces, perhaps, but we are *made* to see by Pope's imagination. Our attention, as we read the *Dunciad*, is directed not only at the world of Dulness, but also, and perhaps even more so, at Pope's masterfully inventive and energetic imagination. This is an aspect of the poem that modern commentators have neglected,[104] preferring to look through Pope's art to the world described or to Pope's moral judgment of it.[105] But eighteenth-century critics, chief among them Joseph Warton, praised the poem not for its heroic challenge to the onrush of Dulness but for its "nervous and spirited versification" and its "poetical beauties," in short, for its art.[106]

---

solution of the world when "one universal ruin spreads abroad" (Young, *The Last Day*, Bk. I). The topic became so popular in the 1720s and 30s that the *Gentleman's Magazine* ran a contest in 1734 for the best poem on the last four things. For a brief summary of this minor genre, see David Morris, *The Religious Sublime* (Lexington, Ky., 1972), pp. 117-23. For other literary echoes, see Jones, "Pope and Dulness," pp. 154-57.

[104] Leavis is an honorable exception. He writes briefly and suggestively of Pope's "creative triumph" in *Dunciad*, Bk. IV, and of the "predominance of creativeness, delighting in the rich strangeness of what it contemplates": Leavis, *The Common Pursuit* (London, 1952), pp. 91, 94.

[105] Of recent critics, Howard Erskine-Hill comes closest to this aspect of the poem; for example, "Pope seems to revel in and amplify the nonsensical world he now imagines." But his emphasis lies elsewhere, on Pope's ambiguous attitude to the creations of dullness," that is, not on Pope's inventive, creative power. Thus he notes that the narrative of II.331-36 (Smedley in Fleet Ditch) "comes to us through a dunce's imagination; it is in the first instance Smedley, not Pope, who raises the low subject by beautiful words and classical allusion": Erskine-Hill, *Pope: The Dunciad* (London, 1972), pp. 31, 32. The section of his little book from which I quote is a modified version of his "The 'New World' of Pope's *Dunciad*" (see n. 24 above).

[106] See Bowles's notes in his edition of *The Works of Pope* (London, 1806), v, 256; Walter Harte, *An Essay on Satire* (London, 1730), p. 6; Ruff-

Because of the decorum of the poem, Pope is not permitted the opportunity to celebrate his powers except in altered forms. Thus poetic invention, in which he manifestly delights, produces a "new world" of unnatural wonders (III.233-48). The *process* of invention too can only be seen in the teeming chaos of a dunce's cracked brain,[107] where Dulness

> sees a Mob of Metaphors advance,
> Pleas'd with the madness of the mazy dance:
> How Tragedy and Comedy embrace;
> How Farce and Epic get a jumbled race;
> How Time himself stands still at her command,
> Realms shift their place, and Ocean turns to land.
> Here gay Description Aegypt glads with show'rs,
> Or gives to Zembla fruits, to Barca flow'rs;
> Glitt'ring with ice here hoary hills are seen,
> There painted vallies of eternal green,
> In cold December fragrant chaplets blow,
> And heavy harvests nod beneath the snow.
>
> (I.67-78)

This is an instance, says Warton, "of great power and elegance of Style on a subject that with much difficulty admits of either." The whole of this description, says Bowles, "is finely worked up, and exhibits the hand of a master."[108] The passage is a triumph of art—and of the artist. It may also be a description of the workings of Pope's art in the poem, for he too jumbles farce and epic, imagines an inverted world where ugliness is beauty and dulness wit.

Such invention exhibits indeed "the hand of a master." Our attention is directed again and again in the poem from

head, *The Life of Alexander Pope* (London, 1751), p. 371; an anonymous contemporary's *Essay on the Dunciad* (London, 1728), p. 25; and especially Joseph Warton's notes to the *Dunciad*, printed in his *Essay on the Genius and Writings of Pope* and in his edition of Pope's *Works* (1797). See especially Warton's notes to II.35-44, 387-428, III.233-48, IV.183-88, 294, 301.

[107] The scene is also a womb; see above, p. 232.

[108] Warton's note in his edition of Pope's *Works* (1797); Bowles's note in his edition of *The Works of Pope* (1806).

the world of the dunces to its imaginer and artificer.[109] "The *Poem was not made for these Authors, but these Authors for the Poem*."[110] Whatever their origin, the dunces fulfill their destiny in the *Dunciad*. For all that they are recognized historical phenomena, victims inherited from Dryden and Swift, actors already, in Pat Rogers's fine phrase, "typecast for their role,"[111] our pleasure in them comes not in a stock response to typecast stage dunces. Rather, we *almost* forget the dunces-as-actors and are caught up in the play being played, Pope's play. If Pope has not in fact made them, he has remade them, remolded "ductile dulness," exercised an artist's prerogative and control, and thus declared his supremacy. The poem, said Johnson, is one of Pope's "greatest and most elaborate performances." In it he "shewed his satirical powers."[112]

[109] Pope himself reflected on the presence of the epic poet in his work. In the Preface to his *Iliad* he noted that "we oftner think of the Author himself when we read *Virgil*, than when we are engag'd in *Homer*. . . . *Homer* was the greater Genius, *Virgil* the better Artist. In one we most admire the *Man*, in the other the *Work*. . . . When we behold their Battels, methinks the two Poets resemble the Heroes they celebrate: *Homer*, boundless and irresistible as *Achilles*, bears all before him, and shines more and more as the Tumult increases; *Virgil* calmly daring like *Aeneas*, appears undisturb'd in the midst of the Action, disposes all about him, and conquers with Tranquillity" (*Poems*, VII, 8, 12). (Pope here follows Dryden, who remarks in the *Preface to Fables* that the "very heroes" of Homer and Virgil "show their authors.") I have recently found support for my view in a fine essay by Michael Rosenblum, "Pope's Illusive Temple of Infamy," in *The Satirist's Art*, ed. H. Jensen and M. Zirker (Bloomington, Ind., 1972), pp. 28-54. As Rosenblum notes, "*The Dunciad* returns us to the figure of the satirist at work on the poem."

[110] "The PUBLISHER to the READER," *Poems*, V, 205. Pope here parodies Le Bossu's Aristotelian remarks about the primacy of action over character: "the *Action* is not made for the *Hero* . . . ; on the other hand, the *Hero* is only design'd for the *Action*" (*Treatise of the Epick Poem*, trans. "W. H." [1695], II, i, in *Le Bossu and Voltaire on the Epic*, ed. Stuart Curran [Gainesville, Fla., 1970], p. 54). Pope alludes to Le Bossu elsewhere in the *Dunciad*; see *Poems*, V, 50-51, 70, 254, 256.

[111] Rogers's valuable book, *Grub Street: Studies in a Subculture* (London, 1972), provides rich documentation about the *reality* of Grub Street but fails to give enough emphasis to Pope's transforming imagination.

[112] "Life of Pope," p. 145. Pope draws attention to the difficulty of his task, and his success in accomplishing it, in Cleland's letter: "To his Poem those alone are capable to do Justice, who . . . know how hard it is (with

The natural comparison here is with Swift and *A Tale of a Tub*. As Johnson wrote in perplexed admiration, the *Tale* "exhibits a vehemence and rapidity of mind, a copiousness of images, and vivacity of diction."[113] Characteristically, Johnson touches a central nerve. Even readers who are dismayed by the apparent bleakness of Swift's vision come away from the *Tale* with wonder and excitement at the fertility and energy of Swift's wit. Indeed, it is sometimes thought that the only genuine "positive" in *A Tale of a Tub* is Swift's own "self-assertion" (Leavis's phrase), his imagination displaying and celebrating its powers. Leavis writes acutely of the "spectacle of creative powers . . . exhibited in negation and rejection."[114] We are particularly aware of the artist's creative powers in *A Tale of a Tub* and *The Dunciad*, not only because of the brilliance of wit and the fantastic inventiveness of imagination, but also because these powers are set off against a contrasting ground, the maddened dull vagaries of schismatics, hacks, charlatans, and pedants. Yet there remains a difference between the celebrations of the witty mind's power in Swift and Pope. Mental energy in the *Tale*, even at its most exhilarating and impressive, always edges near to a kind of dangerous excess. The soaring exuberant fancy may easily plummet to the "Bottom of Things," or fall "like a dead Bird of Paradise." Similarly, in the *Dunciad* Dulness is busy, bold, and anarchic, and cracked brains breed wild nonsense and mental monsters. But Pope seems more concerned to ridicule the indulgence of fancy in dull men than to warn against the danger of his own creative imagination.

If Pope triumphs by creating, he also triumphs by de-

---

regard both to his Subject and his Manner) VETUSTIS DARE NOVITATEM, OBSOLETIS NITOREM, OBSCURIS LUCEM, FASTIDITIS GRATIAM" (v.19). That is, "to give novelty to what is old, brilliance to the common-place, light to the obscure, attraction to the stale." Pope here cites Pliny's *Natural History*, Preface, Par. 15. I give the Loeb translation. Pope omits Pliny's phrase, "novis Auctoritatem" ("authority to what is new") as not to his purpose.

[113] Johnson, "Life of Swift," in *Lives of the English Poets*, ed. G. B. Hill, 3 vols. (Oxford, 1905), III, 51.

[114] Leavis, "The Irony of Swift," in his *The Common Pursuit*, pp. 80, 86.

stroying. Again, Swift provides a similar case. "Swift's way of demonstrating his superiority is to destroy, but he takes a positive delight in his power, . . . the genius delights in its mastery, in its power to destroy, and negation is felt as self-assertion."[115] "This poem," Pope remarked to Swift about the *Dunciad*, "will rid me of those insects . . . if it silence these fellows, it must be something greater than any Iliad in Christendome" (*Corr.*, II, 481). But once more the pleasure in destruction is in part a pleasure in his own *powers* of destruction. Again Johnson hits the mark: "He delighted to vex them [the dunces], no doubt; but he had more delight in seeing how well he could vex them."[116] It is perhaps this imagined delight which led Pope's readers to a recurrent image of the poem: the *Dunciad* as a prison into which Pope has "put" his dunces. Contemporaries complained that they had been unfairly put in, or trembled to offend Pope for fear that they would be put in.[117] Or, like Fielding, they laughed at the way Pope had "imprisoned Moore in the loathsome dungeon of the *Dunciad*."[118] The image has persisted in the minds of Pope's critics. "His presence is as strongly felt in many of his poems as a jailer's in his jail: a strong reason why he is never absent from his

[115] Ibid., pp. 80, 85.

[116] Quoted in Boswell, *Life of Johnson*, ed. G. B. Hill, rev., L. F. Powell (Oxford, 1934), II, 334.

[117] Pope's sister speaks of the rage of "some of the people that he had put into his *Dunciad*": Spence, I, 116. The bookseller Osborne told Johnson that "when he was doing that which raised Pope's resentment, that he should be put into the *Dunciad*": "Life of Pope," p. 187. Cleland's letter wonders how the dunces, "after they had been content to print themselves his enemies, complain of being put into the number of them?" (p. 16). Pope himself may have been responsible for the currency of the phrase. In the list of attacks on Pope, first printed in 1729, he refers to Breval's *Confederates*, "for which he is *put into the Dunciad*," and Blackmore's *Essays*: "It is for a passage in . . . this book that Sir *Richard* was *put into the Dunciad*" (p. 210).

[118] *Tom Jones* (1749), Bk. XII, Chap. 1. Compare Warton's disapproving recognition of Pope's skill at binding monsters: "To pull out these Literary Cacus's, incendia vana vomentes, from their dark dungeons and deep retreats, was a truly Herculean (though not very Heroic) labour" (note to *Dunciad* III.152, in Warton's edition of Pope's *Works*).

Dunciad is because it is he who has put in all the other living writers."[119]

Pope himself may have had some sense of building a dunce's prison.[120] Since the dunces are regularly associated with both poverty and madness, they are by eighteenth-century standards appropriately punished by confinement.[121] But Pope's own image for the poem seems to have been a monument, related to a prison but richer because it combines the ideas of burial dungeon, permanent "bondage" in stone or metal (that is, dunce as statue; for example, Cibber's "brazen, brainless brothers"), and preserved memorial. "In this Monument they [the dunces] must expect to survive" ("Publisher's Preface"). Cibber himself complains of a gentleman unfairly set in "a Nich in a *Dunciad*."[122] Johnson probably had the image of a monument in mind when he remarked that "whoever his criticks were, their writings are lost, and the names which are preserved are preserved in *The Dunciad*."[123] Ruskin viewed the poem not as a memorial but as "the most absolutely chiselled and monumental work 'exacted' in our country."[124] Such praise would no doubt have gratified Pope, who told Spence that the poem "cost me as much pains as anything I ever wrote,"[125] but he seems also to have savored the poem as a

[119] Geoffrey Tillotson, *Pope and Human Nature* (Oxford, 1958), p. 146.

[120] Rogers, *Grub Street*, pp. 292-95, notes the prominence in the poem of images of confinement and punishment.

[121] Debtors were of course imprisoned. On confinement as the standard treatment for lunatics in the period (both imprisonment and bondage in chains or straitjackets), see Michel Foucault, *Madness and Civilization*, trans. Richard Howard (New York, 1965), esp. Chap. 2. On the connection between dulness and madness, see David Morris, "The Kinship of Madness in Pope's *Dunciad*," *Philological Quarterly*, 51 (1972), 813-31.

[122] *Another Occasional Letter from Mr. Cibber to Mr. Pope* (London, 1744), p. 11, printed in *Cibber and The Dunciad, 1740-44* (New York, 1975).

[123] "Life of Pope," p. 136. Compare the related images of the fly or grub in amber (*Epistle to Dr. Arbuthnot*, 169-72) and the "monsters preserved in the most costly spirits" (Bowles's note to *Dunciad* IV.1, in his edition of Pope's *Works*, V, 256).

[124] Ruskin, *Complete Works*, ed. E. T. Cook and A. Wedderburn, 39 vols. (London, 1903-1912), XX, 77.

[125] Spence, I, 147.

monument of a different kind, a memorial of his friendship with Swift and a record of his friends and enemies.[126]
Swift warned that in answering and naming dunces Pope
might succeed only in keeping alive what would otherwise
die and be justly forgotten.[127] But it was perhaps Pope's
aim all along to display his ability to perpetuate these "sons
of a day" (II.307), very unpromising poetic material, by
immuring them in an eternal monument, a "temple of infamy."[128] To make a Cibber or a Theobald, let alone a
Smedley, live in his numbers even "one more day" (I.90) is
indeed a paradoxical proof of creative power. The poem
finally stands as a monument to Pope's own satiric powers
of control. The epigraph to the 1743 edition, infrequently
reprinted and rarely remarked, reads:

> Tandem Phoebus adest, morsusque inferre parantem
> Congelat, et patulos, ut erant, indurat hiatus.[129]

It is taken from Ovid's account in the *Metamorphosis* of

[126] See above, pp. 220-21. Pope's enemies picked up the monument
image and turned it against him. "If this Monument, as he calls it, should
last; let the present Age inform him . . . that it will stand only as a Monument of his Infamy": *Pope Alexander's Supremacy and Infallibility examin'd*
(London, 1729), p. 2. In the *Epistle to the Little Satyrist of Twickenham* (London, 1733), Pope will live "in endless Fame, / An everlasting Monument of
Shame" (p. 10). The subtitle to Henley's *Why How Now, Gossip Pope?* (London, 1736; 2d ed. 1743) refers to "That Monument of his own Misery and
Spleen, the Dunciad."

[127] See Swift's notes on his own rule of not delivering the names of his
attackers to future ages and his remarks on Pope's contrary practice, in
Swift, *Prose Works*, ed. H. Davis, 14 vols. (Oxford, 1939-1968), v, 201.
Elsewhere, Swift encouraged Pope to record the names of dunces; see
Swift's *Correspondence*, ed. H. Williams, 5 vols. (Oxford, 1963-1965), IV, 53.

[128] Pope's term (*Poems*, v, 312), perhaps taken over from Dennis, who
claims in *Remarks on Mr. Pope's Rape of the Lock* (1728) that Pope's *Temple of
Fame* "will, as long as 'tis remember'd, be to A. P--E the Temple of Infamy" (p. vii). David Morris suggests attractively that Pope may have "intended his poem to darken with age," so that the dunces might "slip
through the gloom with the impersonality of ghosts, identified only by the
heavy biographical footnotes which Pope plants like tombstones at the
bottom of the page": Morris, "The Kinship of Madness," pp. 815-16.

[129] Warton complained in his edition of Pope's *Works*, v, 72, that "it is
difficult to see the propriety and justness of this application from Ovid."

Phoebus's intervention to save the exposed head of Orpheus: "But Phoebus at last appeared, drove off the snake just in the act to bite, and hardened and froze to stone, just as they were, the serpent's widespread, yawning jaws."[130] What can this mean but that Phoebus Apollo, patron of poets, enables Pope to enchain the power of Dulness, to arrest those "momentary monsters," the dunces, by transforming them to a stony monument wherein they are forever imprisoned and remembered? Phoebus and the poet remain,[131] not "the modern *Phoebus* of *French* extraction," worshipped by the dunces as their "own true Phoebus" (III.323, IV.61 and n.), but "the ancient and true *Phoebus*" (IV.93 and n.) and the still-singing poet.

The Triumph of Wit

Although the action of the *Dunciad* is "the Restoration of the Empire of Dulness in Britian,"[132] its counterplot is the triumph of Wit. Its "principal Agent" is the Mighty Mother, but its secret agent is Pope himself, persistently present—as man and poet in the critical apparatus, as shadow-hero to Cibber, as narrator, as presenter and master of the show, as creative imaginer and transformer, as keeper of a mighty prison or monument. Is this secret triumph perhaps Pope's "deep Intent" (IV.4)? Not so secret, perhaps, for Pope supplies enough clues. The poem, says the "Publisher to the Reader,"

[130] Bk. XI, 58, 60. Pope inexplicably omits line 59, "arcet et in lapidem rictus serpentis apertus." I use the Loeb translation. Except in the 1743 quarto, this couplet also appeared at the end of Ricardus Aristarchus's dissertation. For the motto Pope originally planned to use, see n. 7 above.

[131] Cf. "What then remains? Ourself" (I.217). I have found corroboration of my reading in Rosenblum's "Pope's Illusive Temple of Infamy," p. 51, and in two more recent essays: J. V. Regan, "Orpheus and the *Dunciad*'s Narrator," *Eighteenth-Century Studies*, 9 (1975), 87-101, and R. G. Peterson, "Renaissance Classicism in Pope's Dunciad," *Studies in English Literature*, 15 (1975), 431-45. See also Geoffrey Tillotson's remark that "the *Dunciad* freezes the grimace on the face of Dulness": Tillotson, *On the Poetry of Pope*, 2d ed. (Oxford, 1950), p. 38.

[132] Warburton's note to I.1, in *Poems*, v.

is styled Heroic, as being doubly so; not only with respect to its nature, which according to the best Rules of the Ancients and strictest ideas of the Moderns, is critically such; but also with regard to the Heroical disposition and high courage of the Writer, who dar'd to stir up such a formidable, irritable and implacable race of mortals. (p. 205)

Dennis caught the hint immediately and wielded his bludgeon: "Thus Pope all at once makes himself the Hero of his wonderful Rhapsody, and stiles his Folly, his Impudence, his Insolence, and his want of Capacity to discern and to distinguish, high Courage."[133] Dennis's tool is as blunt as Pope's wit is sly. Instead of brashly naming himself a modern Odysseus, Pope merely hints at it.[134] Ricardus Aristarchus might be speaking of this aspect of the *Dunciad* when he compares it with a surviving "ancient *Dunciad*," one of Euripides' "Satyric Tragedies," whose subject, he notes, is "the unequal Contention of an *old, dull, debauched, buffoon Cyclops*, with the heaven-directed *Favourite of* Minerva, who after having quietly borne all the monster's obscene and impious ribaldry, endeth the farce in punishing him with the mark of an indelible brand in his *forehead*."[135] Euripides no doubt wrote of Odysseus in the cave of Polyphemus, but the "*old, dull, debauched, buffoon Cyclops*" is also Cibber, who "translated the Italian Opera of Polifemo" (III.305n.), whose forehead is prominent ("Cibberian forehead, and Cibberian brain" [1.218]), while the "*Favourite of* Minerva" (or Athena) is the wise and wily Pope, who effortlessly ends

[133] Dennis, *Remarks upon the Dunciad*, p. 12, printed in Dennis, *Critical Works*, ed. Hooker, II, 375-76.

[134] Note the Scriblerian remarks on the poet's inventive resourcefulness: "if we consider that the Exercises of his *Authors* could with justice be no higher than *Tickling, Chatt'ring, Braying*, or *Diving*, it was no easy matter to invent such Games as were proportion'd to the meaner degree of *Booksellers*" (*Poems*, v, 107); "on due reflection, the maker might find it easier to paint a *Charlemagne*, a *Brute*, or a *Godfrey*, with just pomp and dignity heroic, than a *Margites*, a *Codrus*, a *Flecknoe*, or a *Tibbald*" (ibid., 49). Here Pope joins company with Homer, Juvenal, and Dryden.

[135] *Poems*, v, 255-56; Pope's emphasis.

the "unequal Contention" by marking the monster with the "indelible brand" (compare the permanence of a stony monument) of "Dulness" and so fixes him in our minds. We might thus have hints of another "Mighty Mother and her Son," the secret powers of the poem.[136] And if Pope is the favorite of Minerva,[137] then the owl (sacred to Minerva and often represented with her) displayed so prominently on the poem's title page and in the headpiece to Book I may assume extra significance.[138] Although the owl, fa-

[136] Pope is "willing to approve himself a genuine Son" (IV.1n.). His note to "Great Mother" at 1.33 (1728 edition)—"*Magna Mater*, here applyed to *Dulness*"—hints at the power of the true Magna Mater, a counterpresence to Dulness. The Emperor Julian allegorizes her as an intelligible and generative principle (an "intelligible" god, "the source of the intellectual and creative gods") and associates her with Minerva (Athena): "I recognize the kinship of Athena and the Mother of the Gods through the similarity of the forethought that inheres in the substance of both goddesses" (*Works of the Emperor Julian*, trans. W. C. Wright, 3 vols. [London, 1913-1923], I, 463, 499, 501). Athena is also the "mother of the virtues"; see Robert M. Adams, *The Roman Stamp* (Berkeley, 1974), p. 42. Pope links Minerva and the "Mighty Mother" in a note to IV.606, where he comments that "the great Mother composes all, in the same manner as Minerva at the period of the Odyssey."

[137] It may be significant that in the *Odyssey* Minerva puts the suitors to *sleep* so that Telemachus may escape (*Odyssey* II.444-47). The dunces who fall asleep at the end of Book II apparently lack "Ulysses' ear with Argus' eye" that might keep them awake (*Dunciad* II.374). But Pope—so the line hints—has the power to listen to dulness without being overcome, and thus deserves to be "Judge of all present, past, and future wit" (II.376). For a discussion of some possible affinities between Pope and Ulysses, see above, pp. 48-49.

[138] In the 1728 frontispiece, an owl sits on an altar of dull books with a scroll (marked "THE DUNCIAD") in its mouth. On the title page of the *Variorum*, an owl sits atop a pile of books loaded on the back of an ass. In the headpiece to Book I (1729), a scowling fierce owl is flanked by a pair of asses. An owl also appears in the headpieces to Books I and III in the 1735 edition. See the complete description of the plates in E. F. Mengel, "The *Dunciad* Illustrations," *Eighteenth-Century Studies*, 7 (1973-1974), 161-78. On the other hand, Pope may simply be adopting the traditional and recently employed images of dulness. In Blackmore's *The Kit-Cats* (1708), the "Temple of the God of Dulness" is graced by the "formal Owl" and the Ass, both "dear to the God": J. Means, "Sir Richard Blackmore and the Frontispiece to the *Dunciad* Variorum," *Scriblerian*, 6 (1974), 101-2. See also Alan McKenzie, "The Solemn Owl and the Laden Ass: The Iconography of the Frontispieces to *The Dunciad*," *Harvard Library Bulletin*, 24 (1976), 25-39.

mously stupid, is usually interpreted as a symbol of Dulness ("her bird" is "something betwixt a Heideggre and owl" [1.290]), it may also hint at the presence of Minerva, the goddess of mental alertness, and her favorite, the poet. Thus an owl perched on the back of an ass is perhaps redundant duncery, but it is also a hint of wit astride and scourging dulness. An owl atop a pedestal of dull books (the 1728 frontispiece) likewise may hint at witty triumph. Like a Roman victor, the owl stands atop a pillar with enslaved enemies beneath his feet. A couplet from the early *Temple of Fame* uncannily prophesied this triumph. Pope's own "rising Name" (the owl holds in his mouth a scroll entitled "THE DUNCIAD") is erected on the "Basis" (that is, the pedestal, foundation, lowest part of a column) built from "the fall'n Ruins of Another's Fame" (519-20).[139]

Pope left other reminders that victory in the unequal contention, apparently to be won by the force of brute numbers and dull-witted strength, goes in fact to the cunning. The 1728/29 version of the *Dunciad* concludes with Settle's prophecy and the sublime vision of "universal Darkness." One notes at the end of the prophecy the prominence of the names of Boyle, Gay, Swift, and Pope himself. The lines pretend to prophesy their decline and destruction (Swift mired in Irish politics, Pope in translating), but as the notes to the passage bring out, they in fact declare the multiple triumphs of Pope and his friends in the two or three years immediately preceding the 1728 *Dunciad*. In 1727 "the Portico of *Covent-garden* Church had been just then restored and beautify'd at the expence of *Richard* [Boyle] Earl of *Burlington*; who at the same time, by his publication of the designs of that great Master [Inigo Jones] and *Palladio*, as well as by many noble buildings of his own, revived the true Taste of Architecture in this Kingdom" (III.328n.). Pope refers here to the *Designs of*

---

[139] I owe the connection between the *Temple of Fame* lines and the 1728 frontispiece to Donald Fraser, "Pope and the Idea of Fame," in *Alexander Pope, Writers and Their Background*, ed. Peter Dixon (Athens, Ohio, 1972), p. 350.

Inigo Jones, published by Burlington and William Kent, and he no doubt knew of Burlington's plans to bring out a sumptuous edition of Palladio's *Fabriche Antiche* (1730).

As for unrewarded ("unpension'd") Gay, in 1728 he had honorably refused a "pension" from Walpole. He had also just written "the celebrated *Beggar's Opera*; a piece of Satire which hit all tastes and degrees of men, from those of the highest Quality to the very Rabble. . . . The vast success of it was unprecedented, and almost incredible. . . . Furthermore, it drove out of *England* the *Italian Opera*, which had carry'd all before it for ten years." So reads Pope's note to III.330, hardly a sign that he feared the imminent triumph of Dulness. Swift's successes in these years of course needed no reminder. Pope in fact does not mention the recent *Gulliver* (1726), but the earlier *Drapier's Letters* (1724-1725). Swift had been so victorious in the ironically denigrated "Hibernian Politicks" that he defeated the English scheme and became a popular hero. Pope himself makes an entrance at the climax of the prophecy, his fate "ten years to comment and translate." The line may hint at Pope's unhappiness at so many years of translation, but had he not completed "the noblest version of poetry which the world has ever seen, . . . a performance which no age or nation can pretend to equal"?[140] It is important to note too that the triumphs of Pope and his friends in these years were not coterie successes, but in each instance pleased or reformed an entire "kingdom," "all tastes and degrees of men." He need hardly draw attention to these lines as "his Irony" (III.332n.).

At the close of Book III comes another reminder of Pope's triumph. In the three-book version, the prophecy of "universal Darkness" is neatly, almost impudently, framed by a Virgilian parody: " 'Enough! enough!' the raptur'd Monarch cries; / And thro' the Ivory Gate the Vision flies." When commentators contrast the 1728 and 1743 *Dunciad*s

---

[140] "Life of Pope," pp. 119, 236. Johnson's remarks refer specifically to the *Iliad* (1715-1720), but he later notes that "the same general praise may be given to both translations."

they often suggest that Pope's pessimism has increased with the years, that the saving qualification (just a false dream) disappears when the lines are transferred to the end of Book IV. But the difference between the two versions may be less than has been imagined. The "Ivory Gate" couplet in each version acts as a reminder of authorial control. With a flick of his wand, Pope denies the vision's truth and, more important, reiterates his Virgilian parody and establishes again a context in which the classics—the *Aeneid* and Pope's own masterful use of it— manifest their easy supremacy over the rabble of dunces. In 1743 the couplet appears at the end of Book III, and the poem as a whole closes with another, equally brief reminder of Pope's control: the curtain suggests that, after all, it was but a show.

Finally, as Dulness makes her speech at parting in Book IV, charging her dunces to advance her cause, Pope's note provides a hint of his perspective. A reader should not object, he says, that the dunces are incited to engage in the merest trivia, "to personate Running-Footmen, Jockeys, Stage Coachmen, &c.":

> But if it be well consider'd, that whatever inclination they might have to do mischief, her sons are generally render'd harmless by their Inability; and that it is the common effect of Dulness (even in her greatest efforts) to defeat her own design, the Poet, I am persuaded, will be justified, and it will be allow'd that these worthy persons, in their several ranks, do as much as can be expected from them. (IV.584n.)[141]

[141] This note should be balanced against Pope's numerous suggestions that Dulness and dunces in fact *do* constitute a real threat; see, for example, Book IV as a whole. See also the note at III.333: "Do not thou, gentle reader, rest too secure in thy contempt of these Instruments [for such a revolution in learning, or despise such weak agents as have been described in our poem, but—1729 edition] remember what the Dutch stories somewhere relate, that a great part of their Provinces was once overflow'd, by a small opening made in one of their dykes by a single *Water-Rat*." As modern interpreters have put such emphasis on Pope's warnings of impending chaos, I have not thought it necessary to repeat them.

Again the note catches the opposition of "the Poet," justified in his successful design, and Dulness, who defeats her own design.

Pope's hints did not go unnoticed. In the minds of his friends and supporters, at any rate, the poem celebrated Pope's triumph. "It will indeed be a noble work," Bolingbroke wrote to Swift just before the 1728 version was published. "The many will stare at it, the few will smile, and all his Patrons from Bickerstaff to Gulliver will rejoice to see themselves adorn'd in that immortal piece."[142] Ruffhead, adopting the Scriblerian suggestions of Pope's heroic labors, notes that

> to tell of his quarrels with every unworthy adversary, would be like describing the various annoyances that Hercules encountered in wading through the fenns of Lerna, from every snake, and toad, and beetle, which he brushed off with his club. Let it suffice to say, that by the Dunciad he totally subdued that many-headed monster that had long annoyed him with its hissing.[143]

Early readers agreed: Richardson read the poem as Pope's triumph over "insects of a day";[144] Johnson thought Pope enjoyed his "victory over the Dunces with great exultation."[145] Cibber saw that the intention of Pope's "voluminous Labor" was to present "a most compleat and magnificent Picture of the militant Church, and *Pope* triumphant!"[146]

Thus the *Dunciad* contains both plot and counterplot, both principal agent and hidden hero. It sings both the triumph of Dulness and the triumph of Wit, it celebrates the powers of a Mighty Mother, but also the powers of Pope

---

Rather, I have put my stress (perhaps excessively) on the poem's counterplot. Pope would appear to be (and want a reader to be) in two minds about the threat that Dulness posed to the supremacy of true wit. Perhaps the dunces are individually contemptible but collectively threatening.

[142] Swift, *Correspondence*, III, 264.   [143] Ruffhead, *Life of Pope*, p. 351.
[144] Richardson, *Selected Letters*, ed. J. Carroll (Oxford, 1964), pp. 56-57.
[145] "Life of Pope," p. 150.
[146] *Another Occasional Letter from Mr. Cibber to Mr. Pope*, p. 11.

himself. "Books and the Man, I sing." Pope notes that "the very *Hero* of the Poem hath been mistaken to this hour."[147] "The Man," his notes hint, is both Cibber the Laureate, who helped corrupt the town by importing a Smithfield taste, and Walpole, whose hands presented this poem of Smithfield to King George II. But the man may also be Pope himself, creator of the Smithfield fantasy, a man of letters and yet the adversary of a world of dull "Books," as Aeneas was both a bearer of "arms" and a "man" who came to end the struggle of arms and to create empire.[148]

The magnificent self-assertion in the *Dunciad* fulfills at once Pope's pleasure in artistic mastery and his need to bear personal witness to moral and literary standards.[149] (No doubt it fulfilled also the less lofty need utterly to astound his enemies.) It springs in part from the same impulse that led him to the heroic declarations of the Horatian poems: "Yet there was one who held it in disdain." As in the *Epilogue to the Satires*, Pope imagines the utter triumph of moral chaos, and yet he props against that triumph the determined efforts of a mighty poet. In the *Dunciad* (even in its four-book form), perhaps more than in the Horatian poems, Pope exults in his satiric strength.

[147] Bentley's introductory note to Book I (1743), in *Poems*, v.

[148] Note that Pope may hint at his own role as hero by including James Ralph's silly remark in *Sawney* (1728) that *"The Man who brings"* refers to "our Poet himself, as if he vaunted that *Kings* were to be his Readers (an Honour which tho' this poem hath had, yet knoweth he how to receive it with more Modesty)": Pope's note to I.1 (1728 edition).

[149] By contrast, the dunces' self-assertion (they "see all in *Self*," are "Wrapt up in Self" [IV.480, 485]) is really the abandonment of the self's intellectual and moral consciousness, which constitutes identity, to mere sensation. On this point, see Martin Price, *To the Palace of Wisdom* (Garden City, N.Y., 1964), p. 228. The self-loving dunce loses his "mind" (his brain is "extracted" [IV.522]) and retains but " the human shape" (IV.528n.). He yields to all external pressure, becoming a "slave to Words," "vassal to a Name," "dupe to Party" (IV.501-2). When a dunce drinks the Cup of Self-Love, he forgets "his former friends, / Sire, Ancestors, Himself" (IV.518-19). See Alvin Kernan, "The *Dunciad* and the Plot of Satire," in *Essential Articles*, pp. 795-802, on the spread of dulness as a contraction of life.

I began by noting that the *Dunciad* is perhaps more complexly self-revelatory than the *Horatian Imitations*. For in it Pope is able to recognize and give full play to several powerful and partly conflicting forces in his imagination: his visionary impulse, manifesting itself in both rich fantasy and prophetic gloom; his darkest fears about the decay of culture; his confidence and pleasure in the power of wit. In this many-layered poem Pope appears as the Friend of Virtue (the "best self"), as the partly moral Champion of Wit, and even as the imaginative reveler in duncery. No poem in his work is more richly and variously self-expressive.

Index

LIBRARY OF CONGRESS CATALOGING IN PUBLICATIONS DATA

Griffin, Dustin H.
    Alexander Pope, the poet in the poems.
    Includes index.
    1.   Pope, Alexander, 1688-1744.   2.   Poets, English—
18th century—Biography.   I.   Title.
PR3633.G7   821'.5   78-51167
ISBN 0-691-06371-0